THE
HISTORY OF
HONDURAS

ADVISORY BOARD

THE HISTORY OF HONDURAS

Thomas M. Leonard

The Greenwood Histories of the Modern Nations
Frank W. Thackeray and John E. Findling, Series Editors

AN IMPRINT OF ABC-CLIO, LLC
Santa Barbara, California • Denver, Colorado • Oxford, England

Library of Congress Cataloging-in-Publication Data

Leonard, Thomas M., 1937–
   The history of Honduras / Thomas M. Leonard.
      p. cm. — (The Greenwood histories of the modern nations)
   Includes bibliographical references and index.
   ISBN 978–0–313–36303–0 (hard copy) — ISBN 978–0–313–36304–7 (ebook)
1. Honduras—History. 2. Honduras—Politics and government. 3. Honduras—Social conditions. I. Title.
F1506.L48   2011
972.83—dc22   2010041398

ISBN: 978–0–313–36303–0
EISBN: 978–0–313–36304–7

15 14 13 12 11   1 2 3 4 5

This book is also available on the World Wide Web as an eBook.
Visit www.abc-clio.com for details.

Greenwood
An Imprint of ABC-CLIO, LLC

ABC-CLIO, LLC
130 Cremona Drive, P.O. Box 1911
Santa Barbara, California 93116-1911

This book is printed on acid-free paper ∞

Manufactured in the United States of America

*For Yvonne
and
Tom, Bob, Randy,
Eddie, David, and Stacy*

Contents

Series Foreword

The *Greenwood Histories of the Modern Nations* series is intended to provide students and interested laypeople with up-to-date, concise, and analytical histories of many of the nations of the contemporary world. Not since the 1960s has there been a systematic attempt to publish a series of national histories, and as series advisors, we believe that this series will prove to be a valuable contribution to our understanding of other countries in our increasingly interdependent world.

Some 40 years ago, at the end of the 1960s, the cold war was an accepted reality of global politics. The process of decolonization was still in progress, the idea of a unified Europe with a single currency was unheard of, the United States was mired in a war in Vietnam, and the economic boom in Asia was still years in the future. Richard Nixon was president of the United States, Mao Tse-tung (not yet Mao Zedong) ruled China, Leonid Brezhnev guided the Soviet Union, and Harold Wilson was prime minister of the United Kingdom. Authoritarian dictators still controlled most of Latin America, the Middle East was reeling in the wake of the Six-Day War, and Shah Mohammad Reza Pahlavi was at the height of his power in Iran.

Since then, the Cold War has ended, the Soviet Union has vanished, leaving 16 independent republics in its wake, the advent of the computer age has radically transformed global communications, the rising demand for oil makes the Middle East still a dangerous flashpoint, and the rise of new economic powers like the People's Republic of China and India threatens to bring about a new world order. All of these developments have had a dramatic impact on the recent history of every nation of the world.

For this series, which was launched in 1998, we first selected nations whose political, economic, and socio-cultural affairs marked them as among the most important of our time. For each nation, we found an author who was recognized as a specialist in the history of that nation. These authors worked cooperatively with us and with Greenwood Press to produce volumes that reflected current research on their nations and that are interesting and informative to their readers. In the first decade of the series, more than 40 volumes were published, and as of 2008, some are moving into second editions.

The success of the series has encouraged us to broaden our scope to include additional nations, whose histories have had significant effects on their regions, if not on the entire world. In addition, geopolitical changes have elevated other nations into positions of greater importance in world affairs and, so, we have chosen to include them in this series as well. The importance of a series such as this cannot be underestimated. As a superpower whose influence is felt all over the world, the United States can claim a "special" relationship with almost every other nation. Yet many Americans know very little about the histories of nations with which the United States relates. How did they get to be the way they are? What kind of political systems have evolved there? What kind of influence do they have on their own regions? What are the dominant political, religious, and cultural forces that move their leaders? These and many other questions are answered in the volumes of this series.

The authors who contribute to this series write comprehensive histories of their nations, dating back, in some instances, to prehistoric times. Each of them, however, has devoted a significant portion of their book to events of the past 40 years because the modern era has contributed the most to contemporary issues that have an impact on U.S. policy. Authors make every effort to be as up-to-date as possible so that readers can benefit from discussion and analysis of recent events.

In addition to the historical narrative, each volume contains an introductory chapter giving an overview of that country's geography, political institutions, economic structure, and cultural attributes. This is meant to give readers a snapshot of the nation as it exists in the contemporary world. Each history also includes supplementary information following the narrative, which may include a timeline that represents a succinct chronology of the nation's historical evolution, biographical sketches of the nation's most important historical figures, and a glossary of important terms or concepts that are usually expressed in a foreign language. Finally, each author prepares a comprehensive bibliography for readers who wish to pursue the subject further.

Readers of these volumes will find them fascinating and well-written. More importantly, they will come away with a better understanding of the contemporary world and the nations that comprise it. As series advisors, we hope that this series will contribute to a heightened sense of global understanding as we move through the early years of the twenty-first century.

Frank W. Thackeray and John E. Findling
Indiana University Southeast

Preface

The plane banked sharply, and I mean sharply, to its left around a medium level mountain chain, and then leveled off to fly directly through what appeared to be a short canyon and on to the airport's runway. The plane screeched to a halt just before the runway's end, and a 75-foot drop on to a busy roadway. As they had before and would do so in the future, the passengers gleefully applauded the pilot for executing a safe landing. And well they should have. The pilot had just guided his craft safely into the world's second most dangerous airport, Toncontín, sitting in the heart of Honduras's bustling capital of Tegucigalpa. Over the next 30 years there would be countless landings and take-offs at Toncontín or the more placid Ramón Villeda Morales Airport, some seven miles from downtown San Pedro Sula in northern Honduras.

On that warm spring afternoon in April 1981, at Toncontín, Ernesto Icaza welcomed me to what he then believed to be his temporary home away from Nicaragua. 30 years later, Ernesto and his brothers Favio, Jr. and Juan Carlos are successful businessmen, residing in San Pedro Sula with their own families and parents. I met Ernesto that previous January when he enrolled in my seminar on United States-Central American relations at the University of North Florida.

Obviously, we had a lot to talk about, and so did his father Favio. The elder Icaza had been a large and successful cotton grower near Chinandega, Nicaragua, who initially favored the Sandinistas in their drive to oust the dictator Anastasio Somoza. But when the Sandinista National Liberation Front (Nicaragua) (FSLN) seized his crop duster as a potential threat to the security of the state, Favio lost his idealistic hopes for Nicaragua and packed his family off to Houston, then Miami, and finally back to Honduras, where he found comfort in an exiled Nicaraguan community. In addition to the Icaza family, my research soon brought me into contact with Mario Argueta, a Honduran scholar of first repute. Mario continuously assisted me in locating materials relative to my research on United States-Central American relations and like the Icazas, welcomed me into his home. As with the Icazas, there is no shortage of conversation with Mario. There is some irony in the fact that Mario comes to the United States National Archives and other U.S. repositories to gather materials about his country, while I go to Honduras to learn about the impact of my country's relations with it.

Owing to the Icaza family and Mario Argueta, the circle of contacts, many of whom are now good friends, widened quickly. The list varies widely to include professionals, business managers , small business proprietors, skilled workers, university types, and journalists, a group of people that Latin Americanists habitually label the middle sector. Although wealth varies among the group, they are not part of the elite family group and are far from the difficult life of the country's poor, but they do understand the narrow range of national politics and want to make the system more representative and participatory. Like the upper class, the middle sector has little interest, if any, in the welfare the poor, those numerous Hondurans (including Garifunas and indigenous Mayans), that eke out a living on ravaged soil or are employed as hired hands in the agri-business sector, or perform the unskilled tasks in the manufacturing, transportation, and service sectors of the economy. Many others caught in the binds of poverty are unemployed. Added to this mix of individuals are Nicaraguans, Salvadorans, Guatemalans, and Costa Ricans encountered while residing in Honduras. This cross section of people was encountered while living or visiting for a time in Tegucigalpa and San Pedro Sula or when traveling throughout Honduras. Whether it were from Tegucigalpa southwest to Amapala on the Gulf of Fonseca, or northeast from the capital to San Pedro Sula and thence northwest to Santa Rosa de Copán, or along the North Coast from Omoa to Trujillo and beyond into Olancho Province, people gave generously of their time to inform this *gringo* about whatever was on their mind about life in Honduras, from politics to refrigeration, from poor transportation to education, from lack of jobs to attractive young women on the beach.

All of this is to say that I became fascinated with Honduras, its people, its history, its politics, and its society; which prompted me to quickly accept John Findling's offer to write a history of Honduras for Greenwood Press's series *Histories of the Modern Nations*. I welcomed the challenge and only hope that the final product satisfies Findling's expectations, at least in a small way.

The first challenge in writing any manuscript is organization. Beyond the chronological approach required by Greenwood Press, how does one structure the study of a complex nation? What theme or themes should be pursued? What are the essential questions that must be addressed? While the list of issues can be unending, two basic assumptions became the framework of this volume. First, the world has experienced time periods or blocks of time that share similar characteristics. This is true for the study of Latin America in general or Honduras in particular and is evident in the chapter breakdown set forth in this book. Following from the first premise are a series of questions as a nation moves through these time periods: how did the Honduran experience compare with other Latin American nations and what lessons did the country learn from the events of a given time period? Did they impact positively or negatively upon the country's economic, political and social structures? In other words, how were the cross-section of Hondurans personally encountered over 30 years, and their ancestors, affected by the nation's historical experience? Or, as American philosopher George Santayana observed that those who do not learn the lessons of history are condemned to repeat them. Put differently in the title of the final chapter; the more things change, the more they stay the same.

Prior to Columbus claiming the territory for Spain in 1504, Honduras was inhabited by various Native American, or Indian groups. The Mayans were the most notable, but their civilization was already in decay when the Spanish finally established the semblance of administrative control over the colony in 1572. In theory, the Spanish designed their colonial system to serve the interests of the mother country. In application, all rules were made in Spain, and the crown's representatives in the New World enforced them. Thus, an argument can be made that as a result of the independence movement in the early nineteenth century, Honduran *criollos* replaced the Spanish *peninsulares* as the government administrators of the new nation and that throughout the nineteenth century; these elites struggled for political power among themselves at the expense of all other Hondurans. Owing to a lack of mineral wealth and a large Indian population to convert to Catholicism, Spain paid minimal attention to its new colony on the Caribbean coast of Central America. The lack of economic opportunity also kept foreign entrepreneurs from Honduran shores throughout the nineteenth century. Clearly, during these two time periods, the Honduran people endured a stagnant social system; and their future offered no hope of economic opportunity.

Honduran leaders accepted the liberal economic principles popular with Latin American governments in the late nineteenth century and contributed to the development of the banana industry by U.S. owned companies during the first half of the twentieth century. Cuyamel, Standard, and United Fruit companies received generous concessions to operate in Honduras. Through bribes and corruption, the fruit companies formed an informal alliance with the ruling elite. Neither group had any reason or interest in altering the Honduran political and social structures that served them well. Not until 1944, did the system come into question, and with increased violence it was again attacked in 1954 and 1968 and again during the Central American wars of the 1980s. The *status quo ante* became the norm in Honduras at the conclusion of each event.

With the end of the Cold War in 1991, Honduran political leaders accepted the neoliberal economic principles that gripped the entire world at the time and again opened Honduras to foreign investment. The book's final chapter describes Honduras during the last 20 odd years and posits two interrelated questions: Is it fair to say that the impact of neoliberalism contributed significantly to the Honduran political crisis of 2009–2010? Or was the crisis another symptom of the country's historic experience?

This approach and the conclusions that it presents are not to say that they are cast in stone. Not all of you, the readers, will agree with the interpretation of events or conclusions this volume presents about Honduras. In fact, I would welcome the challenge so that we can engage in lively conversations just as I have had with Hondurans about their own country.

Acknowledgments

Many individuals assisted with making this volume possible. A special note of appreciation goes to series co-editor John Findling for affording me the opportunity to undertake the assignment for ABC-CLIO press. There, the patience, and skillful work of Ms. Kaitlin Ciarmiello and her staff guided the work through the editorial and production process. Two long time friends and mentors, retired professors Lester D. Langley (University of Georgia) and Ralph Lee Woodward, Jr. (Tulane University), always provided guidance for the placing of singular historical events into a contextual framework. Mario Argueta, a prolific researcher and writer at the *Universidad Nacional de Honduras* in Tegucigalpa, provided insights that enabled me to better understand the Honduran perspective. A deep sense of gratitude goes to the librarians and especially for this project to Paul Mosley, at the Thomas G. Carpenter Library at the University of North Florida for kindly dealing with my excessive requests for assistance and obscure materials. Most of all to my late wife, Yvonne, who for over two generations provided indeterminable encouragement, patience, and understanding that made all things possible and, to our six children–Tom, Bob, Randy, Eddie, David, and Stacy–who continue to provide comfort and pleasure. To these seven individuals, this volume is collectively dedicated.

Thomas M. Leonard
Distinguished University Professor Emeritus
University of North Florida
Jacksonville, Florida
April 20, 2010

List of Acronyms

ALBA	The Bolivarian Alliance for the Peoples of Our America
BANADESA	National Development Bank
BANTRAL	Central Bank of Honduras
CACM	Central American Common Market
CDC	Caribbean Defense Command
CET	Common External Tariff
CIA	Central Intelligence Agency (United States)
CONDECA	Central American Defense Council
CONSUPLANE	Supreme Council of Economic Planning
CREM	Regional Center for Military Training
DR-CAFTA	Dominican Republic-Central American-Free Trade Agreement
ECLAC	Economic Commission for Latin America

EU	European Union
EUCA	The United States of Central America
FAO	Honduran Worker's Organization
FMLN	Farabundo Martí National Liberation Front (El Salvador)
FSH	Honduran Syndicate Federation
FSLN	Sandinista National Liberation Front (Nicaragua)
GDP	Gross Domestic Product
IACHR	Inter-American Commission on Human Rights
IADB	Inter-American Development Bank
ICJ	International Court of Justice at The Hague
IMF	International Monetary Fund
INA	National Agrarian Institute
MNR	National Reformist Movement
NAFTA	North American Free Trade Agreement
NSC	National Security Council (United States)
OAS	Organization of American States
OIAA	Office of Inter-American Affairs
PCH	Communist Party of Honduras
PDC	Christian Democratic Party
PDRH	Democratic Revolutionary Party of Honduras
PINU	Innovation and Unity Party
PLH	Liberal Party of Honduras
PNH	National Party of Honduras
PRC	People's Republic of China
PUN	National Union Party
SOUTHCOM	United States Southern Command
UFCO	United Fruit Company

UNC	National Union of Peasants
UNFAO	United Nations Food and Agricultural Organization
UPCA	United Provinces of Central America
USAID	United States Agency for International Development
USIA	United States Information Agency

Timeline of Historical Events

435–950	The Mayan city of Copán flourishes.
763	At Copán, Altar Q depicts the reputed founder of the Mayan civilization, K'inich Yax K'uk' Mo' handing the symbolic baton of office to Yax Pasah, the last dynastic ruler.
1502	During his fourth voyage to the New World, Christopher Columbus lands on the North Coast of Honduras.
1524	Spanish establish first Honduran colony at San Gil de Buenavista.
1538	Spanish authorities assassinate Indian leader Limpera ending Indian mass resistance to Spanish colonization of Honduras.
1548–1700	Honduras falls under the administration of the Audiencia of Guatemala.
1788	British are expelled from the North Coast.
1797	Approximately 5000 black Caribs, also known as Garifuna or Garinagu, are exiled from St. Vincent Island to Roatán Island off the eastern coast of Honduras. The Garifuna define themselves by language and culture, rather than any country or territiory.

1821	On September 15, Honduras declares its independence from Spain but remains under Mexican authority.
1823	On July 1, Honduras becomes a member of the United Provinces of Central America along with Costa Rica, El Salvador, Guatemala, and Nicaragua.
1827–1842	Honduran F. M. ruled over the United Provinces of Central that included the five nations of contemporary Central America.
1839–1840	Guatemalan Rafael Carrera defeats Morazán's army, and with it, the United Provinces of Central America disintegrates.
1839–1841	U.S. amateur archaeologist John Lloyd Stephens and British sketch artist Frederick Catherwood become first white men to visit and report on the Mayan ruins in Central America and Mexico.
1842	Death of Francisco Morazán, Central American statesman and soldier.
1848–1849	U.S.–British rivalry over Tigre Island in the Gulf of Fonseca leads to the 1850 Clayton-Bulwer Treaty limiting transisthmian canal options.
1848–1895	Honduras experiences conservative–Liberal political rivalry that brings the country several constitutions.
1854–1856	Honduras joins military forces with other Central American governments to defeat the U.S. based filibusterer William Walker, and to prevent him from forcing a Central American Unionunder his leadership.
1859	The British cede Roatán Island, 40 miles off the mainland, to Honduras.
1860	September 12, U.S. filibusterer William Walker is executed by a Honduran military firing squad at Trujillo.
1880s	Liberal governments grant favorable concessions to U.S.-based mining companies. Washington Valentine, one of the most successful entrepreneurs, becomes known as the "King of Honduras."
1891–1900	Harvard University Peabody's Museum conducts first survey of Mayan site at Copán.
1899	First banana concession is granted to the Vaccaro Brothers, later to become the Standard Fruit Company. The United Fruit Company is established by the merger of the Boston Fruit Company and the Tropical Trading and Transport Company.

1902	Dissident members leave the Liberal party to establish the Honduran National Party (PHN).
1907	U.S. marines land in Honduras to protect U.S. lives and property in the violence that accompanies the overthrow of President Manuel Bonilla. It is the first of five such landings over the next generation.
	The United States hosts the first Central American Conference that endeavors to outlaw revolutionary or other illegal governments in Central America.
	Samuel Zemurray forms the Cuyamel Fruit Company.
1911	President Manuel Bonilla is overthrown by a group of U.S. mercenaries assembled by Samuel Zemurray and led by Lee Christmas.
1912	United Fruit Company begins its operations in Honduras with the construction of the Tela railroad.
1917	Honduras joins the majority on the Central American Court of Justice to void the 1914 Bryan–Chamorro Treaty that permitted the United States to construct a canal with a terminus in the Gulf of Fonseca that bordered Honduras, El Salvador, and Nicaragua.
	The first Honduran labor strike against Cuyamel Fruit Company is suppressed by the military.
1920	A labor strike by banana workers in the La Ceiba area reveals the disparity of interests between the workers and the companies.
1921	The Honduras Workers Federation is formed.
1923	Second Central American Conference is hosted by the United States in an effort to prevent anyone associated with an illegal change of government from becoming head of state and to control the size of local militaries to avoid their use in support of ruling elites.
	Tiburcio Carías Andino wins the presidential election but is prevented from taking office. This results in a civil war in which U.S. marines again land to protect American lives and property.
1929	United Fruit Company purchases Cuyamel Fruit Company.
	The Honduran Worker's Syndicate is established.
1932	Tiburcio Carías Andino begins a 16-year dictatorship.
1933	U.S. President Franklin D. Roosevelt announces the Good Neighbor Policy, whereby the United States will no longer

	interfere in the internal affairs of Latin American nations, including Honduras.
1941	Honduras declares war on Japan on December 8, 1941, and on Germany and Italy on December 13.
1944	President Carías survives public protests against the extra-constitutional extension of his presidency until 1949.
1941–1945	At the conclusion of World War II, the Honduran economy is in poor condition due to loss of its markets, the United States and Europe, for its primary products.
1948	As promised Tiburcio Carías is not a presidential candidate and steps aside in favor of his protegé, Juan Manuel Gálvez.
1954	Some 60,000 banana workers strike for three months against the U.S.-based United Fruit Company and other land owners to gain improved working conditions
1956	Military officers overthrow Supreme Head of State Julio Lozano Díaz.
1957	Ramón Villeda Morales is elected President. His six-year term is characterized by social and agrarian reform programs that improve the quality of life for working class.
1960	Honduras is a founding member of the Central American Common Market (CACM).
1962–1972	Honduras participates in the Alliance for Progress, a U.S.-sponsored program designed to improve the quality of life for the lower classes in order to stunt the appeal of communism
1963	Shortly before completing his presidential term Ramón Villeda Morales is ousted in a military coup and replaced by General Osvaldo López Arellano, who sets in motion a generation of military rule.
1964	Honduras joins with El Salvador, Guatemala and Nicaragua to form the Central American Defense Council (ODECA).
1969	On June 27, diplomatic relations between Honduras and El Salvador are broken due to a soccer game. El Salvador and Honduras fight a four-day Soccer War when fans bring out long-simmering tensions during World cup qualifying matches. Some 3,000 people die in the four-day conflict.

1974   Hurricane Fifi strikes Honduran coast, killing an estimated 10,000 people, destroying homes and infrastructure. North Coast banana plantation forced to temporarily close.

1975   United Brands pays unnamed government official $1.25 million, reportedly President Osvaldo López Arellano, to avoid paying $7.5 million in taxes. López is overthrown and replaced by Juan Alberto Melgar Castro.

1977   Honduran military arrives in Standard Fruit railroad cars to destroy Las Isletas banana cooperative.

1980   1969 Soccer War officially ends with signing of a peace treaty mediated by U.S. President Jimmy Carter.

United Nations Educational, Scientific and Cultural Organization (UNESCO) declares Copan a World Heritage Site.

1981   Roberto Suazo Cordoba is elected president; first civilian to hold that office in 20 years.

Argentine military train *Contras* for clandestine war against Sandinistas in Nicaragua.

1982–1989   United States increases military presence in Honduras; increases military assistance to Honduran armed forces; and conducts war games with Honduran military as part of U.S. policy to overthrow Sandinistas in Nicaragua and to support government in El Salvador defeat Farabundo Martí National Liberation Front (FSLN).

1984   In a struggle over control of the military, Air Force Brigadier General Walter López Reyes ousts Army General Osvaldo GustavoÁlvarez as commander-in- chief of the armed forces.

1985   Foreign Minister Edgardo Paz Barnica indicates Honduran policy change when he announces that the *Contras* are no longer welcome in the country.

1989   Following three years of negotiations led by Costa Rican President Oscar Arias, on August 8 at Tela, Honduras the five Central American Presidents sign an agreement bringing the Central American conflicts of the 1980s to an end.

1990   President Rafael Leonardo Callejas declares a general political amnesty that frees from incarceration an estimated 2,000 members of seven leftists organizations

| | In light of Violeta Chamorro's presidential electoral victory in Nicaragua, thousands of *Contras* depart Honduras for home. |

1990–1994   During his presidential term, Rafael Collejas (National Party) implements neoliberal economic reforms.

1990–1998   Street gangs and death squad groups multiply leading to significantly increased urban violence.

1992   United Nations High Commission on Refugees repatriates last of estimated 30,000 Salvadoran refugees that date to wars of the 1980s.

Congress approves legislation that weakens the land distribution program that dates to the 1962 agrarian reform program.

At The Hague, the International Court of Justice rules in favor of Honduras on its long standing border dispute with El Salvador.

1993   Congress grants legal status Democratic Unification Party comprised of former guerrilla groups.

1994–1998   President Robert Reina (Liberal Party) implements a harsh crackdown program that momentarily reduces urban violence.

1996   A new sculpture museum opens in Copan National Park, Honduras, with exhibits of Mayan work.

Testimony before U.S. Congress verifies that several U.S. brands—Kathie Lee Gifford, Eddie Bauer, J. Crew and K-Mart—of using underage girls in sweatshop conditions in their Honduran *maquiladora* plants.

An estimated 4,000 Garifuna marched on Tegucigalpa to demand property rights.

1997   Chorti tribal leader Candido Amador is assassinated near the Copan ruins following a meeting with local landowners regarding 35,000 acres of land promised the tribe by the Spanish colonial government in the eighteenth century.

U.S. aid to Honduras had dropped to $28 million from a high of $229 million in 1985.

1998   Transparency International ranks Honduras in the bottom five of the world's most corrupt governments.

An estimated 9,000 people lose their lives to Hurricane Mitch, one of the Caribbean's deadliest storms on record, which pounded Central America between October 22 and November 9, 1998.

Around 33,000 homes are destroyed, and another 50,000 are damaged. Approximately 70 percent of the country's agriculture is wiped out. The cost of the damage is estimated to be $3.8 billion.

1999 The Honduran legislature votes to put an end to the 41 years of military autonomy, putting the military under civilian control.

2000 Honduras joins with El Salvador and Guatemala to conclude a free-trade agreement with Mexico.

2001 Amidst charges of corruption, Ricardo Maduro (Liberal Party) is elected president of Honduras.

2002 Congress elects Justice Vilma Cecilia Morales as the first woman to head the Supreme Court.

2002 President Carlos Roberto Flores restores Honduran diplomatic relations with Cuba.

2003 Amidst escalating urban violence Honduran legislature passes an anti-gang law. Gang leaders now face nine to twelve year prison terms.

Thousands of protestors in cities and towns throughout Honduras demand that the government not renew a debt-payment agreement with the International Monetary Fund (IMF).

2004 On May 28, Honduras joins its Central American neighbors (Costa Rica, El Salvador, Guatemala, and Nicaragua) in signing a free-trade agreement with the United States. The subsequent adherence of the Domincan Republic to the pact provides for the acronym: CAFTA-DR Free-Trade Agreement

Federal troops are dispatched to south-central Honduas to assist local police in suppressing a clash between loggers and environmentalists.

2005 The seven Central American nations (Belize, Costa Rica, El Salvador, Guatemala, Honduras, Nicaragua, and Panama) agree to create a rapid-response force to combat drug trafficking, terrorism and other regional threats.

Liberal Party candidate Manuel Zelaya wins November presidential election with campaign promises to reinvigorate the economy by eliminating government corruption.

2006 In his inaugural address President-elect Zelaya promises to fight against corruption, and also promises to help criminal and gang members to become active members of society.

2007 After a 45-year hiatus, Honduras appoints an ambassador to Havana that completes the restoration of diplomatic relations with Cuba.

2008 Honduras joins the Bolivarian Alternative of the Americas (ALBA), created in 2004 by Cuba and Venezuela to counter the U.S. policy of free trade agreements with individual Latin American and Caribbean countries.

2009 A United Nations survey reports that homicides in Honduras more than doubled from 2,155 in 2004 to 4,473 in 2008.

President Manuel Zelaya announces that a nationwide poll will be held on June 24, 2009, to determine if a constituent assembly should be convened.

President Zelaya announces that he will ignore a Supreme Court ruling ordering him to reinstate a military chief he fired.

A group of military take President Zelaya from the Presidential Palace and have him sent into exile in Costa Rica. Congressional leader Roberto Micheletti is appointed interim president until the end of Zelaya's legal term on January 27, 2010.

On June 30, the United Nations adopts a resolution calling on all 192 U.N. member states to only recognize Zelaya's government in Honduras, and not any other.

On July 3, as some 200,000 demonstrators march both for and against the return of Zelaya, interim-President Roberto Micheletti declares new elections would be held on November 29.

The Organization of American States (OAS) suspends Honduras on July 4 participation in the organization because of an earlier military coup.

On July 6, the Honduras' interim government shuts down its main airport and blocks the runway, in order to prevent Zelaya from returning to the country.

On July 12, the interim government lifts a curfew that had been in place since the ouster of Zelaya.

On July 24, from the Nicaraguan side of the Honduran border, ousted President Manuel Zelaya calls upon his countrymen to resist the coup-installed government.

Following a week long walk from various parts of the country, an estimated 10,000 Hondurans arrive in Tegucigalpa on August 11 to demonstrate on behalf of ousted President Zelaya.

On August 26, nearly two months after the overthrow of President Manuel Zelaya, the Central American Development Bank freezes Honduran credits at a time when many other multi-lateral agencies and foreign governments placed a hold on Honduran aid projects.

The United States cuts off millions of dollars in aid to Honduras on September 3. In response, Interim Pres. Roberto Micheletti vows that President Zelaya would not return, even though international pressure is mounting.

In Honduras Zelaya sneaks back into the country on September 21 and finds safe haven in the Brazilian embassy to avoid threatened arrest.

Porfirio Lobo (National Party), a conservative rancher, defeats fellow prosperous businessman old guard politicos, Elvin Santos (Liberal Party), in the November 27 presidential elections.

Honduras' president-elect Porfirio Lobo asserts on December 8 that he wants amnesty for ousted President Zelaya and for all of those involved in the June 28 coup that deposed him.

On January 27, Porfirio Lobo is sworn in as the new president of Honduras, ending the many months of political and civil instability.

Lobo provides safe passage to Zelaya, who left his refuge at the Brazilian Embassy and flew to exile in the Dominican Republic.

On January 28, one day after taking office, President Lobo declares Honduran bankruptcy and appeals for international financial assistance to help his nation recover from six months of diplomatic isolation.

2010   On March 4, Secretary of State announces that the United States will soon financial assistance to Honduras and calls upon the Latin American nations to extend diplomatic recognition to the Zelaya administration.

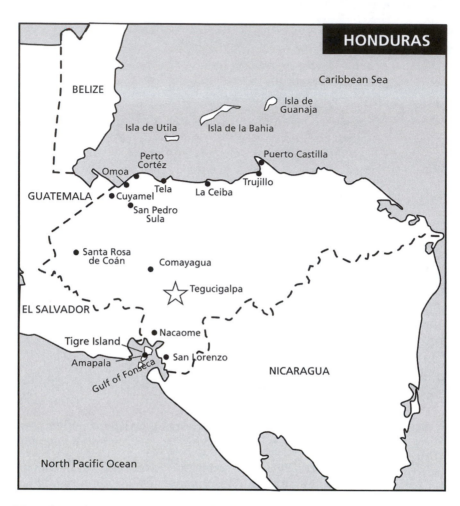

Map of Honduras. (Cartography by Bookcomp, Inc.)

1

Introduction: Understanding Honduras

Totaling 43,277 square miles, Honduras is the second largest country in Central America and approximately the size of the state of Tennessee. It also is one of the poorest nations in the western hemisphere with an extraordinary unequal distribution of wealth. The Honduran economy remains largely underdeveloped with bananas and coffee its major export commodities. In recent years, light industry, particularly in textiles and clothing, has assisted in providing some relief for the unemployed that is officially estimated at 27.9 percent of the 2.5 million person labor force.

GEOGRAPHY

Geography has not been kind to Honduras. A very mountainous country, it is bordered on its north by Guatemala; to the south by Nicaragua, to the southwest by El Salvador, and its entire the Caribbean Sea serves as its eastern border. Honduras touches upon the Pacific Ocean only through the Gulf of Fonseca that shares a border with El Salvador and Nicaragua.

A lingering border dispute with El Salvador is traced to Spanish colonial times when boundaries between the states were not clearly defined. After independence in 1823, the two new nations argued over control of the Gulf of Fonseca (including the islands of *Meanguera* and *El Tigre*) and approximately another 300 square miles of the shared border between Honduras and El Salvador. Although the land conflict dated to the seventeenth century, not until the aftermath of the 1969 Soccer War did the first breakthrough appear. According to the 1980 Treaty of Lima that officially ended the conflict, the governments at Tegucigalpa and San Salvador agreed to submit the border dispute to the International Court of Justice (IJC) sitting at The Hague, Netherlands. On September 11, 1992, the IJC granted control of El Tigre Island to Honduras, Meanguera to El Salvador, approximately 100 square miles of the disputed mainland territory to Honduras, and the reminder to El Salvador. Citizenship of the people living in these territories was to be subsequently determined by a joint commission. The ICJ also ruled that the Gulf of Fonseca is a condominium over which El Salvador, Honduras, and Nicaragua share control. The ruling also provided for a division of control over the Gulf at a future date, should the nations wish to do so. No matter the final outcome, if there is one, the ICJ guaranteed Honduras access to the Pacific Ocean from its mainland enclaves through the Gulf of Fonseca.

Three distinct topographical features characterize the Honduran terrain, an extensive interior highland that comprises approximately 80 percent of the country and two coastal lowlands, one on the Pacific and the other on the Caribbean. The rugged mountain ranges of the interior highlands are difficult to traverse and to cultivate. The soil is poor and, in fact, Honduras lacks the volcanic ash that is found elsewhere throughout Central America that provides for rich and fertile soil. Until the early twentieth century, mining and raising livestock were the primary economic pursuits of the people in the region.

Numerous flat-floor valleys of various sizes are scattered throughout the interior highlands. The vegetation of the valleys supports livestock, and in some instances, commercial agriculture, while subsistence agriculture is pursued by those residing on the mountain slopes. Towns and villages are scattered throughout the valleys, including the nation's capital, Tegucigalpa.

A prominent feature of this region is the depression that stretches from San Pedro Sula in the north, south through Comaguaya, then to the southwest along the Salvadoran border, and into the Gulf of Fonseca. This depression is home to the majority of the Honduran people.

The main street of a rural village located near the town of La Ceiba on the Honduran Caribbean coast. (Thomas M. Leonard Collection.)

The Pacific coastal lowlands occupy a strip of land averaging approximately 16 miles in width on the north shore of the Gulf of Fonseca. Its fine-grained and fertile soil washes down from the mountains that hug the coastline, but the terrain and climate make agriculture nearly impossible. Instead, the Gulf is rich in fish and mollusks, the swampy mangroves along the shoreline are a natural home for shrimp.

The Caribbean lowlands are more popularly known as the North Coast and over time it became the most economically exploited region of Honduras. The central area of the lowlands is east of La Ceiba, is only a few miles wide, but then expands as it goes westward through Tela, San Pedro Sula, and Puerto Cortés to the Guatemalan border. While the latter two cities form the heart of Honduras's industrial and shipping capacity today; historically, the North Coast is known for the production of bananas and other tropical fruits.

The three distinct geographic regions also experience their own climates. The interior highlands have a distinct dry season as is common to all tropical highland locations, but in this region the temperatures decrease as the elevation increases. For example, while Tegucigalpa, which is at an altitude of 3,000 feet above sea level, has an average temperature of 86 degrees Fahrenheit; on a typical April night, at an altitude of 6,000 foot mark in the interior highlands, the

temperature is near zero degrees Fahrenheit. On the Pacific and
Caribbean coastal lowlands year round temperatures average from
82 to 89 degrees Fahrenheit, with a high humidity level. Honduras,
particularly the North Coast, lies within the Caribbean hurricane belt
that contributes significantly to a high annual rain fall count, but
also causes heavy loss of life and physical damage as witnessed by
Hurricanes Francelia in 1969, Fifi in 1974 and Mitch in 1998.

ECONOMY

The economy of Honduras parallels the dichotomy between the
interior mountain ranges and the Caribbean coast. The mining of
silver initially brought the Spanish *conquistadores* to the Honduran
interior. After its independence, foreign companies, North American,
British, and French, slowly took over the abandoned colonial silver
mines. New discoveries in the central valley led to the development
of Tegucigalpa and it becoming the national capital in 1880.
Silver and gold mining reached its peak in the 1880s, accounting for
75 percent of Honduran exports. Thereafter, the amount of ore rapidly
dwindled. Still, silver remained the most valuable export by 1915. By
the 1980s, ore accounted for only 4 percent of the country's exports.
The last large silver mining operation, *El Mochito* west of Lake Yojoa,
closed in 1987. While smaller mines still operate, and prospectors
search abandoned mines and pan the mountain streams, today, the
mining and export of lead and zinc ores have replaced silver in
quantity and value.

The colonial mining experience contributed to the growth of stock
raising, particularly cattle and mules. Beginning in the late 1500s,
cattle *haciendas* occupied the best lands on the grassy floors of the
central valley around Comayagua, Cactamas, and Yoro. Most of these
lands lie infertile today because of overgrazing and misuse. Only
Chuloteca, in the Pacific lowlands, remains as an example of colonial
stock raising. With the introduction of African grasses in the early
twentieth century, cattle and mule grazing shifted to the Caribbean
coast, particularly in the Ulúa and Aguan River valleys. In the 1960s,
meat packing and freezing plants began to appear in various parts of
Honduras. Those in Chuloteca prepared meats for export through the
port of San Lorenzo, and those in San Pedro Sula for shipment through
Puerto Cortés. Despite the growth in the livestock industry, it only
accounts for 8 percent of Honduran exports. In addition, the use of
vast lands for grazing militates against using those lands for the
expansion of food production.

Parts of the Honduran highlands have produced specialty crops since colonial times; the first being tobacco in the Santa Rosa de Copán area. Although cigars produced there earned a good reputation regionally, not until the 1950s did they make their way into the international market, the cigars have been equally well received. Today, Honduran cigars are considered to be a potential export growth industry.

With the introduction of mechanization through the U.S. sponsored Alliance for Progress program in the 1960s, cotton production rapidly expanded, particularly in the Comayagua Valley and Chuloteca area. The initial euphoria over potential growth was doused in the 1970s, as global price for raw cotton plummeted. Thereafter, for the remainder of the twentieth century acreage used for production declined, but still two-thirds of the food production went to the international market. Sugar production traveled the same path. Following a strong uptick in international demand in the 1960s, a decade later a glut of sugar and a change in U.S. sugar import policies prompted this Caribbean lowlands industry to crash.

Today, coffee is the most important cash crop from the Honduran highlands. Salvadoran immigrants introduced the coffee industry to Honduras in the early 1920s after leaving their densely populated homeland. They established small farms of 20 to 30 acres on the mountainous slopes at the lower edge of the cloud cover, where the soil is fertile, and moisture is favorable. After World War II, Honduran coffee made its way into the international market, and by the 1950s, it became the second most important export crop, following bananas.

Until the beginning of the twentieth century, the Caribbean lowlands were disease ridden and sparsely populated with dense forests. Today, their western sectors are home to approximately one-third of the Honduran population and earns about half of the country's export revenue. The commercial banana industry that evolved during the early twentieth century is responsible for the transformation. Initially, North American companies, Cuyamel, Standard, and United, among others, capitalized upon generous concessions offered by the Honduran government. As their giant plantations spread across the North Coast, and the company's control of internal transportation and foreign shipping soon monopolized the industry, the companies extracted further concessions. Until the onset of the Great Depression in 1930s, bananas were the chief Honduran export, but given the concessions, brought little prosperity to the country. The world market collapsed further with World War II, and in the late 1940s, disease wiped out a good portion of the banana plantations. Furthermore, the postwar policies of European nations favored the importation of bananas from their former African and Asian colonies. Beginning in the late 1980s, bananas accounted for approximately 30 percent of all exports.

Some of the Honduran loss in the export of bananas was replaced by coffee, lumber, and increasingly as we come to the present, the growth, processing, and packaging of other tropical fruits such as pineapples and melons, and table vegetables. The new agricultural pursuits also contributed to the expansion or introduction of ancillary industries, including cardboard box making and other containers for shipping.

Across Honduras and especially in the mountain ranges, subsistence farming remains the chief occupation of peasant farmers. This includes the cultivation of food for local consumption. Still using the hoe and machete, the *campesino* harvests maize, beans, sweet manioc, sorghum, and cooking bananas (*plantains*).

In addition to the ancillary food industries, other manufacturing pursuits today include textiles, clothing, chemicals, electronics, and other consumer oriented products and are mostly concentrated in and around Tegucigalpa and San Pedro Sula. With the decline in the banana industry, the banana companies also diversified their operations. Castle and Cook (formerly Standard Fruit) produces soap, cement, and variety of wooden, plastic, and tin containers. United Brands (formerly United Fruit) manufactures rubber, plastics, containers, margarine, and vegetable oil. Because of its proximity to Puerto Cortés and easier access to electric power, today's San Pedro Sula is Honduras's most industrialized city.

PEOPLE

The people of Honduras are largely *mestizo* and are distributed unevenly across the country, most noticeably in the mountainous western and southern highlands. The development of the banana industry brought a large labor force to the Caribbean coast that, today, contains about one-third of the national population. The recent industrialization of San Pedro Sula has grown the city's population to approximately 650,000.

Racially, about 90 percent of Hondurans are *mestizo*, meaning a cross between and/or a descendent of a white/Indian relationship, with a small minority also having black blood. Only 6 percent are considered to be full blooded Indians. Perhaps the blacks and whites comprise 2 percent each of the total population.

A small Garifuna village located along the Honduran North Coast. (Thomas M. Leonard Collection.)

Honduras, save its western portions, rested outside the area of Mesoamerican culture. The scattered pre-Colombian population was largely wiped out by the Spanish. Those who remain today, like the Sumu and Paya river forest people in the northeast, remain outside western culture. Miskito Indians, now often mixed with blacks, live along the Caribbean shore and up the Coco and Patuca Rivers, many as refugees from the 1980s Nicaraguan civil war. Several smaller groups linked to the pre-Colombian Lencas and Mayas dot the interior.

Two distinct black groups live along the Caribbean coast. One consisted of English-speaking descendents of the contract labor brought from Jamaica to work in the banana plantations and today contribute much to the West Indian culture that permeates much of the Caribbean coast. The second group is the Black Caribs, or Garifunas, who migrated out of the Lesser Antilles and now live in small villages and communities along the Caribbean coast.

The Bay Islands that lie off the North Coast of Honduras in the Caribbean Sea are inhabited by an estimated 20,000 people who are a combination of English-speaking whites, blacks, and mulattoes. Their presence can be traced to the 1830s. For those who do not ship with international merchant vessels, work is found in the local fish processing plants or tourist industry.

The Honduran people can be divided into three distinct socioeconomic classes. The elite, or upper class, enjoys privileges and wealth far beyond society's other sectors. Until the arrival of the foreign banana companies in the twentieth century, the elite consisted mostly of large landowners; and to this day, these families still live on the *hacendados* in the country's broad central plain. In addition to economic power, they rivaled among themselves for political power. The elite refused to move into the Caribbean lowlands with the arrival of the banana companies but willingly formed an informal alliance that benefited both and permitted the elite to remain in political power. After World War II, the elite moved into the cotton and cattle export business and, in the process, gained control of lands legally and illegally at the expense of the *compensino* and domestic food production. The elite are not a cohesive group, particularly disagreeing over assistance to the rural poor and unskilled workers.

There is much credence to the argument that the military, as an institution, moved into the elite's ranks after 1954, protecting it and the government from alleged leftist or communist attack. For sure, the military leadership became the government from 1957 to 1982. Today, one can argue that the military ousted President Manuel Zelaya in June 2009 as a protective measure for the upper class.

The middle sector (i.e., the middle class) is not clearly defined by income or occupation. It is an amorphous group that includes small businessmen, white collar workers, skilled labor, professionals, and students who understand the status quo politics of the elite but yet remain largely unorganized to challenge the system.

The poor in Honduras traditionally have lived in rural areas; initially and still today, they live in the mountainous regions along the North Coast, brought there by the banana industry in the early twentieth century. The rural poor and the urban worker account for 80 percent of the Honduran poor, a problem exacerbated by a poor education system. Despite laws requiring children attend school from age 7 to 14, public schools are woefully under funded, under staffed, and under supplied, to say nothing of the technologies needed to meet the requirements of the twenty-first century. Education remains a paid privilege of the upper class.

GOVERNMENT

Government remains the elite's private domain. The 1982 constitution, the nation's 16th since independence in 1823, contains all the proper language regarding separation of executive, legislative, and judicial authority; provisions for the guarantee of civil and human rights; the powers that evolve to the departments (states); and the government's responsibility to provide for the people's welfare. In reality, however, these provisions remain visions of the idealistic rather than ideals to be practiced. In the twentieth century, challenges to political leadership are often explained in constitutional terms, but such statements only conceal the real reasons.

Thus, when the military acted against President Zelaya in June 2009, did it do so to protect the country from his alleged constitutional violations or was it cover for Zelaya's potential threat, real or imagined, to the established order? This *History of Honduras* addresses the two pointed questions and concludes that the latter, not the former, is the reason Zelaya was removed from office.

UNDERSTANDING HONDURAS

History is much more than the recording of facts and figures. It entails an understanding of why events occurred, why political leaders made decisions, and the impact of those decisions on societies. In this sense, we are all products of our past; and as an early twentieth century U.S. philosopher George Santaya observed that, Those who do not learn the lessons of history, are condemned to repeat them. Thus, this volume will place the Honduran experience into the broader framework of Latin American experience, meaning that during sweeping time periods all Latin America shared common characteristics; although their impact often varied widely from country to country.

The first period under consideration focuses upon the Spanish conquest and administration of Honduras and its subsequent break with the colonial government at Madrid, Spain. The Spanish imposition of its centralized government authority, strict adherence to mercantilism, and rigid social structure left indelible marks upon Honduras. Throughout the nearly 320 years of the Spanish colonial period, Honduras remained a distant outpost. Absent of rich metal reserves or other economically profitable primary products to exploit and void of large native American settlements to be converted to Catholicism, few foreign people settled in Honduras; and when they did, it was largely scattered throughout the colony. independence was not a violent experience as in Mexico and Andean South America, the legacies of Spanish rule remained throughout the nineteenth century. Honduran government remained in the hands of landed elites known as *criollos*, people of pure Spanish blood born in the new world; and their descendents squabbled, and often fought, for the right to administer government. There was little difference between these two groups, conservatives and liberals, but they shared the determination to keep the masses, mostly nonwhite *mestizos* from participating in the Honduran political arena.

Toward the end of the nineteenth century, Honduran Liberals came to the political forefront. They accepted the liberal philosophy prevalent in all Latin America at the time. It called for opening the country to foreign investment because Honduras was incapable of financing its own modernization. By investing at the top of the pyramid, the socioeconomic benefits would pass down to the masses. During the same time period, the United States became greatly interested in Central America because of the canal it constructed at Panama. The North Americans concluded that disturbances or foreign threats in this region threatened the U.S. owned and operated canal at Panama. To correct these problems, the United States sought to impose political democracy and financial responsibility upon tumultuous Honduras. While the U.S. owned and operated fruit companies prospered until the onset of the Great Depression in 1930, the U.S. government failed to bring democracy to Honduras. Given scant attention during this time period, however, was the emergence of rural labor as a potential political force.

Tiburcio Carías served as a bridge between the old and new Honduras. Carías preserved the old order and kept the masses in place, often acting as a positivist, rather than implementing social programs on their behalf. Although an ardent pro-Allied supporter for the democratic cause during World War II, Carías maintained order at home as a dictator would, by suppressing his opposition throughout the 16 years of his rule. Within this framework, Carías differed little from other Latin American dictators of his day, particularly those in Central America.

The political protest against the Carías dictatorship at the end of World War II marked the beginning of another change in the Honduran political experience. Whereas analysts correctly attribute the 1944 call for Carías's resignation to the middle sector's desire for a more representative government, the 1954 labor strike and 1968 Soccer War with El Salvador were indicators of the plight of the poor, particularly rural workers. These incidents gave rise to the military as an institution on to itself, rather than serving the oligarchs. Reformers became communists during the Cold War, and there was a need to secure Honduras from the scourge of that ideology.

Finally, at the start of the 1980s, a new wave landed upon Latin America's political-economic shores. First, there was a return to democracy, a confusing term in that how does one define Latin

American democracy? It might be better to suggest that there was a return to civilian government with the military sitting in the shadows, a correct observation for the case of Honduras. The second movement sweeping Latin America starting in the 1980s was the acceptance by governments of the neoliberal or Washington Consensus model. Most simply put, it meant free trade and full legal protections for foreign businesses conducting business operations in any given country. For Third World or developing countries like Honduras it meant increasing the production of its primary products and those for niche markets. As in the late nineteenth century, the benefits would trickle down to the masses. With very few exceptions, this scenario did not play out across Latin America, including Honduras. As this volume suggests, failure of the neoliberal model contributed to the June 28, 2009, *coup d' etat* that deposed President Manuel Zelaya.

In addition to Honduras's internal matters, there remains the factor of external influence or power over the country's domestic economic and political scenes. Whether it was Spanish colonial policy, interference of the United States in the Honduran economic and political arenas during the first generation of the twentieth century, or the post–World War II emphasis upon the real or imagined communist threat, one must consider the impact upon Honduras' maturation process.

Despite the communist threat, real or imagined, Honduran leaders continued to call for socioeconomic reforms, to improve the quality of life for those at the bottom of the social structure. Progress proved minimal, at best. It is easy to assert that the elite has no real interest in reform because it would have to bear the majority of the cost, financially, in political privilege, and social standing, one must also ask if Honduras has the capabilities to lift the nation from its poverty. The country is not rich in natural resources, in fact, in the recent past it appears to be destroying its timber forces. Its primary products are in agriculture that faces stiff global competition. And, although the government claims a high literacy rate for its people, for the most part, the workers are not prepared for the skilled jobs that have emerged in the globalized economy. So, while being confronted with the demands of an ever changing modern world, Honduras is still mired in the political controversies of the past.

2

Indians, Spaniards, and Independence

The Centralists wished to preserve the usages of the colonial system and resisted innovation, every attack upon ... their own prejudice or interests. The Liberals ... cherishing brilliant schemes of reform, aimed at an instantaneous change in popular feelings and customs.[1]

John Lloyd Stephens
U.S. Minister to the United Provinces
April, 1839

During his fourth and final voyage to the New World in 1502, Christopher Columbus briefly stopped at the island of Bonacoa (then known as Guanaja) on July 30 in the present day Bay Islands off the Caribbean Coast of Honduras. There he encountered a large seagoing canoe similar to those he had seen on his second and third voyages from 1493 to 1496 and from 1498 to 1500 when he discovered Dominica, Guadeloupe, Jamaica, and Trinidad. The canoe was as long as a galley made of a single tree trunk and eight-feet wide. In addition to merchandise from

the areas around Cuba, the canoe held several women and children and
25 paddlers. In addition to the apparent wealth, the canoe contained
embroidered and decorative cloth, sleeveless shirts, flint knives, and a
copper melting pot. Columbus sailed on to the Central American mainland, stopping first Point Caxinas where he encountered similar people
and then south to Cape *Gracios á Dios* whose inhabitants were "almost
black in color." At present day Trujillo, Columbus reportedly named
the entire territory Honduras for the deep waters off its coast, a report
challenged by subsequent scholarship. Despite the discovery of new
people and possible wealth, Columbus pressed on, unsuccessfully, in
hopes of establishing a colony at Panama and a transisthmian route to
the Pacific Ocean. The legacy of Columbus's fourth voyage remains with
his son Fernando's cultural and geographic descriptions of the then
virtually unknown Honduran Caribbean coast.

INDIGENOUS PEOPLES

Although the figures cannot be verified, when Columbus departed
for Panama in September 1502, he unknowingly left behind an
estimated 500,000 to 2 million indigenous inhabitants who were divided
into several distinct groups that represented a wide range of cultural
and linguistic backgrounds. While these groups traded and often
fought among themselves, they also had exchanges with other native
groups as far south as Panama and as far north as Mexico; yet on the
eve of Spanish conquest, no large cities remained active. The most
notable and advanced group were the Mayans whose roots could be
traced to Mexico's Yucatán peninsula and to Guatemala's Petén region
during the preclassic period from about 2000 B.C. to 250 A.D. The
Mayans reached the apex of their development during the classic
period from about 250 A.D. to approximately 900 A.D. and continued
their existence until the arrival of the Spanish. At the height of the
Mayan civilization, cities were densely populated; and they produced
one of the world's most culturally advanced societies.

Beginning in the fifth century A.D., Mayans spread into Honduras's
Río Montagua Valley where they constructed the ceremonial center of
Copán near the present day city of Santa Rosa de Copán and near
the Guatemalan Mayan site, Quirigua. During the next three and
one-half centuries Copán developed into a major cultural center and
the leading regional center for art and astronomical studies at which
the Mayans were quite advanced. The portrait stelae placed along the
processional paths in the city's central plaza, the adjoining acropolis
and other buildings are filled with stonecraft that is among the finest

Stela 3 was erected by Chan Imix K'awii or Smoke Imix, who ruled over Copan from 628 to 695 A.D. The stela is located in the Copan Valley and is part of the Principal Mayan Group for the Period. (Thomas M. Leonard Collection.)

surviving in all Mesoamerica. Like most other Mayan sites, Copán included a large ball court, the second largest found in Central America. At its peak in the late classic period, a prosperous class of nobility, scribes, and artisans were among Copán's 30,000 inhabitants as evidenced by the number of cut stone residences. Copán also contained one of the longest Mayan hieroglyphic inscriptions (1,500 to 2,000 glyphs) ever discovered and can still be seen today. Copán's agricultural and cloth goods spread into southern and eastern Honduras and northeast to the Yucatán and north into central Mexico.

Copán descended into ruin after 822 A.D., the last dated hieroglyph. The lack of data prevents supporting firm conclusions about the civilization's decline. Among the many suggestions given for Copán's collapse are agricultural disasters that include soil depletion, overuse of land, and climatic changes; unsustainable population growth; and foreign invasions and internal warfare. While high priests and rulers responsible for the art, astronomy, mathematics, and hieroglyphs vanished, much of the Mayan lower class remained in the area but did not retain the meanings of the inscriptions or the reasons for the city's collapse. The city's population dwindled from approximately 20,000 people in the fifth century to less than 5,000 in 900 A.D.

During the time of the Spanish conquest of Honduras, Copán was long covered by rainforests while colonials learned of the site. Diego García de Palacio came upon Copán in 1570, but the site remained unknown to the outside world until the early nineteenth century. Guatemalan Juan Galindo's description of the ruins appeared in 1835, and it sparked the interest of subsequent U.S. Minister to Central America and amateur archaeologist John Lloyd Stephens and his British sketch artist, Frederick Catherwood,to visit Copán during their 1839–1840 trips to Guatemala, Honduras, and Mexico's Yucatán Peninsula. Stephen's and Catherwood's two volume study, *Incidents of Travel to Central America, Chiapas and Yucatán*, marked the beginning of Mayan studies by modern American and European scholars.

Between 1891 and 1900, Harvard University's Peabody Museum of Archaeology and Ethnology conducted surveys and excavations of Copán, the first in modern history. In 1934, Sylvanus G. Morley struck a deal with the Honduran government that provided the Carnegie Institution in Washington one half of the artifacts discovered at Copán in exchange for Peabody's excavations and restorations conducted periodically through the early 1970s. Thereafter, the government of Honduras sponsored *Projecto Copán* to continue the Peabody's work. Today, a national museum within the park site houses an excellent collection of artifacts uncovered at Copán. In 1980, the United Nations Educational, Scientific, and Cultural Organization (UNESCO) designated Copán as a World Heritage Site.

The emphasis placed upon the Mayan site at Copán overshadowed the fact that numerous other indigenous groups also resided within the boundaries of contemporary Honduras. Many of these peoples came from Mexico, including the Toltecs, who migrated into western and southern Honduras. Among the most notable groups were the Toltec-speaking Chorotega, who established themselves near the present day Honduran city of Chuloteca, approximately 35 miles east of the Gulf of Fonseca. Maize was the staple crop of their agricultural society, augmented by beans, squash, and cactus fruits. Legend attributes the Toltec decline to civil conflict., The Nahua-speaking Pipil, whose language related to the Aztec tongue, migrated into present day El Salvador in the late seventh century, then eastward into the Copan area of Honduras, on to the Caribbean coast, and south along the Gulf of Fonseca in the southwest of Honduras. The Pipil successfully challenged the Spanish conquest until defeated in

June 1525. Today, an estimated 2,700 Pipiles reside outside the public limelight in southwestern El Salvador and Honduras.

The area east of Trujillo was occupied by the Pech, the Miskito and the Sumu Indians. The Pech, identified in the historical literature as the Paya before the 1980s, inhabited all of the Honduran Atlantic coastal area from Aguán River to the Cabo de Gracias a Dios. During the colonial period, the Spanish pushed the Pech inland, forcing many into religiously controlled communities. In 1805, on the eve of independence, the Black Caribs, or Garifuna, forced the Pech from their last waterfront community at the mouth of the Aguán River. Today, an estimated 2,500 Pech remain in Olancho Province.

The Miskito Indians date to the late seventeenth century when a group of indigenous peoples integrated with freed or escaped African slaves at the mouth of Río Coco River that forms the Honduran-Nicaraguan border. With time's passage, the Miskito expanded as far south as the San Juan River in Nicaragua and north along the Honduran coast to Puerto Lempira. While trading with the British and Caribbean pirates, the Miskitos always resisted Spanish authority, a resistance that carried over to Nicaragua following Central America's independence in 1821. The Sumu were the second largest indigenous group along the Mosquito Coast of Honduras and Nicaragua. As the Miskito Indians expanded inland during the seventeenth century, they demanded tribute from the Sumus and often captured and enslaved them. The Sumu continually moved inland so that by the mid-nineteenth century they resided in isolated villages along rivers in the Honduran rainforest. An estimated 1,000 Sumu remain in Honduras today.

Two other indigenous groups of note existed in Honduras before the Spanish conquest, the Lencas and the Jicaque (Xicaque). The Lencas reportedly came from Colombia but whose language shows little relationship to other indigenous groups. They settled in west-central and southern Honduras. Spanish colonial reports refer to the Lencas as a community, but the generalization of the term as a cultural, language, and ethnic group is attributed to U.S. journalist, diplomat, and amateur archaeologist Ephraim G. Squier who traveled throughout Honduras in the 1850s. Originally residing in small fortified towns, the Lencas fell victim to the Spanish *repartimiento* labor system when they were converted to Catholicism and otherwise hispanisized. After independence, small communities of Lencas again appeared in the mountainous and rural areas of Honduras. The Jicaque, whose language roots are the subject of scholarly debate and with whom Columbus reportedly made initial contact with in 1502, was spoken by the Indians residing along the northwest coast of Honduras and as far south as the Olancho Valley. Their culture is similar to that of the Sumo and Miskito. The Jicaques lost their lands at the beginning of the nineteenth century when the Spanish made settlement grants on the Atlantic coast to the Black Caribs and again in the early twentieth century to the U.S. banana companies. Today approximately 19,000 Jicaques live in Yoro Department, but only two groups, totaling some 400 people, living in Montaña de la Flor, retain the original language and culture.

Among the other remains of pre-Colombian societies that archaeologists have examined are located in the Aguan, Naco, and Comayagua Valleys, around Lake Yojoa and sites now located beneath the Cajon Dam.

The Spanish Conquest of Honduras

For two decades following Columbus's 1502 voyage that touched upon the Honduran Caribbean coast, there was little exploration of that region. At that time, more important to the Spanish were the large and organized Native American societies and their vast wealth in Mexico and Peru. Hernán Cortéz departed Cuba for Mexico in February 1519. From his landing at today's Veracruz on Mexico's Caribbean coast, it took Cortés two years before overtaking the Aztec Empire because its ruler Montezuma was stoned to death by his own people at Tenochtitlan on July 1, 1520. Six years earlier, in 1513, Vasco Nuñez de Balboa crossed the isthmus at Panama, becoming the first European to cast eyes upon the Pacific Ocean from the Americas. Nineteen years later, in 1533, Juan Pizarro defeated the Chief of the Inca Empire, Atahualpa at the Andean city of Cajamarca. The vast parameters of Spain's New World empire were outlined. Honduras became an outpost in this vast land expanse.

In 1508 Spanish navigators Juan Díaz de Solís and Vicente Yáñez Pinzón apparently touched upon Honduras during their explorations along the Caribbean coast, but their interests took them to the north. During the second decade of the sixteenth century expeditions from Cuba and Hispaniola reportedly encountered people on the *Islas de la Bahía*. Spain's interest in Honduras deepened after Gil González Dávila's 1523 expedition discovered the Gulf of Fonseca on Central America's Pacific coast and today borders the countries of Honduras, El Salvador, and Nicaragua. A year later, four separate expeditions commenced the conquest of Honduras. In 1524, two rival expeditions began. González Dávila and Cristóbal Olida each sought to carve out a piece of territory for his own rule. In 1524, clashes between the two military groups prompted Hernan Cortéz to dispatch troops under the command of Francisco de Las Casas to suppress the rival commanders ambitions, but subsequently, Cortéz himself marched south with approximately 3,000 troops to restore his own authority. The situation within Honduras became more complicated with two additional expeditions, one led by Pedro de Alvarado from Guatemala and the other by Hernando de Soto from Nicaragua.

Olida seized the initiative with the capture of Dávila and Las Casas, but they quickly turned the tables of fortune. Dissidents within the Olida's army switched their loyalty to the two captors, who then captured Olida and executed him. Although subsequently condemned for their actions by a Mexico court, neither Dávila nor Las Casas were punished for their crime. Cortéz arrived in Honduras in 1525, quickly reestablished order, and imposed his own authority over the rival Spanish factions and some indigenous groups. Cortéz established the coastal town of Trujillo and from there proclaimed his authority over the colony of Honduras without knowing its size. Cortéz, however, did not meet much success in establishing other communities. After proclaiming his mission a success and naming his cousin Hernando de Saavadra governor of the colony, Cortéz returned to Mexico on April 26, 1526. Saavadra quickly established the department of Olancho and the township of Frontera de Caceras, but his efforts reignited strife among the Spanish rival groups.

On August 30, 1526, the *audiencia* (court of justice) appointed Diego López de Salcedo the first royal governor of Honduras and ordered all other Spanish adventurers to leave the territory. But the volatility continued. López's harsh policies drove the indigenous groups, previously pacified by Cortéz, into open revolt. López suffered further humiliation in 1528 during an attempt to extend his authority over Nicaragua. After his release from a Nicaraguan prison, López returned to Honduras in 1529. He died the following year. By 1534, the colony stood on the verge of collapse owing to the renewed fighting between the Spaniards and widespread indigenous resistance and revolts, accompanied by the decimation of the Indian population through disease, mistreatment, and their exportation in large numbers to the Caribbean Island sugar plantations.

At this point, the Spanish authorities divided the region into two provinces: Honduras-Higueras with the latter encompassing the western portion of the province. Attracted by the prospects of gold and to keep Higueres from being abandoned, Pedro de Alvarado, accompanied by native Guatemalans, entered the depressed province in 1536. Alvarado soon established a profitable gold and silver mining business that contributed to the need for a labor force that translated into the further exploitation of the indigenous population. The Native Americans increased their resistance to enforced labor until a significant uprising in 1537 led by young Lenca chieftain known as Lempira, whose name and image grace today's Honduran currency. Higueres was soon aflame in revolt as Lempira's success encouraged other Indian groups to rise up and rally behind Lempira in his battle against the Spanish authorities. From his fortification atop *Peñol de Cerquín*, Lempira successfully resisted all Spanish attacks upon his fortress for six months while his troops burned Comagaya, forcing its inhabitants to flee to Gracias that came under threatened attack, along with the towns Puerto Caballos (today known as Puerto Córtez) and Trujillo. Finally, in 1538 Spanish authorities lured Lempira into peace negotiations, designed as a cover for the Indian leader's assassination. The resistance movement rapidly disintegrated following Lempira's death. It also accelerated the decimation of the Native American population under Spanish control, which in 1539, stood at an estimated 15,000 people. Two years later, approximately 5,000 remained. Honduras was now under Spanish control, although no more than 200 Spaniards resided in all Honduras, and only an estimated 50 settlers resided in the largest community, Trujillo.

SPANISH COLONIAL ADMINISTRATION

Spanish political jurisdiction over Central America, including Honduras, developed slowly. Unaware of the vastness and the complexity of their New World discoveries, authorities in Madrid introduced governmental institutions as the colonies developed. Initially, a Vice Royalty was established over a large portion of territory, the first being the Vice Royalty of New Spain. It included all of Mexico north of Chiapas to the northern interior provinces: an undefined Central America, the Caribbean, and the Philippines. In reality, the Viceroy's authority was limited to Mexico, in the three outlying regions, political power rested with local authorities. Rivalries among the spokesmen for authority in each of these places contributed significantly to the early political turmoil throughout Central America, particularly in Honduras and Nicaragua. Their personal rivalries coupled with geographic and transportation barriers slowed regional unification efforts in the sixteenth century. As a result, several independent centers of political power emerged: Santiago de Guatemala; Ciudad Real, Chiapas; Comaguaya, Honduras; León and Granada, Nicaragua; and Panama City and resulted in decentralization that drifted downwards to the town councils (*ayuntamientos*). By 1530, the provinces of Chiapas, Guatemala, Honduras, Nicaragua, and Panama acted independent of each other, and the municipalities within distanced themselves from the provincial central government. Spanish administrators in Madrid recognized that the appointed governors such as Pedro Alvarado in Guatemala, Pedro Arías Avila in Nicaragua and Panama, and Diego López de Salcedo in Honduras became powerful and personalistic dictators whose claim to rule rested with their conquests and contributed to their independence from Spanish authority. To correct this mistake, a 1542 law established an *audiencia* that stretched from Mexico's Yucatán Peninsula to Panama with its capital at Gracías a Dios in western Honduras where Pedro Alvarado's discovered gold. There, a tribunal consisting of an appointed president and three judges were to administer the vast Central American territory. Administrative authority was transferred to Antigua, Guatemala, in 1548; and from then until 1570, administrative authority over Honduras passed between Panama and Guatemala as governors consistently faced charges of graft and corruption. Finally, on May 23, 1572, Diego de Herrera arrived at Trujillo and from there to San Pedro Sula to assume his place as governor and *alcalde mayor* of Honduras. Still, the move to Antigua reaffirmed the subordination of Honduras as a province within the *Audiencia*/Captaincy General of Guatemala until Central America's independence in 1821.

The *audiencia* consisted of a president and usually three judges appointed by the Spanish government and responsible to the Viceroy in Mexico City. The *Audiencia* of Guatemala, subsequently known as the Kingdom of Guatemala comprised the five nations of Central America–Costa Rica, El Salvador, Guatemala, Honduras, and Nicaragua–then known as *provincias*. An appointed *gobernadore*, again a Spaniard, was charged with overseeing the implementation of Spanish regulations within the province and with representing the colonists to the *Audiencia* de Guatemala. A *cabildo or ayuntamiento* (town council) graced each Spanish speaking community. Composed of landowners from the surrounding area, the *cabildo*, implemented the laws passed down from above and legislated the few laws that applied to the local community. Until the eighteenth century Bourbon reforms, the *cabildo* provided the only opportunity for the local landed elite to participate in government. The Spanish crown also appointed a *corregidor* to each community: a *corregidor de los españoles* for the Spanish cities and townships and a *corregidor de los indios* for all Indian settlements. The *corregidor* served as an overseer to insure that Spanish laws were implemented and that taxes were properly assessed and collected for the crown.

Spanish law clearly prevented its New World authorities,from the rank of viceroy down to *corregidor*, from being residents of their area of responsibility or to engage in local economic activity. Given the distance from Spain to Mexico City thence to Guatemala City and on to Honduras and its outlying communities, coupled with transportation difficulties between each central city, the strict control that Spain envisioned over its New World colonies failed to materialize. Instead, bribes kept authorities from imposing all laws as written, justices paid to make the correct rulings, and taxes avoided, all to the benefit of local landed elite and the few merchants. By the time the War of Spanish Succession ended with the Peace of Utrecht in 1714, Spain's New World Empire was void of effective government and near financial bankruptcy.

The Roman Catholic Church, an integral part Spain's government and society, was planted in the New World. In the Spanish conquest of the New World, a cleric of a religious order accompanied the *conquistador*. This was done when Columbus landed at Trujillo in 1502, causing many analysts to claim this to be the first bishopric of Honduras. Others fix the date at 1524 with the establishment of modern Trujillo. There it remained until its transfer to Comayagua in

The Church of Dolores, also known as the Church of Pain, is a structure of baroque architecture that dates to 1732 and anchors Tegucigalpa's central park. It served as the center of Catholicism in Spanish colonial Honduras. (Thomas M. Leonard Collection.)

1560 and remained there throughout the colonial period. The bishop reported to and accepted the authority of the Archbishop in Mexico City. Two types of clergy came to the New World: regular and secular. The regular clergy included all priests, friars, and monks who were members of religious orders. The secular clergy consisted of clerics and priests who administered the daily affairs of parish life and fell under the administrative control of the Spanish monarchy. Because they lived out in the world, the term secular came to apply. Pope Adrian VI granted the religious orders all powers necessary to convert the indigenous to Catholicism; and in Central America, including Honduras, this practice fell largely to the Dominicans, Franciscans, and to a lesser degree, the Jesuits.

The clergy moved quickly to establish parishes, convents, and missionary centers for the conversion of the indigenous to Catholicism and to minister the needs of Spanish residents. The clergy became the protector of human rights for the indigenous and, over time, assumed responsibility for education and medical care. However, not all was harmonious between the various orders. Continuous territorial disputes further embittered the relationship between the Dominicans and Franciscans. The regular clergy received a salary from the Spanish government. Despite the steady income, these clergy became jealous of the secular priests who 'relied upon the donations of their parishioners and for ministering the sacraments of the church such as baptism, confirmation, and marriage. The income for the latter quickly outpaced that of the former. As an institution the church also became a banker and with time's passage, a wealthy banker. Free from the crown's oppressive taxing system the Church accumulated sufficient funds to become a lending agency, particularly to the Spanish and *criollo* elite. Long term loans, at high interest rates, enhanced the church's wealth. The church demanded land as collateral for loans. The church could seize the land for nonpayment of the loan or inherit the property upon the borrower's death. These properties were either sold at higher prices than the loan value or rented. Either way, the church's coffers continued to fill, causing consternation among the Spanish and *criollo* residents of the colony. Much of the wealth went for the construction of new churches, convents, monasteries, and charitable institutions. Despite Honduras being the poorest of the provinces in the Kingdom of Guatemala, these funds contributed to the construction of 145 religious buildings on the eve of Honduran independence in 1800. During the 152 years from the establishment of the *Audiencia de Guatemala* in 1548 until 1700, when the French Bourbons ascended to the Spanish throne, Honduras steadily declined in importance to the Spanish colonial economic system, built around the principles of mercantilism that dictated colonies existed solely for the benefit of the mother country.

The initial mining centers were located around the town of Gracias near the Guatemalan border. As these mines petered out in the early 1540s, they were replaced in importance by those located to the east in the Guayape River Valley where both gold and silver were found. The new found wealth gave rise to Comayagua and decline of Gracias as the focal point of Honduran life. The concomitant demand for increased labor led to increased conflicts with Indians that contributed to the decimation of Native Americans and led to the importation of African slaves. By 1545, an estimated 2,000 slaves lived in Central Honduras. Subsequent gold deposits were found near San Pedro Sula and the port of Trujillo, but neither sight contributed significant wealth to the colony.

Beginning in 1569, new silver strikes in the interior briefly revived the economy and led to the founding of the town of Tegucigalpa, which soon rivaled Comayagua as the most important town in the province. The city's growth prompted King Phillip II to appoint Juan de la Cueva the first Alcalde Mayor of Tegucigalpa with instructions to report directly to the audiencia at Guatemala City. The immediate effect was to divide the country politically.

The silver boom peaked in 1584 but declined markedly thereafter, contributing to another provincial economic depression. Several problems hampered the Honduran mining industry: the lack of capital investment funds, the shortage of a consistent and large labor base, and the location of mines in difficult terrain where one often found a limited size of the gold and silver deposits. Added to these realities was the Spanish government regulations and incompetence. For example, mercury, vital to the production of silver, was constantly in short supply; and at least on one occasion an entire year's supply was lost through the negligence of officials. Other economic pursuits of sixteenth century Honduras included cattle raising for local consumption; cultivating sarsaparilla used for medicinal purposes; and indigo, a dyewood that made its way into the European markets. By 1700 Honduras stood as a poor and neglected backwater in the Spanish colonial empire with a scattered population of mestizos, native people, blacks, and a handful of Spanish rulers and landowners.

The Spanish *conquistadores* did not intend to perform the backbreaking labor necessary for mining and agriculture. Immediately, they turned to the Native Americans and exploited Indian labor through the Crown's *encomienda* system. Beginning in 1503, the Crown granted *encomiendas* to the *conquistadores*, their soldiers, and other officials. As the Spanish population in the New World expanded over time, many became *encomenderos*, who were responsible for the conversion to Catholicism and the labor and welfare of the Indians residing within a specified territory. The *encomendero* became more concerned with extracting labor than with the conversion and welfare of his charges. The system proved brutal for the workers, and as early as 1510, clergy began protesting to the Crown about the cruel treatment of the Indians. The Dominican priest Bartolome de las Casas dedicated his life to correcting the Indian abuse. The Laws of Burgos in 1512 and 1513 and the New Laws promulgated in 1542 were designed to protect the human rights of the Indians. Although the laws failed to achieve their objectives, the *encomienda* became less used. It was replaced by the *repartimiento* by which a Spanish *conquistador*, government official, or New World Spanish citizen received the right to supervise the work of the indigenous worker in mining, farming, and public works, but like the *encomienda*, work conditions and worker's treatment were harsh. Indigenous communities provided 2–4 percent of their population for this purpose. As the Honduran mines became exhausted by the late 1500s, the Spanish and their *criollo* descendents turned to agriculture. The *haciendas*, large estates with a lot of land, replaced the *encomienda* and provided the indigenous the opportunity to work for a wage and housing. But again, the wages were poor, living conditions at the subsistence level, and the laborer at the mercy of the *hacendado*. Survivors of this system comprised the Honduran lower class.

The Spaniards initially envisioned Trujillo to be the port city from which Spanish vessels would bring the Honduran gold, silver, and other products back to the mother country. However, Trujillo's inaccessibility to the interior provinces and the inability to defend the city from pirate attacks prompted the Spanish to look elsewhere. Hernán Cortes explored the Honduran north coast in 1524; and 12 years later, Pedro de Alvarado founded the town of *Puerto de Caballos* (Port of Horses) on the southern shore of the body of water known as the Laguna de Alvarado. By 1536, Omoa remained a small *pueblo de indios* a part of a *repartimiento* that included the nearby Indian town of Chachaguala. By the 1580s, Omoa was no longer a viable village.

In 1752, Omoa was revived and became a functioning town with government buildings, a church, a hospital, military barracks, and warehouses. The Spanish constructed the fortress at Omoa between 1756 and 1779 to protect the Central American coast from pirates and to serve as the embarkation point for shipping to Spain the silver cargos that originated in San Miguel and Tegucigalpa. Ironically, the fort's construction ended after the pirate threat had ended. At the end of the eighteenth century, Omoa had a diverse population that included Spanish, Indians, enslaved Africans, mulattos, and free blacks.

Omoa remained Honduras's most important port until after independence in the early nineteenth century. Owing to the growth of the banana industry that dominated the Honduran north coast enterprises in the 1880s, Puerto Córtéz emerged as the country's primary port, and nearby San Pedro Sula as the nation's chief commercial center. Today Omoa is a small fishing village dwarfed by the fortress, now a national museum.

In the late sixteenth century and continuing through the early nineteenth century, Dutch, French and, particularly English pirates, or corsairs, sailed the Honduran Caribbean coast with the intention to intercept ships carrying gold, silver, and other materials back to Spain. The more aggressive British established a footing along Roatán's northern coast. In 1600, Spanish authorities estimated that approximately 5,000 British pirates lived on the island of Roatán. which served as a major launching point upon Spanish commercial vessels.

Mahogany and other hardwoods initially attracted the British to Honduran coastal regions soon spread inland and developed into a thriving industry. In addition to lumbering, many of the rural villages engaged in trading and the production of pitch. Among the major British settlements established during the colonial period included those at Gracías a Dios and at the mouth of the Río Sico on the southeastern Caribbean coast. The British presence ended with the 1786 Anglo-Spanish Convention that provided for the recognition of Spanish sovereignty over the Caribbean coast. Still, on the eve of Honduran independence in 1800, an estimated 4,000 people resided in the Río Sico area.

Significant changes came to Spanish America following the conclusion of The War of Spanish Succession (1701–1714) that secured the French Bourbons on the throne in Madrid for the next century. Philip V and his successors, Carlos III and Carlos IV, introduced reforms designed to tighten political control in order to provide more efficient government administration and to insure that all appropriate tax revenues were collected in the vast New World empire that included Honduras. Most of the changes that affected Honduras came in the latter part of the eighteenth century.

The most notable political change was the appointment of an *intendente* placed in charge of an administrative unit called an *intendencia*, which could include one or more provinces. In 1786, an *intendente* was appointed to Comayagua and two years later, in 1788, the territories of Comayagua and Tegucigalpa were combined under the directorship of a singular *intendente*, testimony to the sparse population and economic unimportance of the region.

The *intendente* came to the New World to insure the applications of all colonial laws at the expense of the viceroy and the *audiencia* president/captain-general. Within his geographical domain the *Intendentes* replaced the *corregidores*, and he oversaw the local treasury, the collection of taxes, and promoted agricultural and other economic activities. With fiscal powers that gave them a say in almost all administrative, ecclesiastical and military, *intendentes* were conceived by the Bourbon kings to be a check on other local officials, who in the past couple of centuries had come to gain their position through the sale of offices or inheritance.

The Bourbons liberalization of trade had little impact upon underdeveloped Honduras. In 1717, the Crown began dismantling the Seville-Cádiz trade monopoly with the New World. In its place individual trading companies were established designed to increase trade between Spain and the colonies. Furthermore, the Free Trade Act of 1778 opened New World ports to inter-colonial trade and, in effect, was to reduce Central America's commercial dependency upon Mexico. Other Bourbon economic reforms established state monopolies on liquor and tobacco to control consumption, to keep it out of contraband trade, and to insure tax collections. With the lowering of export taxes, planters were encouraged to increase and to diversity their crop production.

While these reforms are credited with increasing the amount of trade through the Bay of Honduras, they had little impact upon Honduras, owing to the smallness of its market size that could not consume large quantities of imports and had limited materials to export; but the policy changes contributed to road building projects that connected the Honduran north coast with its interior.

By the beginning of the eighteenth century, Church presence came to symbolize the wealth, influence, and prestige of the institution. Throughout the Kingdom of Guatemala, the Dominicans held the largest estates and were assumed to be the richest order. The Franciscans, the Augustinians, and the Mercidians followed. The Jesuits, holding large estates elsewhere throughout the Spanish New World, were less conspicuous in Central America. The Bourbons set out to check clerical, particular the regular clergy, influence over society during the first half of the eighteenth century. The first decrees limited the construction of new monasteries, seminaries, and convents and directed the orders not to accept novices until they reached adulthood. The Crown also eliminated or drastically decreased taxes and other levies used to support the Church, particularly in Indian villages. The most damning anticlerical measure was the expulsion of the Jesuits from the New World in 1767.

The Bourbons also introduced other reforms that had little or no success. For example, in response to a smallpox epidemic in 1780, the Spanish government directed the implementation of a vaccination program that met with partial success at the time. There is little evidence that the Crown's 1799 directive that all communities of more than 100 residents construct elementary schools at tax payers' expense was ever implemented in Honduras.

Guatemala received Central America's first printing press in 1660, but like those in Mexico City, Puebla, and Lima, ecclesiastical printings accounted for most of its publications until the end of the eighteenth century. Still, through the elite's travels abroad or via Spanish translations, key works of The Enlightenment's critical thinkers made their way to Central America, including the writings of Rousseau, Smith, and Voltaire.

The Road to Independence

When the French dictator Napoleon I placed his brother Joseph in the chair of the Spanish monarchy in 1808, he unexpectedly set in motion a chain of events in Spanish America that led to its independence from Madrid by 1826, save Cuba and Puerto Rico. In Seville, Spain, a Liberal junta was formed to declare its support for the deposed Ferdinand VII, an act followed by some in Spanish America, notably Buenos Aires. Following the restoration of Ferdinand VII to the Spanish crown in 1815, much of the New World's privileged *criollo* citizenry were not anxious to return to Spanish authority. While the path to independence took a different path in each of the colonies, Buenos Aires again set the example. On the southern fringe of Spain's New World Empire, the Rio de Plata region quickly acclimated to self-rule after 1808; and following the restoration of Ferdinand VII, an 1816 congress, representing the provinces of Rio de Plata, convened in Buenos Aires where it declared its independence from Spain. The pattern was set and soon played out elsewhere in Spanish America. By 1826, all but Cuba and Puerto Rico became independent nations.

The Central Americans, including Honduras, did not fight for their independence, but they quarreled about its path. Three issues, all an outgrowth of the colonial experience, characterized the argument. First, there was the question of equal political rights for the *criollos* at the expense of the governing *peninsulares*. Next, came the question about the relationship between the individual states and the central authorities in Guatemala City and finally the question of any relationship to Mexico. The final issue was of church-state relations. The debate over these issues became the framework for subsequent political parties.

The Honduran path to independence evolved slowly, and not everyone joined in. For example, on the eve of the nineteenth century, a good number of Hondurans remained loyal to Spain. On December 23, 1796, when news of Spain's declaration of war on Great Britain reached Comayagua the whole colony mobilized to protect the coasts from a British invasion. Arms and soldiers were sent to Trujillo where the defenders repelled the British. Again in 1808, when Napoleon I deposed Spanish King Ferdinand VII, there was significant sentiment for remaining loyal to the king and to his restoration in December 1813. The Hondurans stood on the sidelines, respectively, in November and December 1811, when uprisings in El Salvador and Nicaragua stood as the first abortive attempts in Central America to break from Spain. Reflecting the same attitude, when the king decided on March 7, 1820, to re-invoke the constitution of 1812, the governmental leaders in Honduras gave their support.

Despite loyalty to the Spanish crown, not all Hondurans were satisfied with their colonial status. Although absent a printing press, materials from Guatemala made their way to Comayagua and Tegucigalpa and exposed the communities to discussions about free trade, representative government, the U.S. and French revolutions, and eventually some news of the insurrections elsewhere in Latin America. On June 18, 1797, the government asked the king for complete separation from Guatemala and called for the creation of Honduras as a semi-*audiencia*. At the same time, many Honduran intellectuals went beyond this to envision complete independence from Spain. The first Honduran public demonstration against Spanish authority came on January 1, 1812, in Tegucigalpa in response to the Spanish effort to prevent the spread of revolutionary ideas by insuring the continuance in office of Spanish officials. Around 100 men, armed with knives and clubs, gathered from the city districts of La Plazuela, San Sebastían, and Comayagüella to prevent this policy from taking effect. Father Cura D. Juan Francisco Márquez intervened and persuaded the municipal council from resorting to armed repression. The demonstration indicated two important popular trends: (1) the desire for independence or semi-autonomy from Spanish authoritarianism and (2) the unacceptability of special privileges granted to Spaniards over Hondurans. In response, the municipal council voted not to elect any more Spaniards to the *alcaldías* and for 1812 named Hondurans to these positions.

In 1814, shortly after King Ferdinand VII's restoration, Spanish authorities squelched an antigovernment uprising in Guatemala City but not before it spread to Tegucigalpa where a parish priest led a group of *criollo* residents, armed with machetes and sticks, in a march to the city plaza where they demanded greater participation in government. After refusing to consider the demand, the governor ordered the military to suppress the protestors. Although considered a minor event in the scope of colonial administration, the protest illustrated the conflict between *peninsulares* and *criollos*. As with the Mexican clergymen Hidalgo and Morales, the parish priest better understood the plight of the disenfranchised. In Mexico that meant Indians and *mestizos*, in Indian-barren Honduras, it was the *criollo*.

Criollo political protest also applied to the special privileges of the Catholic Church and the church's officials. The Church's administrative clergy did not support any political change that might threaten theirs or the institution's special privileges: freedom from taxation; special courts, extensive landholdings, control of education and other social institutions. Like the political protests and protesters, the government at Guatemala City ordered that these protestors be abruptly and brutally silenced. Guatemala Governor José D. Bustamante's assertions that the political protestors intended to behead priests, rape nuns, and desecrate altars was soon repeated by the archbishop and regional bishops. Officials called for their imprisonment and deportation. Such actions failed to achieve the objective. Coupled with the Inquisition's restoration in the Kingdom of Guatemala in 1817, the allegations against the reformers only encouraged continued and intensified the anticlerical backlash across the region. Central America's Declaration of Independence on September 15, 1821, contained anticlerical rhetoric that called for the stripping of all archbishops and bishops of their titles and the use of the word padre when referring to all male clerics.

The immediate impetus for Honduran independence came on March 1, 1820 when Augustín de Iturbide was declared ruler of Mexico, and he announced the Plan of Iguala, a rather vague document that planned to make Mexico City the center of New World power and bring Ferdinand VII or another member of the royal family to preside over it. Roman Catholicism would be the official religion. Mexico's action prompted the convening of a congress of Central American *criollos* who declared their independence from Spain, effective on September 15 of that year.

Although the September 15, 1821, declaration did little more than announce Central America's independence from Spain, it did ignite arguments within the five Central American states that reflected the legacies of its colonial status. The debates within Honduras mirrored those across the isthmus. For example, the *criollos*, who had been long jealous of the special privileges granted to the *peninsulares*, wanted to insure their own position in political power at the expense of the lower classes. Annexation to Mexico was the most contested issue. Many Honduran *criollos* favored the Mexican linkage because the Mexican constitution's advocacy of free trade portended a solution to Honduras's economic plight. Yet the same *criollos* viewed the outlawing of slavery as a potential cause for local Indians and *mestizos* to demand greater political and economic rights and social privileges. In Honduras, the more conservative city of Comayagua favored annexation, while the more liberal city, Tegucigalpa, opposed it.

The debate reached a new height on September 28, 1821, when the Governor of Comayagua, José Gregorio Tinoco de Contreras received copy of the Act of Independence signed in Guatemala City on September 15, 1821. The Central American hand was forced on October 19, 1821, when Iturbide declared himself as the emperor and invited Central America to remain within his empire. The Central Americans now had to determine whether or not to accept Iturbide's invitation. Tinoco called a meeting of the leaders of secular and ecclesiastical institutions in Comayagua, who voted their allegiance to whatever government Mexico might form. Tinoco then strongly urged the leaders of Tegucigalpa to follow suit and threatened an armed invasion of the city if compliance did not quickly follow.

Tegucigalpa's *cabildo* refused and charged Francisco Aguirre with mobilizing forces for the town's defense. One of the individuals answering the call was Francisco Morazán, who would go on to become one of Central America's early political leaders. Fearful of conflict, however, the Tegucigalpa *cabildo* called for an open meeting to discuss the subject and promised to abide by the wishes of its citizenry as expressed by the municipal councils. This proved unsatisfactory. After the 23 municipal councils contended that only the general congress could determine the relationship to Mexico; 104 of the delegates voted for union, 11 consented but with various qualifying conditions, 32 agreed to follow Guatemala, while many others made no decision at all. The group's leading spokesman, Dioniso de Herrera drew up the measure expressing this vote and sent it on Guatemala City. Until some formal arrangement could be concluded, Honduras existed as an independent nation. But independence was short-lived, for the conservative leaders in Guatemala accepted Mexican annexation on January 5, 1822. Only after Itrurbide's coronation as Emperor of Mexico, did the disgruntled Tegucigalpa council reluctantly express its loyalty.

The need for a constitution establishing the formalities of the new Mexican empire necessitated another election. Representatives to the Congress at Mexico were elected on March 10, 1822, including four from Comayagua and three from Tegucigalpa. Many considered José Cecilio de Valle to be the most notable Honduran representative. He arrived in Mexico City on July 28, and promptly elected a member of the constitution committee and subsequently vice president of the assembly. Despite pledges of loyalty to the Emperor, Iturbide suspected del Valle of working with the adherents of independence, particularly the representatives from El Salvador. The constitution was never completed because the ever suspicious Iturbide dissolved the Congress on October 31, 1822, and proceeded to rule as an absolute monarch. Opposition pressure continued and forced Iturbide to resign on March 19, 1823, and along with his family, he fled to Italy, bringing to an end Honduras's experience with the Mexican Empire.

Finally, on July 1, 1823, the Central American constituent assembly declared the region's absolute independence from Spain, Mexico, and any other foreign nation, including North America. The assembly also called for the establishment of a republican system of government.

United Provinces of Central America, 1823–1838

José Cecilio de Valle convened the constituent assembly's initial meeting on June 24, 1823, in Guatemala City. Other delegates arrived in September. Of the 41 initial delegates, only he and Francisco Aguirre represented Honduras. After declaring the region's independence from Spain, Mexico, and the United States on July 1, the delegates selected a three man board to exercise executive power over the assembly. Among the initial problems confronting the assembly was the request from Francisco Antonio Márquez, a newly arrived delegate from Tegucigalpa. He requested that his city and Comayagua be recognized as separate states. After the Assembly defeated the plan, the Honduran delegates agreed to alternate the capital between the two cities but provided no details on how this would be accomplished.

The assembly then appointed a committee with the primary task to prepare a constitution that would unite the five disparate states. The committee included most of Honduras' impressive intellectual elite: Pedro Molina, José Francisco Barrundia, Mariano Gálvez, Matias Delgado, and José Cecilio de Valle, considered by many the most distinguished member of the group. Each was familiar with the works of Voltaire, Rousseau, and other eighteenth century liberal French philosophers; the course of the French Revolution; and the formation of the United States. In addition, Barrundia exchanged letters with U.S. President James Monroe.

Preparing the constitution proved to be a most difficult task despite the fact that many of Central America's leading *criollo* families were linked by marriage, educated at many of the same Church institutions, and engaged in commerce with each other. Coupled with their experiences under Spain's Kingdom of Guatemala, the *criollos* shared the belief and need to form a unity government among them. Still, these similar experiences contributed to the concerns about the authority of a central government over individual states and towns within those states. This, along with other issues that divided the *criollos* contributed to the development of two political parties: conservatives and liberal. Conservatives favored a centralized government based upon aristocratic leadership, the maintenance of church privileges, including its control over education, hospitals and other social service activities. In contrast, the liberals favored a decentralized government, a less privileged church and economic development as witnessed in the United States and western Europe. Both groups shared a disdain for the Native Americans and, slightly less so, for their *mestizo* cousins. The conservatives were more adamant about keeping the indigenous people in their traditional and subservient positions. In contrast, liberals desired the elimination of an indigenous society by incorporating it into the national, Hispanic culture.

Although the liberals comprised a majority of the assembly delegates, their goal of a Federalist system of government met legitimate conservative challenges regarding communication and transportation, an informed citizenry, and economic development. The conservatives pointed to the Chilean and Colombian models as examples of Federalism's failure. The conservatives also dismissed the United States as a proper Federalist example because it had a long term experience at participatory government before its independence. By contrast, Central America immediately emerged from authoritarianism that only permitted minimal government experience for a few of its residents, a fact that limited the number of people prepared to participate in government administration. And there was the immediate need to pacify those outlying districts already in anarchy. Finally, the conservatives objected to the limited powers of the executive, election of judges, and the extension of suffrage.

In response, the liberals asserted that Central America needed to adopt a modern framework of government in order to prosper and advance its citizenry. With a stake in government, the liberals argued that the masses of the people would quickly become politically educated and result in a government more responsive to society's needs.

These conflicting ideas played out during meetings of the liberal-dominated constituent assembly gathered in Guatemala City. When the committee completed its work on November 23, 1824, it was a mixture of the 1812 Spanish constitution, the 1789 U.S. constitution, and British, French, and Portuguese doctrines. It assigned the federal congress with legislating powers on matters of common interest and the right to central taxing. The federal government also retained power over civil, commercial, and criminal law. The federal congress was empowered to legislate on matters of mutual interest, including a federal taxation system. But, the federal government's taxing power was restricted by the proviso that allowed the individual member states to voluntarily contribute money to cover the cost of the federal debt. Another executive limitation rested with the congressional right to override senate vetoes, but the president had no veto powers.

The legislative branch was designated as the government's most dominant branch, with members of the House of Representatives determined by population and the Senate by state, both elected by popular vote. In addition, the constitution assigned the House the most significant powers of government: pass laws, levy and collect taxes, declare war and make peace, regulate foreign and interstate commerce, and decide when the president could use the state militia. In contrast, the Senate could not initiate legislation but could amend legislation coming from the House. The Senate was empowered to advice and consent with the president on appointments and removal. The Senate also nominated for presidential approval all diplomatic personnel and treasury and military officials, and indicted, prosecuted, and removed any of these appointments upon proving their malfeasance in office.

Elected popularly within each state, the president and vice-president served four year terms, with eligibility for reelection. The president's most significant power was as commander-in-chief of the army. Technically in complete charge of Honduras's relationship with the United Provinces of Central America, the senate served as a check upon his actions. In all other areas, presidential powers were severely restricted. For example, he could appoint government officials only from a list of nominees generated by the senate, and to remove any appointed government official, the president needed a two-thirds senate vote of approval. The president was directed to consult with the Senate on all matters of foreign affairs. On administrative matters, the president needed to consult with the House regarding the meaning of the laws and then with the Senate regarding the procedures of application. In addition to presenting the Congress with an annual report, the president was on-call to provide the legislature with any administrative data it might request. The president could not leave the capital without congressional approval, nor could he leave the country for six months after his term in office.

Without defining their jurisdiction and powers, Supreme Court justices were to be popularly elected. In practice, it became the court of last resort regarding the interpretation of the constitution, laws passed by the congress, and disputes between citizens of different states. The court soon exercised its authority involving diplomatic representatives and in criminal cases involving government officers that the Senate could prosecute. The Supreme Court also assumed administrative powers for the president's nominees to the lower courts and served as a watchdog over the conduct of all lower court judges.

The 1824 constitution also guaranteed the people freedom of speech, assembly, free ingress and egress, full control over private property, and trial by jury. The document voided the death penalty except in cases of assassination or premeditated homicide and crimes against the public order. However, the constitution did not provide for religious freedom, instead establishing the Catholic faith as the only one acceptable throughout the provinces.

The constitution also included two measures designed to insure support from the states' upper class: abolition of slavery and establishing Catholicism as the state religion were direct appeals to the conservative and liberal reformers.

At the state level, an assembly would be elected and determined by proportional representation, whereas the state senate consisted of two representatives from each department. Otherwise, the five states were free and independent regarding internal and administrative matters.

The committee's final product, signed on November 15, 1824, and put into effect on February 6, 1825, became the basis of Honduras's subsequent 13 instruments of government through the 1936 constitution. For the visionaries of the day, like Spanish America's liberator Simón Bolívar and the Honduran Liberal Francisco Morazán, the appeal of a federal-democratic government, coupled with Central America's location for a transisthmian canal, political stability would bring foreign capitalists and, concomitantly, wealth to the region. Like all Central Americans, the Hondurans rejected Spanish central authority; contemporary critics thought that they would be more willing to accept federalism at home and as participants in the United Provinces of Central America (UPCA).

The local reality was vastly different. In 1825, an estimated heterogeneous 137,000 people resided in Honduras. Largely uneducated and spread over a vast and poorly connected territory, their daily concerns were more important than the theories and structure of government. The debate over those issues remained among the matters discussed by the elite class.

Francisco Morazán and the End of Central American Unity

The initial Honduran enthusiasm for unity faded within two years after the implementation of the 1824 constitution. In fact, its 13-year experience in the United Provinces was characterized by strife and disunity. As the government at Tegucigalpa resisted authority from Guatemala City and refused to pay taxes to support it, the conservative center at Comayagua and all outlying districts, no matter their political philosophy, resisted Tegucigalpa's authority. Nor did Honduran gold and silver miners and indigo and cochineal producers want their products subject to the authority of government in Guatemala City. The Honduran state government issued its own currency to be used in international trade, a move that paralyzed foreign commerce and disrupted banking operations. By 1836, the Honduran frustration with government was evidenced on June 11, when the Honduran Assembly rejected the proposed constitutional changes made by Chief-of-State Joaquín Rivera and considered by many to be the most complete and more reflecting the Central American reality at the time. By that time, 1836, the UPCA was in disarray.

The most far-reaching political crisis occurred at the initial meeting of the general assembly at Comayagua on April 5, 1826, when interim head of state Dionisio d Herrera read a paper summarizing previous government actions and outlining a program for the future. Arguing along traditional conservative and liberal lines, the assembly failed to discuss the plan or its administration. The conservatives asserted that Herrera held only a temporary appointment as head of state and demanded new elections. In response, Herrera offered to resign. Rather than accept that and prepare for elections, the assembly dissolved itself.

Amidst the subsequent tension, Herrera set out to quell the revolutionary spirit that gripped the nation. Stating that the violence might spill over into other Central American provinces, the UPCA head of state and conservative, José Manuel Arce ordered troops into Honduras where he teamed up with the vice headof state José Justo Milla to defeat the Honduran forces at Comayagua on May 9, 1827. Arce's real intention, however, was to destroy the Liberal Party and, toward that end, sent the captured Dionisio to imprisonment in Guatemala.

Among the liberals who escaped the captor's net was Francisco Morazán. Born a mestizo, probably of Corsican decent in Tegucigalpa in 1789, where his background and education did not provide any special training that would be needed in the important role Morazán played in Central American history. He fled to Nicaragua where he assembled an army to return home and oust the invading forces in the Battle of La Ceiba on November 11, 1827. By 1829, Morazán became head of the UPCA and during the next four years sent federal troops into Honduras to maintain political order.

At the national level Morazán turned the federal congress into rubber stamp for his liberal policies, including the installation of José Francisco Barrundia in the presidency. The federal congress declared all laws it passed since 1826 null and void. Conservatives came under immediate attack: their properties confiscated, government salaries retracted and threatened with exile should they militate the new government. The church also fell victim to the government's wrath, being forced to remove clergy opposed Morazán and to mint into coin large amounts of the church's silver reserve. Then in July 1829, on orders from Morazán, President Barrundia directed that Archbishop Ramón Casáus and almost all members of the Franciscan, Dominican, and Recollet missionary groups be exiled to Havana on the grounds of intriguing against the state. The federal government then set out to confiscate all properties of the priestly orders, except the Bethlemites who remained outside politics. In response, as might be expected, the number of young men entering the priesthood dropped significantly. In addition, the federal government halted the recruitment of nuns. The liberals did not intend to destroy religion, but to reduce, if not eliminate, Church influence in politics and in the everyday life of the masses. State reports reveal wide spread prosecution of conservatives and confiscation of their properties.

The conservative and the Church did not succumb quietly. They resisted the loss of prestige and influence, to say nothing of wealth. In Honduras, revolution broke against the Morazán regime, hopeful that Spanish or British assistance would some come to their rescue. In Honduras, the Governor of Omoa, Ramón Guzmán, seized the fort, raised the Spanish flag, and dispatched ships to Cuba to retrieve the exiled Archbishop Casáus and reinforcements. Another conservative seized Trujillo and marched into the interior. These rebellions were suppressed in 1832 and the Cuban reinforcements seized. That same year, 1832 Morazán's army crushed a secessionist revolt in El Salvador.

Neither the military victories in 1832 nor Morazán's return to the presidency in 1835 insured the future of the United Provinces of Central America. Increasingly, the individual states refused to pay tax assessments to the central government. At the same time, individuals refused to pay any taxes, a factor that contributed to the states keeping customs duties for their own use rather than the needs of the central government. The turmoil led to the convening of a constituent assembly in 1835 that produced a document similar to the 1824 constitution, except for the declaration of religious freedom. Only Costa Rica and Nicaragua ratified the document.

Conservatives and church officials frequently played upon the emotions of the uneducated Indians and mestizos to support their cause. This happened in 1835 when Morazán encouraged foreign colonization to help modernize Central American society and to contribute to the uplifting of the Native Americans. Not only were these foreigners non-Catholic, they would bring a new culture that threatened the very existence of the ancient based societies. Although these charges ignited protests from the poorer people that increasingly could not be controlled by federal forces, an outbreak of cholera that began in 1837 served as the catalyst to bring the UPCA to an end.

In the midst of this turmoil, a semiliterate charismatic *mestizo*, Rafael Carrera emerged. Initially supported by a group of Indians and clergy, by 1838 his followers included a cross section of people opposed to the liberal reforms of President Gálvez. Morázan's federal army engaged Carrera's guerrilla force on several occasions but could not defeat him because at the same time, Morazán confronted uprisings throughout Guatemala. On February 2, 1838, Carrera's troops entered Guatemala City. The Gálvez government collapsed, and only a handsome bribe and supply of arms and ammunition convinced Carrera to leave the city and its inhabitants unharmed. By the end of 1839, Costa Rica, Honduras, and Nicaragua had withdrawn from the UPCA. Only El Salvador technically remained a part of the union. Morazán remained in El Salvador for a brief time before departing for Costa Rica, where his life finally ended before a firing squad on September 15, 1842, the twenty-first anniversary of Central America's independence from Spain.

When newly appointed U.S. Minister John Lloyd Stephens arrived in Guatemala in the spring of 1839, he made an honest effort to make contact with a Central American government. Failing that and agreeing with the British Minister Frederick Chatfield, Stephens notified authorities in Washington that a Central American government did not exist. He then prepared the papers still housed in the U.S. legation for shipment home and planned his departure to the Mayan communities that lie to the north of Guatemala City.

§ § § § §

Several factors contributed to the dissolution of the United Provinces of Central America in 1839. Included was the lack of training and experience in public affairs, a weakness in all Latin America but particularly true in Central America. Because the region lacked natural wealth for the Spanish to exploit, few colonists came to the area; and most of the administrators were of lesser quality than those found, for example, in Mexico City or Havana. Spain's administrative structure provided very limited opportunities for local *criollos* to participate in government, and lacking commodities demanded in the Spanish commercial system, Central America produced few businessmen. Yet, it was representatives of these three who comprised the oligarchic leadership during the 15 years of the United Provinces, a group mistrusted by all other residents throughout the region, including Honduras. The close State-Church relations during the colonial period were another problem that all Latin America confronted. While other Latin American nations moved slowly towards separation of Church and State in the immediate post-independence years, Francisco Morazán attempted to move rapidly, an effort that only stiffened church and conservative resistance to change. Nor were the leaders prepared to implement liberal political reforms; the past framework of government served the elite well. Nor were the light-skinned *criollos* prepared to share politics, economic opportunity, or social life with the darker-skinned residents, be they the indigenous people, blacks, *mestizos*, or mulattos. But given Central America's poor communication and transportation systems, a stronger centralized government would not have worked well either. Simply put, in 1840, Central America was a collection of small towns and villages, isolated from each other. No sense of nationhood existed. Honduras stood as a primary example of such underdevelopment.

NOTE

1. John Lloyd Stephens, *Incidents of Travel in Central America, Chiapas and Yucatán* (Toronto: Dover Publishing Company, 1969, 2 volumes; reprint of 1841 edition by Harper and Row), I, 196.

3

Conservatives and Liberals

If a political party is to be defined as a voluntary association, organized for the purpose of achieving control of government through legal procedures ... then political parties have existed in Honduras since the 1890s. If, to this definition is added the possession of an effective guiding philosophy, then political parties probably have never existed in Honduras.[1]

Foro Hondureño
January and February, 1939

The collapse of the United Provinces of Central America in 1838 brought to the forefront across Central America the legacies of Spanish administration and several characteristics to the internal dynamics of the five republics. Politically, the conflict between conservative and liberal ideologies became apparent before 1822, and, over the next four generations, this political conflict would continue. Part of the argument focused upon the issue of centralization and decentralization of government power. The unwillingness of the individual states to support the central government of the United Provinces significantly contributed to its downfall. After 1838, the debate continued in each individual nation: What powers should remain with the central government and what should devolve to the provincial and township governments? Conservatives also pressed to continue the special privileges of the Catholic Church: the right to tithing and to owning property, exemption from state taxation, use of its own special courts, to inherit property, to control hospitals and education, and to be the keeper of vital statistics. In contrast, the liberal argued that these privileges should either be curtailed or abolished. Despite the few political differences among them, both parties represented the elite property owners and business leaders who argued that the right of government service remained their privilege well into the twentieth century and that they would use the military as an instrument to secure that position. Politics became a domain of the elite families at the expense of the masses. Beyond politics, the Central Americans had to find their way in the international market. Both conservatives and liberals agreed to this, but the former favored reconnecting with Spain, while the liberal sought new trading partners.

Throughout the nineteenth century, Honduran politics shared these characteristics, but in a country less populated, more poor and devoid of wealth, understanding the discord between the provinces and among those groups that sought power—landowners and merchants, civil, military and religious leaders—became more difficult. Honduras lacked a unifying force among the groups competing for power. The turbulence became a weakness in the nineteenth century that resulted in Honduras being dragged into other inter and intrastate conflicts and in becoming a victim of maneuvering by foreign powers, usually the United States and Great Britain.

THE CONFLICT FOR PRESIDENTIAL POWER, 1838–1876

Independence did not bring any immediate improvements to Honduras. Geography was part of the problem. Honduras had slightly less than 147,000 residents spread over a country consisting of 43,277 square miles, approximately equal to the size of the state of Tennessee. Its two largest cities, Comayagua and Tegucigalpa, were home to approximately two-thirds of those people, but nonwhites outnumbered those of pure Spanish decent (*criollos*). The other nearly 50,000 people lived in the 87 hermit villages or towns scattered across the country, where they worked their small farms and cattle ranches. Cattlemen, with large herds, dominated the savannas of eastern Olancho Province and the southern plains of Choluteca. These groups had little contact or issues in common with the Amerindian, *mestizos*, and peasants that dominated the western borderlands with El Salvador and Guatemala or with the nonwhite mahogany tree cutters on the North Coast. These isolated laboring groups usually connected to their neighbors by little more than foot paths and to the larger towns by mule or with Comayagua, Tegucigalpa, or San Pedro Sula and beyond to El Salvador and Guatemala by dirt and unkempt roads.

Under these conditions, from 1842 to 1876, Honduras suffered economic stagnation, social decline, and arbitrary government. Disillusioned with the failure of union and with centralized government at home, Morazán's lieutenants retreated to isolated ranches, beginning a Honduran tradition that still calls a landowner "colonel" and accepts local, feudal rule more readily than centralized government. For years to come, Honduras was to have two types of generals: the one officially appointed by the government and the other a self appointed *gritado*, or *caudillo*, who ran his own small army and was responsible to no one but himself. Conservative governments controlled all Central American governments, starting in the 1840s; but in Honduras, they were unable to promote stability, let alone Morazán's version of Western liberalism.

On May 30, 1838, the Central American Congress removed President Francisco Morazán from office and announced that the individual states could declare their sovereignty and establish their own governments. The United Provinces of Central America collapsed. For Morazán, the devout advocate of Central American unity, fate proved to be unkind. Still under attack from separatists in the Union's last capital, San Salvador, and from the outside by Honduran separatist Francisco Ferrera and Guatemalan *caudillo* Rafael Carrera, Morazán fled San Salvador for Costa Rica and then on to Peru. There, Morazán raised both money and troops for a return to Costa Rica, where supporters made him chief-of-state on July 10, 1842. Subsequently, in response to Morazán's call for the reestablishment of a Central American union, the Costa Rican congress appropriated funds for an army to achieve that goal. Morazán's conservative opposition met the challenge. After forcing him to retreat to Cartago, the two armies engaged in 66 hours of battle before the Morazán was captured. Morazán's end came before a firing squad on September 15, 1842, the twenty-first anniversary of Central America's declaration of independence from Spain. Having lost its chief union spokesman of the day, the Central American states then set upon their individual courses.

From the start, Honduras lacked strong ideological underpinnings. Morazán and his liberal colleagues took the ideals of liberalism and Central American union to their graves. Honduras did not have strong conservative spokespersons who provided political leadership. In the absence of political leadership, conflict became the norm, not the exception. Tegucigalpa remained the center of liberalism and Comayagua, conservatism. Men of means in both cities and throughout the country—retail merchants and their larger counterparts who traded with commercial houses in Guatemala and Belize, mine operators, cattle ranchers and small farmers, government bureaucrats, and military men—attempted to come to grips with the devolution of power to the provinces at the expense of the central government; while at the same time, each group attempted to protect its own interests.

On January 1, 1839, three months after Honduras declared its independence on November 15, 1838, a new state constitution was formally adopted. It provided for the usual three branches of government—executive, legislative and judicial—and contained extensive provisions for protecting individual rights, the longtime crusade of Francisco Morazán and his liberal followers. The new nation's initial president, Francisco Ferrera demonstrated excellent leadership qualities during battles against Cuban and Spanish forces along the Honduran North Coast in 1831, and it was significantly enhanced in 1839 when he joined forces with the Guatemalan Chief of State Rafael Carrera to drive Morazán temporarily from Central America and associating himself with the Honduran independence. The National Assembly again elected Ferrera president of Honduras on December 30, 1841, to a two-year presidential term and again to a four-year term on February 23, 1843. The Honduran Assembly elected Ferrera president in 1847, but he refused to serve. What followed Ferrera set the pattern for Honduras's nineteenth century political history. Eight other acting presidents and four council of ministers governed the country until February 12, 1847, when Juan Lindo Zelaya took over the presidential office for a five-year term that he completed on February 1, 1852.

Lindo was born into a landowning family in Tegucigalpa, Honduras. Lindo received his early education in Mexico and subsequently earned a law degree from the University of San Carlos in Guatemala in 1814. Five years later, Lindo was appointed the interim colonial governor of Honduras and in 1821, the Honduran constituent assembly reappointed him to post and as the representative of the Province of Comayagua to the 1821 Central American congress, where he voted in favor of annexation to Mexico. During the fifteen year life of the United Provinces of Central America, Lindo served as a representative to the Honduran assembly and to the 1838 constituent assembly where he voted for Honduran separation from the UPCA. Following the collapse of the UPCA, Lindo briefly served (1841–1842) as President of El Salvador, where he established the *Colegio de Asunción*, that became the University of El Salvador in 1847, and ordered the construction of schools, at public expense, in every township with a minimum 150 residents. Lindo returned to Honduras in 1842 and five years later, with the support of Honduran conservatives and conservative Guatemalan Head of State, Rafael Carrera, Lindo became president of Honduras on February 12, 1847, and held office until July 16, 1848, as required by the new February 4, 1848 constitution. His second term began that same day and lasted until January 1, 1852. One of Lindo's notable accomplishments illustrates the blurring of conservative-liberal ideologies in the early nineteenth century. In 1847, he directed the opening of the University of Honduras with a revised curriculum that included the study of law and philosophy. Analysts attribute such accomplishments to liberals, not conservatives such as Lindo.

In February 1848, Lindo put a new constitution in operation. The product of a conservative administration, the new constitution replaced the 1839 document, but it did not represent a break with the country's ideological past. The new the constitution provided many significant liberal concepts. For example, it retained guarantees for individual rights while adding provisions against double jeopardy and self incrimination. It did, however, reflect the land holding elite's desire to secure power for themselves by adding a land holding qualification for voting eligibility and creating an upper house to the legislative branch of government. Furthermore, only the land owning elite could participate in the selection of a president, although the chamber of deputies selected his vice president. Up to this time only the chamber of deputies could initiate legislation, but now the senate could introduce bills into the lower house The senate also gained the right to alter legislation as it emanated from the chamber. And the president and his ministers now could introduce legislation to the chamber of deputies.

In addition, the scope of the presidential authority in the legislative process was enlarged to include to include the authority to introduce legislation in the chamber of deputies and the power to appoint, discipline, and remove cabinet ministers, military commanders, most central government officials, and departmental political chiefs. The constitution added a council of state to serve as a buffer between the president and the legislature. Comprised largely of presidential appointees, the council included only three legislators: one senator and two deputies. While the council served in advisory capacity to the president regarding legislation, administration of laws and finance and defense of the country, it also became the body to field complaints from citizens about government officials.

Effectively, the 1848 constitution not only enhanced the central government's power and authority but also that of the president. Voting qualifications not only limited participation in politics but insured that the government consisting of the elite would serve their interests.

The third conservative president of significance in the generation and one-half since the collapse of the United Provinces was José Santos Guardiola, a member of a prominent Tegucigalpa family. He presided over Honduras from 1857 to 1862, after engineering the overthrow of Guardiola's predecessor, José Trinidad Cabañas. Guatemalan strongman Rafael Carrera had Guardiola installed as President of Honduras. Guardiola assumed a second term on July 2, 1860. Guardiola's administration was one of the most liberal in Honduran history, despite he being a member of the conservative party because it provided for press and expanded individual freedom of expression, expanded suffrage to include members of the smaller landowning middle sector, and regularized church-state relations. Economic conditions, however, continuously spiraled downward, forcing Guardiola to issue copper coins. For his efforts to limit church influence, Guardiola ran afoul of the Bishop of Honduras, Msgr. Miguel del Cid, who excommunicated Guardiola on December 26, 1860. Pope Pius IX not only overturned the decision but also replaced del Cid with Jesus Zepeda. Guardiola's continued anticlericalism erupted into the *Guerra de los padres* in April 1861, which in turn contributed to Guardiola's assassination on January 11, 1862. For the next four years, Honduras endured political chaos.

During the turmoil of Honduran politics in the late 1850s through the early 1860s, Latin America experienced a significant political change that continued into the twentieth century: liberals returned to political prominence. The movement accelerated in Central America following the death of Guatemalan strongman and conservative Rafael Carrera in 1865. Similar to liberals across Latin America in the nineteenth century, the Central American liberals believed in progress and economic development directed from the government downward through society. They sought to integrate their economies into the global market to acquire the benefits of advanced civilization and to promote material improvement. In practice, Central America's late nineteenth century political leaders appeared as images of Mexico's Porfirio Díaz. The Central American leaders set up republican dictatorships in which they centralized authority, rigged elections, and controlled governmental and nongovernmental institutions, all in an effort to maintain themselves in power. Heads of government drew support from the landowning elite who often benefited as a group from the government's economic policies and personally, through appointments to government and military offices. The nascent middle sector also supported the system because of expanded economic opportunities and was always concerned with the potential restlessness of the uneducated and unskilled masses below them. For the most part, the republican dictators modernized their military establishment and police forces that were often used to silence political opposition and maintain the political order.

Honduras followed the broad framework on its liberal path, but a path more hesitant and twisted. Politics remained a struggle between elite families, while the promises of modernity and prosperity for other social sectors remained elusive. Honduras first liberal President since Francisco Morazán was José Trinidad Cabañas, who assumed the office on March 1, 1852. A *criollo* from Tegucigalpa, Cabañas received his childhood education in Comayagua and went on to earn military honors as a supporter of Francisco Morazán. He also was involved in the internal affairs of El Salvador, Guatemala, and Nicaragua prior to his selection as President of Honduras. As president, Cabañas encouraged expanded coffee and timber production for export purposes but gained the landowners ire by imposing export taxes on those products to support the government construction of elementary schools throughout the nation. Cabañas' penchant for involvement in Guatemalan internal affairs, however, contributed to his downfall. Guatemalan President General Rafael Carrera provided the catalyst for change when his troops defeated Cabañas's army in the Battle of Masagua on October 6, 1855. Cabanas's loss provided Hondurans with the courage to oust him from the presidency on October 18, 1855.

Following Guardiola's assassination on January 11, 1862 five different individuals occupied the Honduran presidential chair until March 18, 1864 when another conservative José Medina took the oath office. Medina became the most dominant figure in Honduran politics until 1876. Medina oversaw the implementation of the 1865 and 1873 constitutions that further narrowed the public's participation in government. At the same time, the documents strengthened presidential power. According to the new documents, henceforth, property qualifications for holding office ranged from 1,000 pesos in value for legislative and the supreme court membership, to 5,000 pesos in value for the president. The constitution also stipulated that land ownership was a requirement for citizenship but that citizenship could be suspended for nonpayment of debts or taxes.

The most significant procedural change strengthened the presidency at the expense of the legislature. The president gained authority over the police and the military, finance and incorporation, and the right to draft commercial, mining, civil, and penal codes. Members of the supreme court, who were presidential appointees, joined the president and his ministers with the right to draft legislation.

The 1873 constitution replicated the previous document except for granting the president extensive wartime powers and the Supreme Court the right to criticize congressional laws and suggest ways to square them with the constitution.

On paper, the 1873 provided the legislature with some control over presidential nominations. The legislature was empowered to certify one's eligibility to hold the presidency and to approve supreme court nominations and the promotion of military officers from the rank of brigadier general upward. In the reality of nineteenth-century Honduran politics, however, the legislature did not challenge the president. As the Honduran leadership struggled with the implementation of new constitutions, liberals came to political power in neighboring countries between 1871 and 1885; Gerardo Barrios, Francisco Dueñas, Santiago Gonzálaz, Andrés del Valle, and Rafael Zaldívar in El Salvador and Miguel García Granados, and Justo Rufino Barrios in Guatemala. These men exerted strong influence over Honduran politics. The relationship among the leaders was conflicted and reached a high water mark in 1872 when Guatemalan president Barrios determined to replace Honduran president Céleo Arias with another liberal, Ponciano Leiva. On November 23, 1873 Leiva organized a government at Choluteca and two weeks later declared null and void all acts of the Arias government, including the recently proclaimed 1873 constitution. Following the Arias's military capitulation on January 13, 1874, Leiva convened a national assembly in April 1874 that reinstated the 1865 constitution and made Leiva president of the republic. What had begun as a liberal revolution ended with a conservative president and constitution. Leiva's inability to maintain order, however, prompted Barrios to again intervene, this time naming Liberal Marco Aurelio Soto president on August 27, 1876. Soto would govern until 1883.

Born in Tegucigalpa, Soto was educated at universities in Honduras and Guatemala. At Guatemala's University of San Carlos, Soto studied with future Guatemalan President Justo Rufino Barrios and with Ramón Rosa, who would become a Soto confidante. In the mid-1870s,

Soto served as Barrios' minister of foreign affairs. Barrios supported Soto in the 1876 conflagration that resulted in Soto becoming interim president of Honduras on August 30, 1876, and then constitutional president on May 30, 1877. As a Barrios disciple, Soto and his minister of government Ramón Rosa set out to pacify the country by not prosecuting political enemies by tolerating all opposition groups and cancelling all government forced loans. Once accomplished, Soto implemented a series of reforms that included the establishment of a finance department, a reorganization of the tax code, balancing the national budget, consolidating the public debt, and amortizing it so that it could be paid off. Soto reduced church influence in civil matters by secularizing marriage and instituting compulsory public education. By making promotions more democratic, Soto reduced the military's potential to serve presidential interests. Soto is also credited with the modernization of civil, penal, and customs codes along with regulations governing commerce and mining. Soto is also responsible for the establishment of a national mint and a national library in the newly proclaimed capital city of Tegucigalpa.

With these liberal reforms in place by 1880, Soto and Rosa set out modernize the country. The country's most important towns and many smaller villages were linked by a telegraph grid that also connected Honduras to the United States and Europe. The government began construction of a road connecting Tegucigalpa with the town of San Lorenzo on the Gulf of Fonseca.

Many of the civil and political advances found expression in the new constitution that went into effect on November 1, 1880, one day after Soto declared Tegucigalpa to be the permanent capital of Honduras. The document's first section renewed and guaranteed all of the individual rights found in previous Honduran constitutions and for the first time guaranteed the right of *habeas corpus*. The new document clearly stated that property requirements were not necessary for voting and holding office. Voting for all government offices would henceforth be direct, public, and obligatory for all citizens but the clergy were prohibited from holding public office. In fact, the 1880 constitution declared separation of Church and State with the establishment of compulsory public education and the removal of Church influence in higher education. Military service now became compulsory, but the State absolved itself from any responsibility to property damage caused by any form of civil strife.

The 1880 constitution provided for the direct election of the president to a four-year term and that he could serve only one consecutive second term. The president now had authority over

foreign affairs, the military, and the administration of laws, and henceforth, he was authorized to appoint secretaries of state who had to
countersign every presidential act. The secretaries could attend
congressional debates and discussion, where they would be subject
to questioning by the representatives. The method was a step toward
parliamentary government and a means to secure executive transparency. The congress was empowered to check the president in other
ways such as approving or disapproving of all executive expenditures,
check his war powers by declaring a state of siege, limiting the number
of troops, and reviewing a declaration of war. The congress also
received authority to oversee the implementation and completion of
all government sponsored and supported projects.

In effect, the 1880 Honduran constitution reflected the most
complete expression of progressive political thought in late nineteenth
century Latin America. If implemented, it would have fully altered
the course of Honduran political history.

Under the terms of the 1880 constitution, Soto was elected president
for a four-year term beginning February 1, 1881, but he did not
complete his term in office. On March 10, 1883, Soto resigned his post
ostensibly for health reasons but in reality to the pressure exerted by
Guatemalan strongman Justo Rufino Barrios. The Honduran congress
refused to accept Soto's resignation and instead sanctioned a leave of
absence for the president, who then departed for Europe and the
United States. In the early summer of 1883, Soto learned of rumors that
indicated Barrios would again force a change in the government of
Honduras. Barrios' scathing reply to Soto's written inquiry on July 8,
1883, convinced Soto that he should resign from office in order to save
the country from further violence. Soto's resignation became effective
on August 27, 1893. Another liberal and favored by Soto, Louis Bográn
assumed the presidency on November 30, 1883, and was reelected to a
second term in 1887.

Born into a wealthy and well connected political family in northern
Honduras, Bográn studied at Guatemala's University of San Carlos
before pursuing a military career. He rose to the rank of general, after
which he became involved in national politics and a protégé of Marco
Auerlio Soto. A founding member of the National Party of Honduras
(PHN), as president, Bográn expanded the educational reform program begun by Soto with the establishment of primary and secondary
educational institutions across the country. In addition to the creation
of the National Press, Bográn is credited with the founding of the
National School of the Arts and the Literary-Scientific Academy in
Tegucigalpa. Bográn initiated the scholarly study of the Mayan ruins

at Copán through arrangements with foreign universities. With the exception of a failed military revolt in Tegucigalpa in 1890, Honduras experienced political tranquility for the eight years of Bográn's presidency.

A political storm erupted shortly after the 1891 election won by former President Ponciano Leiva. The conflict's origins rested with Bográn's founding of the Progressive or National Party in 1887 to insure his re-election to the presidency over the Liberal Party's challenger and former president, Céleo Arias. In 1891, Soto was rejected by the Progressive/National Party, which instead, nominated Leiva to run against Policarpo Bonilla, who assumed the leadership of the Liberal Party following the death of Céleo Arias May 28, 1890. Leiva won the openly fraudulent election but served as president for only 20 months before being forced from office on August 7, 1893. Leiva's administration militated against all those who opposed his political philosophy, an intolerance that resulted in the dissolution of the Liberal Party on May 8, 1892, and the deportation of its leadership including Bonilla, Generals José María Reina, Erasmo Velásquez, Dionisio Gutiérrez, and Miguel R. Dávila. The deportations were followed by sporadic uprisings throughout the country that government forces suppressed, after which the remaining liberal leadership went into self-imposed exile in Nicaragua. Leiva's tenuous presidency ended with his forced resignation on February 9, 1893, by General Domingo Vásquez, whose antiliberal attitude was surpassed only by his brutal suppression of them.

During this same time frame, a group of Bonilla supporters organized the liberal forces in Nicaragua for a return to Honduras. Supplied with a constant flow of arms from Nicaraguan strongman and Liberal José Santos Zelaya, the Bonilla-led troops opened the war with an attack upon Choluteca on January 15, 1894, and completed it with the capture of Tegucigalpa on February 22, 1894. Bonilla acted quickly to legitimize his control of Honduras. On April 26, 1894, Bonilla called for the convening of a Constituent Assembly that met for the first time on July 11 and completed its work on October 14, 1893.

Policarpo Bonilla built upon the liberal program of his predecessor Marco Aurelio Soto, including the revision of civil and penal, commercial and mining, and military codes. However, he was unable to convince his fellow politicians to maintain party discipline and to compete fairly in elections. During his administration Bonilla confronted only one revolt, in 1897 when Enrique Soto directed his troops to simultaneously attack La Esperanza and Puerto Cortés. General Terencio Sierra led the government forces in a successful counterattack and utilized his military exploits to become the next President of Honduras on February 1, 1899. Rather than build upon Soto's and Bonilla's modernizing policies, Sierra spent the next four years maneuvering for his own re-election. Although Sierra failed to realize his objective, it may not have mattered. Honduras was on the precipice of significant change.

THE CONTINUED SEARCH FOR CENTRAL AMERICAN UNION

The collapse of the United Provinces of Central America (UPCA) in 1839 did not put an end to the dream of union among the five Central American nations. The same issues that contributed to the collapse of the UPCA remained: the framework of government structures and its philosophy of administration; the question centralized versus decentralized government, the extent of Church privileges, and the search for external commercial markets. One's opinion about these issues usually identified that person as a conservative or liberal.

In the nineteenth century, unification of Central America focused on political pragmatism, not upon the ideals of a Central American union. It was not uncommon for the ruling party of one nation to exile the leadership of political opposition groups to a neighboring state, where the opposition would reconstitute its forces for an invasion of his home state. On other occasions like-minded political leaders would unite forces to impose "one of their own" in the presidential palace of another nation.

Under these new conditions, for two years following the collapse of the UPCA, notes circulated among the Central American governments regarding the possibility of coming together again. While there was interest, no more than two states could ever agree on the location site for a meeting of delegates until March 17, 1842, when representatives El Salvador, Honduras, and Nicaragua gathered in Chinandega, Nicaragua. The Costa Rican and Guatemalan governments refused to send delegates, a shortcoming that would characterize future conclaves. Most distant from the northern capitals, the government at San José did not wish to get involved in the political machinations of its northern neighbors, an attitude that would persist well into the twentieth century. In Guatemala, Rafael Carrera was just beginning to solidify his hold on the country, and he brought with him an isolationist attitude based upon the Guatemalan experiences during the era of the UPCA. The Chinandega Agreement, as it came to be known, established a provisional government of the participating states with a council comprised of a delegate from each state and a majority of the delegates selected statesman and diplomat Antonio José Cañas as its presiding officer. Costa Rica and Guatemala could become members simply by a declaration of adherence to the agreement that intended to create a new federal government. Accordingly, each state was sovereign in every matter not expressly assigned to the central authority; the states agreed not to interfere in each other's internal affairs and to recognize all legal acts and court decisions of the other states. The civil and political rights of all citizens were guaranteed. A member government's request for the extradition of a criminal would be completed immediately except for offenses of political nature. Alliances designed against one or two member states and treaties with foreign powers were prohibited.

A bilateral congress comprised the legislature. The lower house, or assembly, would be comprised of delegates based upon population with one deputy for every 50,000 people. Each member state would have three senators appointed by the individual nation's own senate. The republic's president would be elected to a four year term by an un-described electoral *junta*. Without a vice president, should a presidential vacancy occur, the joint congress was to select a successor; and if the congress were not in session, the senior senator was act as president for the remainder of the term. A three-man Supreme Court would be elected by the two houses of the congress. Customs duties collected at each state's entry ports would be the central government's primary income source. Although the proposed constitution had most vague language, one must remember that while the delegates continued unity of their region, they were victims of a centralized Spanish colonial system and only a less so UPCA. It was an effort to bridge the gap between that past and a more democratic and decentralized system of government for which the Central Americans had no preparation.

Because of the actions of the two non-conference participants the Chinandega Agreement quickly fell apart. The Costa Rican government offered too many qualifications to its vote of approval, while Guatemala rejected outright the proposed agreement, and its President Rafael Carrera and Honduran chief of state Francisco Ferrera also rejected it. Rather than abandon the idea of Central American unity, external pressures such as British designs on the Mosquito Coast, the Mexicans toiling in Soconusco state northwest of and adjacent to Guatemala, and Francisco Morazán conspiring in Costa Rica, prompted delegates from El Salvador, Honduras, and Nicaragua to meet again on July 27, 1842. The most significant changes

from the Chinandega document included a three man executive council rather than a president and an assembly consisting of one member
from each state, ideas previously held dear by the Costa Rican and
Guatemalan governments. Still these two governments rejected
the proposed *Confederación Centroamericana* fearing a loss if state
sovereignty to a central government. The hollow government
continued until 1845.

In the meantime, a third attempt was made in1842 at creating a
unified regional government, this time at a meeting in Guatemala City.
Only Costa Rica abstained from signing the October 7, 1842, agreement that called for the establishment of a centralized government,
which in reality was a defensive alliance. The agreement was
motivated, in part, by the British government's pressure to collect
forced debts and contributions by its citizens to Central America's
warring factions and, in part, with the anticipated efforts by Francisco
Morazán to unify the region under his control. This time, delegate
Pedro Nolasco Arriaga committed Honduras to make common cause
with El Salvador, Guatemala, and Nicaragua in case of an attack and
agreed not to send Honduran troops across a neighbor's border without permission of that government. Furthermore, the signatories
agreed that they would withhold recognition from a government that
attained power by revolution three. In matters of foreign policy, the
governments were to speak and act in a singular voice, hopefully an
economically efficient means to strengthen the Central American
diplomatic position with more experienced governments in Europe
and the United States. At best, however, this was an ad hoc organization
in search of security from the international powers and a means to keep
meddling in each other's internal affairs.

In April 1844, the administrative council of delegates for the *Confederación Centroamericana* received a request from Salvadoran President
Francisco Malespín for military assistance to repel a Guatemalan
invasion force led by Manuel José Arce, his fourth attempt to return to
the Salvadoran presidential palace since 1829. The Salvadorans were
quickly defeated by a combination of armed troops from Guatemala,
Honduras, and Nicaragua after which Honduran troops briefly
confronted troops from El Salvador and Nicaragua for violations of its
own border. When the dust finally settled, Nicaraguan Fruto Chamorro
resigned as supreme delegate of the *Confederación Centroamericana*, and
with it the organization passed into history.

Political tensions that often resulted in military skirmishes between
supporters of conservatives and liberals were a major characteristic
of Central American history, including that of Honduras between

1842 and 1846. During the same time period, the British expanded and tightened their control over their interests along the Mosquito Coast that ran from southern Honduras into Nicaragua. The Central Americans still fretted over the spread southward of Mexican influence. When the United States did not respond to Nicaraguan President Chamorro's 1845 request for help in checking the British, he revived the idea of a Central American federation.

Chamorro repeated previous proposals for three separate administrative units: executive, legislative, and judicial. Each of the five member states would send representatives to the federal congress for five-year terms and that congress would nominate a candidate for chief executive. The existing state court systems would function as the federal judiciary. The proposal also stated that all powers not specifically assigned to the federal government belonged to the states. Finally, each state would contribute two hundred men to form the core of the federal army. Otherwise, Chamorro's proposal was woefully short on details. Before the details could be hammered out, however, it took several months for the governments to agree upon Sonsonate, El Salvador as the initial conference site, just as Chamorro originally suggested.

Because the Central American world had changed significantly since independence 25 years earlier, many contemporaries viewed the Sansonate conclave as the final opportunity for the establishment of a regional federation. Despite a common heritage, the individual states were now beginning to develop separate cultures, customs, interests, and laws. Economic issues such as trade and commerce, banking, currency exchange, tariffs, and the acquisition of new debt, mostly to international banks and commerce houses were in need of attention. And the European governments were now demanding that Central America have a singular voice to represent it in all international matters. Efforts to convene a conference in May, June, and July1846 failed. No more than three delegates convened at any one time, and the Nicaraguan delegate was a no-show on all three occasions. The meeting at Sonsonate began on July 11, 1846, only to be cut short two days later when Salvadoran President Eugenio Aguilar declared a state of siege in response to the violence that erupted between the supporters of the Liberal president's policies and those of the conservative bishop in San Salvador, Msgr. Jorge Viteri. Aguilar won and Viteri vanished to Nicaragua. At the same time, the mostly liberal delegates at Sonsonate disbanded the conference, viewing the Church standing as an obstacle to their fundamental rights.

Following the suspension of the Sonsonate meeting, representatives from Honduras, El Salvador, and Nicaragua met on two different occasions to discuss the possibility of placing themselves under a United States protectorate because of their concern about further British expansion along the ill-defined Mosquito Coast and on Tigre Island in the Gulf of Fonseca that bordered all three nations. The protectorate idea was eventually tabled in favor of yet another conference that convened in Nacaome, Honduras, to create yet another Central American government. Guatemala and Costa Rica, however, turned down invitations to participate; the former preferred to pursue an independent foreign policy, and the latter proclaimed that it would participate once the other four states agreed to a form of government, an unlikely possibility given the region's historical record. Under these conditions on October 7, 1847, at Nacaome, the three participating states agreed to call for a constituent assembly. In March 1848, the governments of Honduras, El Salvador, and Nicaragua ratified a compact concluded by their representatives at the Nacaome meeting. Costa Rica refused to consider the agreement for ratification fretting over the potential new cost for supporting a centralized bureaucracy, executive, and a new court system. Viewing themselves as different from their northern neighbors, the *Ticos* also concluded that a central government's authority as a potential intrusion into their internal affairs. They also vigorously objected to a military draft for a Central American army. In Guatemala, strongman Rafael Carrera still preferred to pursue an independent foreign policy and, therefore, viewed any Central American government as a threat to that objective. The situation became more complicated because, at the same time unity discussions were underway, the Salvadoran government attempted to separate Los Altos state from Guatemala.

From its start, the 1848 agreement was ineffective, but it did not deter the original three, Honduras, El Salvador, and Nicaragua, from trying again. The agreement concluded on November 6, 1852, at León, Nicaragua provided for the regular consultation of their foreign ministers to discuss any foreign threats to the signatories internal security. The foreign ministers also were to consult on matters negatively affecting each nation's internal security and political stability. In other words, this meant suppressing rebellious groups in one country that had designs upon another country. For the same reasons as before Guatemala and Costa Rica refused to consider joining the agreement. This defensive alliance came into being on January 1, 1851, entitled "The National Representation of Central America" whose sessions were held in either León or nearby Chinandega, Nicaragua.

The remaining three states sent the required two representatives who elected Honduran José Francisco Barrundia its first president. The National Representation government failed in its attempt to combine its diplomatic corps so that one diplomat could represent two or three countries in a capital abroad, but the United States and several European governments were not receptive because they did not accept the representation government, really a council of six men, as a duly constituted government representing the three signatory states or in a position to speak for all of Central America.

In an effort to correct the deficiencies of the representation government, in October 1852, Honduran President Trinidad Cabañas convened a meeting of the six delegates in Tegucigalpa where agreement was reached to change the organization's name to "The Republic of Central America." Many of the original articles of cooperation were tinkered with, but the most important additions empowered the republic to use force to bring peace within any of the member states, an article aimed at political exiles who habitually found safe havens across the border where they raised armaments and troops for a re-invasion of the homeland.

The Republic of Central America was short-lived. In 1856, the Guatemalans elected Justo Rufino Barrios President for Life and with it, his ambitions to unite all of Central America under his control. The first step came with his forced installation of Santos Guardiola as President of Honduras. While both men enforced order and stability at home, they also opposed any concept of Central American confederation. Only years later would Barrios revive the concept.

The Central Americans momentarily came together for defensive purposes in 1856 to drive the U.S. filibusterer William Walker from Nicaragua. As elsewhere on the isthmus, Nicaragua was locked in a liberal-conservative struggle for government control. At the invitation of liberals, Walker arrived in Nicaragua in May 1855, ostensibly to secure the liberals in power. A year later, however, he governed Nicaragua through puppet President Patricio Rivas but clearly had designs to unite all Central America under his command. The other governments, all conservative, responded in unison to defeat Walker's army and force his surrender on May 1, 1857.

The ideal of a Central American Union did not die with William Walker's execution by Honduran troops at Trujillo, Honduras, on September 12, 1860. Over the next generation, Central America underwent a political transformation as liberals supplanted conservatives in presidential palaces across the isthmus. In Guatemala, the son of a wealthy northern landowner, Justo Rufino Barrios, epitomized that change.

His policies contrasted sharply with that of former Guatemalan conservative head-of-state Rafael Carrera, but they shared common bonds for their silencing of political opposition and suppressing the indigenous and other members of the lower class. Barrios, Guatemala's president from 1873 to 1885, envisioned himself as head of a Central American Union. In 1876, Barrios called for a meeting of the five states in Guatemala City for the purpose of planning a federal union. While his agenda items reflected debates of the past, Barrios also called for a common defense plan, meaning a federal army and a singular naval fleet, and for a unified foreign policy through the creation of a singular diplomatic corps and foreign office neither of which previously existed in Central America. Once in place, Barrios envisioned that the federal government could construct a common road and communications systems, unify legal and educational systems, and a singular citizenship for the people of the current five republics. During the Guatemala City meeting, Barrios' army was preparing its invasion of El Salvador to install a president more favorable to his own plans. Barrios waited until after the conference ended on May 1, 1876, to install Rafael Zaldivar in the presidential chair in San Salvador. A similar plot placed Marco Aurelio Soto in the Honduran presidency on August 27, 1876. Both were adherents of Barrios's liberal/positivist philosophy and openly supported his dream of heading a united Central America, but the idea quickly faded elsewhere in the region.

Barrios interpreted his 1880 reelection to Guatemala's presidency as a mandate, including his vision of a Central American union under his tutelage. Finally confident of internal support, in January 1883, he sent emissaries to the other four states to state his lofty ideals and to pledge noninterference in their affairs. As could be expected, the Presidents of Honduras Luis Bográn and El Salvador responded favorably, but Costa Rica and Nicaragua again demurred. Unwilling to accept the snub, an emboldened Barrios declared a Central American Union on February 28, 1885, and under the threat of military enforcement, directed the other states to dispatch delegations to Guatemala City for a meeting starting on May 1, 1885, where they would establish a unified government. Again, Honduran President Soto assented, but the other three heads of state resisted. Salvadoran President Zaldivar spearheaded the opposition and persuaded Nicaraguan Adán Cárdenas and Costa Rican Próspero Fernández Oreamuno to join him in a military alliance against Barrios. Apparently, still under the impression that his will could be enforced, Barrios led his forces into El Salvador on March 1, 1885, where he was killed in the Battle of

Chalchuapa on April 2, 1885. Zaldívar attempted to rekindle the unification effort, calling for a meeting on May 15, 1885 in Santa Tecla, El Salvador. As in the past, only the weak and impoverished Honduras accepted the invitation. The meeting never convened.

Ten years later, in 1895, Honduran President Policarpo Bonilla used the expulsion of the British from the Mosquito Coast as the reason to again attempt unification of Central America for defensive purposes. The long-term Mosquito Coast issue best illustrated the vulnerability of Central America to foreign interests. A unionist, Bonilla invited the Central American chiefs of state to a meeting at Amapala, but only Presidents José Santos Zelaya (Nicaragua) and Rafael Antonio Gutiérrez (El Salvador) accepted. On June 20, 1895 three reached an agreement that was promptly ratified by their respective national legislatures. Guatemala and Costa Rica, not represented at Amapala, received invitations to join the newly created *República Mayor* or the Greater Republic of Central America, as it would be known once they voluntarily joined.

Given the ambience of the time, the Republic was charged with responsibility to deal with foreign affairs but little more. Its legislature, comprised of one national delegate and alternate for three-year periods would make decisions by a majority vote. Each year, the legislature would select one of their own to represent the republic in negotiations with foreign nations. The agreement also anticipated a general assembly to be created within three years. It would be comprised of 20 delegates from each member state appointed by state legislatures. Until the general assembly convened, individual states could ratify treaties or agreements concluded with another nation. The assembly would rotate its meetings annually, first at San Salvador, followed in order by Managua and Tegucigalpa.

Subsequently, Presidents Rafael Yglesias Castro of Costa Rica and Manuel Lisandro Barillas Bercián of Guatemala accepted invitations to join the Republic in 1897, their national legislatures rejected any suggestion of participating in a Central American Union.

Although Costa Rica became the first nation to recognize the Republic after its formation in 1895, the United States became the first country to accept a diplomat representing a group of Central American nations in nearly 60 years when, on December 24, 1896, President Grover Cleveland received Minister José Dolores Rodríguez. Cleveland qualified his recognition, however, with the proviso that the United States remained free to deal individually with each Central American nation. Cleveland's successor, William McKinley, changed the Republic's designation to an association not a federation with authority over member states. The new designation, however, did not alter diplomatic exchanges with one minister, representing the Republic's three members, accredited to Washington, D.C. and the United States having one minister accredited to the states that comprised the Republic and another to Guatemala and Honduras.

Delegates from Honduras, El Salvador, and Nicaragua completed a permanent constitution in Managua in June 1898 to replace the provisional 1895 document. The new constitution provided the framework of government–executive, legislative and judicial–but permitted the individual states to continue their own authority over internal affairs. Under the cloud of individual national interests, *Los Estados Unidos de Centro América* (the United States of Central America) came into being on November 1, 1898, only be dissolved by the month's end. General Tomás Regalado engineered a *coup d' etat* in El Salvador and on November 13, 1898, announced the republic's constitution inoperative in El Salvador because it had never been submitted to the people for approval. Neither the Honduran or Nicaraguan government mustered the courage to force Regalado to back down and on November 30 formally dissolved the union.

Responsibility for the dissolution of the proposed 1898 Central American Union quickly fell upon Tomás Regalado, but his actions also served as a reminder of historic Central American fears about a central government that could result in a loss of local authority and of individual rights and of a petty nationalism among the five states that comprised Central America. What Hondurans Francisco Morázan envisioned in 1829 and Policarpo Bonilla attempted to complete in 1895 never reached fruition in the nineteenth century.

§ § § § §

Nineteenth-century Honduran history is a microcosm of the Central American experience during the same time period. The democratic political principles and the guarantee of civil and human rights found in the United States and European models made their way into the several Honduran constitutions from 1842 until 1894, but in practice, the *criollo* land owning elite were the beneficiaries. Only this class of people participated in the political system, and, as continued from colonial practices, the rulers of independent Honduras arduously worked to prevent the lower socioeconomic groups from entering the arena.

The ideal of a Central American Union also continued into the nineteenth century, but the focus often became a defensive arrangement either to protect the conservatives or the liberals in power or, as in the Honduran example, the imposition of like minded individuals into the presidential palace. Similarities in government philosophy served to prevent exile groups of one country from going abroad to amass an army and munitions for return home to oust the existing government. Such arrangements were not always successful. The Honduran leadership never developed a clear vision of where the nation was going and thus often found itself at the center of regional political intrigue.

The failure to mature politically contributed to Honduras's lack of economic development during the nineteenth century. Granted, the nation lacked natural resources to be exploited and the necessary supporting infrastructure, but political leaders were more concerned with their own power than with national development. As a result, on the eve of the twentieth century, Honduras was the poorest and most underdeveloped independent Central American nation.

Devoid of a vibrant tax base, the liberal administrations, despite all their assertions about education, health care, road construction, and the like, simply lacked the money to accomplish the stated goals. The primary source of government income throughout the century remained export tariffs on primary agricultural goods.

With a lack of funding to modernize the nation, Honduras remained a place of relative economic and social backwardness throughout the nineteenth century. The country remained overwhelmingly rural, with only Tegucigalpa, Comayagua, and San Pedro Sula as cities of any size and economic and political importance. The total population in the 1850s was estimated at 350,000, the overwhelming majority of whom were mestizos. By 1914, the population grew to only 562,000.

Opportunities for education and culture were limited at best. Mid-nineteenth century records indicate that Honduras had no libraries and no regularly published newspapers. Two universities existed, although their quality was questionable. By the 1870s, only 275 schools, with approximately 9,000 registered students existed in the entire country. In 1873–1874, the government budgeted the U.S. equivalent of $720 for education but designated solely for the national university. Things did not improve by the end of the nineteenth century.

NOTE

1. *Foro Hondureño* (January and February, 1939), 229. Author's translation.

4

The World Comes to Honduras

You are to gather all the information possible about this new Central South American country ... a position of highest geographical importance–important also by the commercial connections and lodgements on the soil by the British with the neighboring Bay of Honduras and Mosquito Shore.[1]

John Quincy Adams
June 14, 1824

Like most North Americans in 1824, Secretary of State John Quincy Adams was ignorant about Central America but alert to its strategic importance in the greater Caribbean region. In part, U.S. ignorance can be attributed to Spanish colonial policy that closed Central America to foreigners. Only a few outsiders-among them Thomas Gage, Ravaneu de Lusan, John Cockburn, John Roach, and one North American, John Rhodes-recorded the experiences of their travels to this backwater of Spain's New World empire. There are no indications that any North American library held any of their works. Thomas Jefferson, however, did read Alexander von Humboldt's 1808 classic *Political Essay on the Kingdom of New Spain* that covered his travels to Venezuela, Peru, Mexico, and Cuba, but not Central America.

As the Latin American independence movements gained momentum after 1810, Americans gained a fleeting impression of Central America via the infrequent statements made by government officials and newspaper reports that applauded the hemispheric revolution. Americans anticipated commercial opportunities in the independent republics that followed the break from Spain. The absence of warfare across the isthmus compared to that in South America and the events in Mexico also distracted the North Americans from events on the isthmus and its less violent independence struggle.

Given this mutual isolation in 1824, Americans did not understand the political, economic, and social conflicts plaguing Central America such as the legacies of the direct line of authority established by Madrid over its New World colonies. Nor did the Americans understand that local elites used local town councils (*cabildos*) as a means to subvert Spanish authority. In mountainous Central America, the king's emissary learned early the futility of trying to carry out policies that could not be enforced or issuing orders that would not be implemented.

Thus, Secretary Adams' 1824 instructions to Mann were appropriate. The Americans knew little about Central America other than the discarding of the Spanish authorities. The Americans did not know that the Central Americans retained the local economic monoculture. Local *haciendas* produced staple crops such as indigo and cocoa, while ranchers in Honduras produced cattle for locals and for distribution into Nicaragua. The limited market for these exports sustained an important group of landowners and merchants. At the time the Guatemalan Caribbean port served as the central point for shipping staple Central America's products abroad and importing foreign made goods for distribution to the interior markets, a factor that further enhanced the political power of Honduran merchants. Fluctuations in the world market prices, and competition from other supply sources contributed to the emergence of a debtor-creditor relationship between the Honduran merchants and landowners and, to an economic rivalry between Guatemala and the outlying provinces, including Honduras.

With the colonial economy preserved, Central America also retained its rigid social structure. Of the region's estimated 1.6 million inhabitants on the eve of independence, an estimated 100,000 were pure white (*criollos*), about 900,000 pure Indian, about 450,000 *mestizos*, and another 20,000 blacks and mulattoes. Spanish administrators (*peninsulares*) dominated the imperial bureaucracy, but many of their rivals, *criollos*, had become large landowners and successful merchants, gaining social and economic privileges but not political participation. With independence the *criollos* replaced the *peninsulares* as government administrators at both the national and local levels. But, as in the colonial period, the *criollos* ignored the mixed-blood *mestizos* below them and reduced Indians, blacks, and mulattoes to forced labor, debt peonage, and slavery. The Roman Catholic Church, entrenched in Central America, gave its tacit, if not enthusiastic support to this rigid structure.

Central America's colonial experience and isolation severely restricted its understanding of the outside world. A small number of Central Americans may have read the works of Antonio de Aledo Bexar,, Abe Renal, and Abbé Pradt, who provided descriptions of the U.S. economy and geography and some discussion of the country's revolution, constitutional government, and religious toleration. Certainly, most of the early Latin American patriots had read the Declaration of Independence, U.S. Constitution, and some of Tom Paine's writings, but personal contacts between Central Americans and U.S. citizens after the American Revolution were negligible. Most of those who came north were on official business seeking to enlist U.S. support for the fledgling independence movements. A few, such as the Guatemalan scientist José Felipe Flores, returned home to spread their favorable impressions of the United States. Spanish American liberals applauded the great extent of civil and political freedom, religious toleration, social equality, literacy, and the lack of pomp and ceremony. Others understood that the societies of both hemispheres differed greatly and suggested that the federal form of government might not apply to Spanish America. Conservatives, who feared that any changes in the existing institutions would destroy their orderly world and privileged position, remained largely pessimistic about using the United States as a political or social model.

Despite their mutual isolation and ignorance, the United States and the United Provinces of Central America (UPCA) shared three foreign policy objectives: a transisthmian canal, new markets, and opposition to the intervention of a European power in Central America.

The dream of a transisthmian canal was as old as Balboa, the conqueror of Panama; but early Spanish interests in a passageway across Darien or Tehuantepec, the dredging of the San Juan River, collapsed with the wars of independence. Independent Central America revived the dream just as American political leaders and merchants awakened to the canal's significance for the evolution of the nation's worldwide commercial contacts.

Transatlantic imperial rivalries frustrated U.S. trade in the Caribbean for 30 years after its independence in 1783. Similarly, independent Central America was unable to chart its own foreign economic policy.

From the start, U.S. vessels and their crews had fallen prey to British, French, and Spanish gunboats while seeking in the Caribbean, which centered on Cuba, then on Puerto Rico and Venezuela, and by 1817 on Veracruz, Mexico. Through these Caribbean ports, American merchants had limited contact with Central America, yet they anticipated a Central American market for American wares, a notion reinforced by Englishman John Hale, who wrote that the Central Americans "look upon foreign products as miraculous articles." This was especially true in Costa Rica, where farmers used wooden tools, and agricultural development was more than a century behind that of Europe and the United States. Hale foresaw a limitless market for iron shovels and hoes, garden rakes, paint, turpentine, machines for planting cotton, and sawmills. Given the collapse of formerly guaranteed Spanish markets, the limited domestic demand for staples and the lack of a merchant fleet, Central America's exporters found themselves at the mercy of international markets and rivalries.

An immediate issue in the 1820s, as it had been for three decades after the American Revolution, was the concern with foreign intervention in the West. Since its independence in 1783, the United States constantly sought to remove the dangers posed by Britain, Spain, and France in the Western Hemisphere, first, from its border areas and then from the high seas. In 1803, Thomas Jefferson determined "to exclude all European influence from the hemisphere," and persuaded a reluctant Congress to purchase Louisiana in order to secure the American West, the Floridas, and New Orleans against further European intrigue. An 1811 congressional resolution railed against the transfer of the Floridas and Cuba to another European power. A year later, the United States went to war to reaffirm its independence, and more precisely, to rid its southern flank of menacing European influence. In 1819 it completed its absorption of the Floridas, forcing the Spanish to retrench and the British to reassess their imperial strategy in Spanish America.

Thus, in December 1823, when President James Monroe asserted before Congress that the Western Hemisphere was off limits to further European colonization and political ideologies, he was reaffirming the fundamental tenets of U.S. foreign policy based upon its 40 years of international experience since independence. The United States fashioned a coherent foreign policy.

In contrast, Central American foreign policy was not as clearly defined as that of the United States. Certainly, Central Americans were alert to the foreign presence, especially the British whose logging establishments on the Caribbean coast that dated to the early seventeenth century and intruded upon Honduran, Guatemalan, and Nicaraguan territory. With a base at present-day Belize, the British built a string of forts stretching south to Panama. By 1741, British officials in Jamaica regularly appointed a superintendent to Belize and established a virtual protectorate over the Mosquito Indians. From the Mosquito territory, the British carried on illicit trade with Nicaragua and Costa Rica and attacked Spanish shipping and coastal positions in the region. During the American Revolution, the British plan to seize the San Juan River in Nicaragua as a preface to their plan to construct an interoceanic transit route fell victim to the weakness of their own forces in the region, the course of the American Revolution, and the strength of the Spanish response, which included the recruitment of a Central American army. Although the 1783 Treaty of Paris failed to dislodge the British, their interest in the Caribbean coast waned on the eve of Central American independence.

In addition to British presence at Belize, the Napoleonic Wars, which began in 1803, raised across the isthmus the fear of a possible French invasion and disrupted isthmian trade with Spain. The trade problem ignited a debate that split the landholding aristocracy and local merchants. Landholders favored expanded foreign commerce so that the expected profits and taxes could be used to protect the region against foreign attack. Merchants, who wanted to maintain their relationship with Spain, looked instead to Church properties as the source of income for the common defense. The conflicts over foreign commerce and the conflicts over taxation were but two of the issues that carried over into the post-independence period.

In addition to its vulnerability to foreign intrusion, the UPCA lacked a unifying statement like Monroe's. There was no second war for independence as the United States had fought in the War of 1812. The pursuit of markets and quest for security provided no common agenda in the political wars of Central America's first generation of rulers. Unlike the United States, Central America began its independence without a consensus about its position toward the outside world; and, unlike the hemisphere's first republic, it was unable to fashion one.

These experiences, however framed the foreign policy of each for the next 40 years. Honduras fell within the purview of the larger issues.

A GROWING MISTRUST

Thomas N. Mann never reached Guatemala City, the capital of the UPCA in 1824. In fact, only five of the twelve diplomats appointed to Central America between 1823 and 1839 did. Because of the limited and sometimes sporadic transportation, reaching Guatemala City proved an arduous task. After departing from a U.S. east coast port, usually New York, Philadelphia, or Baltimore, the diplomats first traveled to Havana, Cuba, or Kingston, Jamaica, where they awaited another vessel destined for Omoa on the Honduran Caribbean Coast. By mule or horseback, the diplomat then trekked with a group across the mountains from Omoa to Guatemala City. Using the same transportation route in reverse, in 1823, the United Provinces of Central America dispatched two diplomats to the United States: Jose Arce and Juan Manuel Rodríguez in 1824 by Juan José Cañas and in 1835 Juan Galindo. While the Honduran Francisco Morazán served as a focal point of a Central American government, the same was not true for his country with regards to international affairs.

Once in Guatemala City, the U.S. diplomats found a government in disarray, a static social structure dominated by *criollos* that discriminated against *mestizos* and the indigenous, and a culture separated by a broad divide upon the past of Spanish colonialism and a long indigenous history. In 1833 Charles DeWitt observed that ignorance, superstition and corruption characterized all Central American social institutions. Charles De Witt, who did not venture beyond Guatemala City during his five year tenure (1833–1838), consistently dispatched gloomy reports about the UPCA that he correctly predicted would melt away like a piece of ice in the bright sun.

The Central American visitors to the United States considered its institutions as models to be imitated for the region's modernization. In 1822, Salvadorans Manuel José Arce and Juan Manuel Rodríguez informed Secretary of State John Quincy Adams that El Salvador would better advance itself if linked to the United States and not Iturbide's Mexico. The following year, the same two Salvadorans asserted that all of Central America should come under the umbrella of protection as expressed in the Monroe Doctrine. Morazán and his key advisor José Francisco Barrundia unsuccessfully sought to impose the U.S. federal system of government upon Central America and their home state of Honduras. The liberals in Guatemala made the most advances with the adoption of the Livingston Codes, copied from the Louisiana legal system, and in education reforms. But these attacks upon the legacies of Spanish rule contributed to vehement conservative opposition that significantly contributed to the collapse of the UPCA in 1839.

Antonio José Cañas arrived in Washington, D.C., in 1825 confident that U.S. business would underwrite the cost of a transisthmian canal through Nicaragua. Cañas and his Guatemalan contemporary, José

Aycinena, who lived in the United States during its heyday of canal construction in the 1820s and early 1830s, envisioned that such a canal would bring prosperity to the entire region, spur its agricultural and industrial modernization that would produce goods to be marketed in Europe, and make Central America a global maritime center. Europeans would be attracted to the economic opportunities and, once in the region, marry and uplift the indigenous peoples. With little U.S. interest at the time, the anticipated project faded into the background only to be revived when Juan Galindo arrived in Washington, D.C., in 1835. With British, Dutch, and French commercial groups now showing varying degrees of interest in a transisthmian canal, President Andrew Jackson and the U.S. Senate wanted to meet the challenge. Jackson dispatched Charles Biddle to Guatemala, Nicaragua, Panama (then a province of Colombia) and to Bogotá to determine the status of various canal projects. In the meantime, the senate resolved that any such waterway should be open to world traffic and to levy tolls to be used to reimburse the capitalists who constructed it. The Biddle mission was a disappointment. Although he negotiated an agreement in Bogotá for a road-canal connection between the two oceans across Colombia, he visited only Panama on the isthmus because people he spoke with in the Caribbean advised him that such an undertaking was impossible across Central America. There the issue rested for the next decade.

Viable commercial relations proved equally frustrating. When Cañas was in Washington, D.C., he hoped to find new markets for Central American wares and also a source for goods previously purchased from Spain. His arrival coincided at a time when western spokesmen, like Henry Clay, looked to the circum-Caribbean region as a market for goods to be transported through the ports at New Orleans and Mobile. The mutual interests resulted in the 1825 Treaty of Amity and Commerce that provided for complete trade reciprocity. Unfortunately, little materialized. Central American commerce remained a miniscule part of overall U.S. trade. Britain, followed by France, Germany, and Holland continued to dominate trade with the region. The UPCA were in decay at the time of Juan Galindo's arrival in Washington, D.C., in 1835, a fact reenforced by the reports by Charles DeWitt, the U.S. Minister in Guatemala City. DeWitt's replacement, John L. Stephens, a lawyer turned amateur archeologist, arrival in Guatemala City coincided with the collapse of the UPCA in 1839, an event that freed Stephensand his traveling companion, architect and draftsman Frederick Catherwood, to pursue his real interest in the region: exploration of Mayan communities.

Throughout the 1840s, the United States policymakers focused upon expansion to the Pacific Ocean, not Central America despite warnings issued to Washington by U.S. consuls William S. Murphy and Henry Savage about a growing British presence in the region.

Frederick Chatfield arrived in Guatemala City in the late spring of 1834 to represent British interests throughout the region. Chatfield, like Stephens, sought the assignment; but as an experienced diplomat, he viewed the post as a stepping stone to still higher rank in Britain's Foreign Office and aggressively sought to expand British interests on the isthmus. Alerted by Chatfield's reports about San Juan del Norte, Nicaragua, as a possible canal terminus, in 1837, the British government declared that the Mosquito Indians and Territory, including Honduras, be protected against Central American encroachments. In 1840, Chatfield gleefully approved Britain's protection proclamation over the Mosquito Coast and its inhabitants, a direct affront to Honduran sovereignty. In 1839, he persuaded the British Royal Navy to seize control of the Bay Islands off the Honduran North Coast. Two years later, the British superintendent at Belize, Alexander MacDonald, extended his administration over the Bay Islands. Standing alone, politically weakened and with a military force, Honduras was in no position to challenge the British actions.

The Mexican War from 1846 to 1848 ignited some U.S. interest in annexing all territories from the Rio Grande River through Panama in order to bestow the blessings of democracy upon these downtrodden and backward people. The more pragmatic President James K. Polk, however, focused upon the reports of growing British interest across the isthmus. He dispatched Elijah Hise to Guatemala City with instructions to determine what the United States could do to check the British. The first U.S. diplomat assigned to Central America since 1839, Hise arrived on March 31, 1848, and shortly thereafter recommended that the United States use the Monroe Doctrine to thwart British expansion on the isthmus, an idea rejected out of hand by Secretary of State James Buchannan. In violation of his instructions, Hise went on to negotiate a treaty with Nicaragua that provided for a unnamed private U.S. company to construct and operate a transisthmian route, and in return, the U.S. government to protect Nicaraguan territory, a clear reference to the Mosquito Coast. Hise returned home with treaty in hand and to a reluctant president, Zachary Taylor, who never submitted the treaty for congressional approval. The significance of the proposed Hise Treaty rests with the concessions provided to the United States. They served as a harbinger of future U.S. pursuits for a transisthmian canal.

President Taylor replaced Hise with a self-educated and respectable journalist, Ephraim George Squier, who completed an agreement with Nicaragua almost identical to that negotiated by Hise but also specifying that Cornelius Vanderbilt's Accessory Transit Company would construct a river-lake-road transit route connecting Nicaragua's Caribbean and Pacific coasts.

From Nicaragua, Squier moved on to Honduras where he persuaded that government to cede to the U.S. Tigre Island in the Gulf of Fonseca, long considered the western terminus to a Nicaraguan canal. The cessation so infuriated the British Minister Frederick Chatfield that he ordered a British naval ship into the Gulf. But cooler heads prevailed in Washington and London. The Squier Treaty arrived in Washington In October 1849, one month after Secretary of State John M. Clayton (1796–1856) commenced negotiations with the British Minister Sir Henry Lytton Bulwer that resulted in an 1850 treaty that momentarily neutralized each other's interests in Central America. Squier remained in Honduras for several years, during which he wrote extensively about the region and as a partner in the failed effort to build a railroad across Honduras.

The maneuvering by external powers did not conceal the continuing liberal-conservative conflict that characterized Central American politics since independence in 1823. In the 1850s, the political conflict left Nicaragua vulnerable to outside influence. In 1854, a group of Nicaraguan liberals with Honduran assistance, attempted to seize power but failed when Rafael Carrera assisted his conservative allies in Guatemala. The conflict may have momentarily passed into history were it not for Byron Cole, part owner of the Honduras Mining and Trading Company. Cole feared that conservative governments in Guatemala and Nicaragua would bring a similar government to Honduras, which would limit his company's economic opportunities to the betterment of British interests whom the conservatives preferred. In the fall of 1854, Cole convinced Nicaraguan Liberal Francisco Castellón that filibuster reinforcements would guarantee his party's success. Castellón contracted with William Walker. Walker and his 56 followers landed in Nicaragua in June 1855. After initial setbacks, Walker's forces turned the tide that enabled him to persuade the conservatives to sue for peace in October 1855. From November 1855 to June 1856, Walker ruled the puppet presidency of Patricio Rivas. President Franklin Pierce extended recognition to Rivas' regime later that year, an act that prompted the Central American leadership to conclude that the United States had expansion designs upon the region.

By this time, Walker decided to the Americanization of Nicaragua that included, among other things, a declaration making English the official language and fiscal policies meant to attract U.S. colonists, particularly southerners, followed by the revocation of Nicaragua's 1824 emancipation edict. Once in place, Walker announced that he would form a Central American Union under his leadership.

Such concepts drew a harsh response from the other Central American governments, including Honduran liberal dictator José Trinidad Cabañas. Walker's pronouncements prompted the formation of a combined Central American army, financed by Cornelius Vanderbilt and supported by a British blockade of Walker's supply routes. Walker finally surrendered to a British naval officer and abandoned the region on May 1, 1857, and was repatriated to the United States. Seven months later, the undeterred Walker set out again for Central America. This time, the U.S. Navy was waiting in offshore waters. Walker was again stymied.

Walker attempted to return one more time in May 1860. The path was cleared by British interests and diplomacy. At that time, the British were preoccupied with the Crimean War and with the eastern Mediterranean. These complex issues led the British to seek an accommodation with the United States over Central America, a region much more important to the latter than the former. In 1859, London dispatched Charles Wyke first to Guatemala, where he completed a treaty settling the disputed Belizean territory. According to the treaty, Guatemala surrendered its claims to what became British Honduras in 1862 in return for a British promise to construct a railroad connecting northeastern Guatemalan with the Caribbean coast. Wyke moved on to Honduras where he completed a treaty granting Honduras sovereignty over the Bay Islands in return for a Honduran commitment not to cede the islands to any third party and not to interfere with the religion of the British subjects on islands. Britain also abandoned its protectorate over the Mosquito Indians to Honduras. From Tegucigalpa, Wyke went to Managua where he negotiated away British rights over the Mosquito Indians and their territory to Nicaragua.

With the treaty system in place in April 1860, members of the British community on Roatán, the largest of the Bay Islands, approached Walker to discard Honduran rule following the 1859 treaty. Walker accepted the challenge because he saw it as a stepping stone to a larger goal: to join an existing revolt against the current Honduran President, José Trinidad Cabañas. Walker disembarked at Trujillo, Honduras, where he and his forces attempted to hold an old Spanish fort, only to be captured by the British. Reportedly, Walker refused to be turned over to the U.S. authorities and therefore became a prisoner of Honduran troops who executed him before a firing squad on September 12, 1860.

Despite Walker's death and President James Buchanan's 1858 observation that domestic issues prompted the United States to momentarily retreat from Central America, the U.S. Civil War presented some unique problems. Authorities in Washington, D.C., did not want any foreign government to extend recognition and hence legitimacy to the Confederacy. With memories still fresh in their minds from the Walker intrusion, the Central Americans quickly complied and denied Confederate privateers use of their ports, like Omoa and Trujillo in Honduras. Without a naval force of their own, open ports invited attacks and/or blockades by the Union fleet. A most sensitive chord was struck in late 1861 and in early 1862 when Secretary of State William H. Seward persuaded President Abraham Lincoln to approve the relocation of freed blacks to Central America. Seward argued that climatic conditions; sugar, tobacco, and coffee plantations; and the nonwhite demographics of Central America provided an environment that could quickly absorb the former slaves. Honduran President Santos Guardiola joined his presidential colleagues in responding with an emphatic no. He perceived the sending of exslaves to Honduras as a back door way to extend U.S. influence over the isthmus.

Since the late 1840s, the region had become a pawn in United States-British policies. Central America was not consulted in any of the U.S. diplomatic maneuverings at mid-century that led to the Clayton-Bulwer Treaty. In effect, Central American problems were solved by nations outside the region. Coupled with the U.S. government's indifference, at best, to the William Walker affair and attempt to place black freedmen in the region left the impression that the United States were replacing Great Britain as the imperial power on the isthmus.

CONVERGING INTERESTS

For nearly a generation after the U.S. Civil War ended in 1865, official relations between the United States and Central America received minimal attention as each side experienced significant internal changes. Officially, the U.S. State Department continued to publically advocate a Central American union as the best means to overcome political turmoil and provide for economic development. But that appeared as a distant and idealistic goal on the isthmus and one the United States would distance itself from during this time period. The U.S. Minister assigned to all five republics in 1874, George

Williamson, noted that Central American leaders professed the high ideals of unity but were not willing to make the sacrifices to accomplish that goal. A forced potential union that guaranteed continued political conflict best characterized the generation of Central American leaders. Given this conflictive environment, Secretary of State Thomas Bayard announced in 1885 that henceforth the U.S. would work to avoid conflict and attempt to manage the peace across the isthmus.

The maneuverings for union made by Guatemalan President Justo Rufino Barrios between 1871 and his death prompted Bayard's policy statement. In 1871, Barrios, joined by kindred spirits José Maria Medina in Honduras and Santiago Gónzalez in El Salvador, formed a league among the three states to fight their conservative opposition. Medina was particularly concerned with internal opposition to his administration. Little came of this endeavor, but Barrios's proclamation of a Central American Union in February 1885 led to a Guatemalan-Salvadoran war that took Barrios's life on April 2, 1885. His successor, Manuel Lisandro Barilla Bercián, convened a conference in Guatemala City in 1887 that reached several agreements including the recognition of each other's territorial sovereignty and noninterference in each other's internal affairs, both of which fell within the framework of sustaining the political leadership then in power. Honduran President Marco Aurelio Soto approved the pact for that reason. However, there was no interest in reestablishing a Central American Union until 1895 when Honduran President Policarpo Bonilla called for a heads of state meeting at Amapala. Guatemala and Costa Rica declined the invitation, but Bonilla and the other two presidents completed an agreement on June 20 that established loose confederation among them to be called the Greater Republic of Central America. While the states remained independent and acted on their own internal matters, the Republic focused upon foreign affairs. Its Minister to the United States, José Dolores Rodríguez presented his credentials to U.S. President Grover Cleveland on December 24, 1896, with a reminder that the United States still recognized and would deal with the individual Central American states. Central America's political atmosphere remained fluid, and in 1898, General Tomâs Regalado seized control of the Salvadoran government. Always a critic of Central American union, Regalado announced his nation's withdrawal from the agreement one day after seizing power, November 14, 1898, and, with it, ended the nineteenth century efforts to unify the isthmian republics.

Domestic economic changes during the same generation eventually brought the United States and Central America again into a close relationship that conventional wisdom describes as the former's exploitation of the latter, an assertion, however, that is not completely accurate. The United States underwent an industrial revolution in the years after its Civil War. Its consumer products, ranging from women's clothing to agricultural machinery and from the Singer sewing machine to the Bessemer steel process, won accolades at various World Fairs. In 1891, for the first time in its history, the United States exported more manufactured than agricultural products, and at the 1896 Chicago World's Fair, Pabst became the first American and, in fact, non-German beer to win the blue ribbon at such expositions. Concomitant with this economic growth was an ever increasing demand for foreign markets and raw materials, a larger commercial fleet and navy to protect it, and a transisthmian canal to facilitate commerce. Central America fit neatly within this purview. European nations, particularly Great Britain, Germany, and France, similar to the United States, experienced rapid growth in manufacturing that demanded raw materials and new markets for the final products.

The liberals' arrival in presidential palaces across all Latin America by 1880 coincided with the northern hemisphere's so-called second industrial revolution. Latin America fell within the capitalist's purview in many ways. Bankers, bondholders, and individuals found opportunity in developing the infrastructure necessary to support the exportation of Latin American raw materials and agricultural produce and for the importation of consumer goods. The northern capitalists found the Latin American governments, including Central America, most congenial hosts by permitting the duty free importation of materials, most broadly interpreted, necessary for the construction of infrastructure, the lighting of cities, the mining of ores, expanding agricultural production and other economic endeavors. The Latin American governments also promised and kept labor peace. Until its collapse with the onset of the Great Depression of 1930, the Golden Age of Latin America's export based economies brought prosperity to the foreign investors and elites in Argentina with its exportation of beef, wheat, and wool; Chile with nitrates and copper; Venezuela with oil; and Cuba with sugar. In Central America, Costa Rica and El Salvador benefitted from coffee in the late nineteenth century; and in the twentieth century, along with Honduras and Guatemala, they benefitted from bananas, earning the region the collective name "the banana republics."

By 1885, Latin American liberals, including those in Central America, were entrenched in political power across the isthmus. The liberals espoused faith in positivism, a combination of Auguste Comte's sociocracy and Herbert Spencer's Darwinian evolutionary theory. The positivists believed that economic growth and prosperity were necessary before true political democracy could be established. Well into the twentieth century, these republican dictatorships were characterized by their obsession with material development, faith in scientific and technical education, imitation of U.S. and western European values, and increasingly the postponement of democracy and insensitivity to worker's needs.

For its part, the United States intended to capitalize upon the largesse of the liberals. In the 1870s, Minister Williamson's reports on the economies of the five republics became increasingly detailed, not only about market opportunities, but also the legal and political systems relationship to economic development. To advertise their wares, Central Americans participated in world trade congresses, particularly in New Orleans, which soon became the trading gateway to the isthmus. The liberals promoted diversification of agriculture and development of an export economy, mining, transportation, communications, and manufacturing. To attract badly needed foreign capital, the liberals granted generous concessions, modified tax laws, and suppressed labor's demands for increased wages, better working conditions, and an improved quality of life. The foreigners who came to Central America quickly identified and melded with the elite in an informal alliance that included a self-serving need to preserve the existing social and political order.

Honduras lacked favorable growing conditions for coffee production that rapidly developed in the other isthmian republics. An abundance of timber–mahogany, cedar, and rosewood–attracted attention from U.S. companies who extracted the lumber at the equivalent of one lempira per log and the planting of two seedlings to replace every tree cut down. Mining, particularly silver, drew most attention in Honduras. President Marco Aureilio Soto exempted from import duties and all national and municipal taxes on virtually everything need to mine the ore: machinery, equipment and materials, including furniture, European whiskies, and clothes for the mine managers and their families. The exported ore was also exempt from taxation. The mining companies also received timber and water rights on adjacent territories. Soto's successor, President Luis Bográn, instituted the *mandimiento* press-gang labor system to meet the mining industry's labor demands. Mining's ancillary economic activities brought little benefit to Honduras. Merchants imported most of their supplies from New York, and because they were related to mining, came into Honduras duty free. Local hotel, transportation facilities, along with the charcoal and salt industries were considered essential for the mine's daily operation and thus avoided taxation.

Under such favorable conditions, the Honduran government granted a total of 129 mining concessions during the 1880s and another 58 the following decade. Among the earliest U.S. companies to gain access to Honduras was Thomas Lombard's Yuseman Mining Company and Chicago Honduran Mining Company. The most successful was the New York and Honduran Rosario Mining Company, led by Washington S. Valentine, who wielded sufficient political influence into the twentieth century that he earned the title the King of Honduras.

European nations had a marked presence in Central America since the early nineteenth century. The British venture into Central America began on a cold morning in January 1823, when a group of 240 emigrants set sail on the *Honduras Packet* and the *Kinnersley Castle* from Leith (near Edinburgh, Scotland) for the nation of Poyais on Central America's Mosquito Coast, where the émigrés were told they would find rich and fertile soils, a balmy climate, and beautiful, civilized cities. A mixture of urban workers and small rural farmers, they had invested with their life's savings and possessions to purchase bonds that guaranteed them land in their new country. Upon arrival a month later, the weary travelers found three dilapidated eighteenth century buildings sitting among swamps and mangroves, not the idyllic scenes described and pictured in their Poyais guidebooks. The travelers quickly recognized that they had been the victims of one of the most elaborate hoaxes in history. The land they had been sold was nonexistent; the banknotes and guidebooks they carried with them were forgeries; their documents were worthless. Poyais was a fiction designed by General Sir Gregory MacGregor, the Prince of Poyais, a flamboyant and charismatic character who served as a mercenary in Simon Bolivar's army. Only 50 of the adventurers survived the ordeal and returned to the British Isles physically exhausted and financially ruined to live out their lives. For his part, MacGregor served a short prison sentence, after which he lived quietly in Scotland until his death in 1845 at the age of 59. Subsequent British bondholders shared the sunken feeling of the original investors: investing in Central America was throwing good money after bad.

In 1825, the United Provinces of Central America floated a $244,500 bond issue at 8 percent, meaning that the bondholders received approximately $118,990 before the UPCA collapsed in 1839. Frederick Chatfield was the first of several British Ministers to unsuccessfully press for full repayment individual governments. By 1880, British invested $10,601,445 in Central American bonds, $3,222,000 was in

Honduran paper, all of which the government in Tegucigalpa defaulted upon in 1872. During the same time period, British private investors pumped nearly one million dollars in the Honduran economy, 90% of which went into mining and the remainder among the proposed railroad connecting Omoa with Acajutla, El Salvador, and into smaller textile manufacturing operations and consumer goods merchant shops.

The French found Central American society and politics in a state of confusion in the early 1840s, a situation its agents in the region warned that the British would capitalize upon in its desire to dominate regional trade. The British declaration of a protectorate over the Mosquito Coast and its seizure of San Juan del Norte, Nicaragua, were considered the first steps in that direction. To counter British economic interests, a French agent in Central America, Jean-Marie Raimond Baradére sought permission to arrange for the export of Guatemalan tobacco to France. Another French agent, E. Perrín, was convinced that a treaty with Honduras would develop a market for French products and colonials who would bring stability and riches to a nation marred by backwardness and underdevelopment. Also during the 1840s, the British Minister to Central America, Frederick Chatfield, continually argued that British culture, economic development, and politics stood above that of other nations and, as such, was an example for the Central Americans to emulate. The French agents challenged the British assertion with statements about French preeminence as a conveyer of culture, civilization, and Christianity, a tough sell when only some 30 French families, mostly merchants, were scattered across Central America, including Honduras. Nothing came from these suggestions, nor where French efforts in the late 1850s to establish a joint European guarantee of the five republics against U.S. intrusions, but French trade with Central America continued to increase. By the mid-1870s, French naval captains who visited Central American ports reported to Paris that French merchants had earned a good reputation. When French merchant ships stopped calling at Central American ports after 1876, trade leveled off. British, German, and U.S. shippers and merchants were the benefactors.

Like the French, German immigrants to Central America can be traced to the 1840s, followed by another spurt in the last generation of the nineteenth century. Many in the latter group came at the encouragement of the German government to establish businesses to market German manufactured goods. The effort proved quite successful. Most German émigrés settled in Guatemala and Costa Rica, where greater opportunities for business and agricultural pursuits existed.

Honduras, still a nation of far scattered and poorly connected communities that offered limited economic opportunities stood a distant last among the five republics in attracting immigrants.

Frenchman Ferdinand de Lesseps failed attempt to construct a transisthmian canal in 1881 ignited U.S. interests in the project. During the remainder of the nineteenth century, a variety of groups publically demanded the U.S. construction, ownership, and operation of an isthmian canal. Beginning with President Rutherford B. Hayes in 1881, each chief executive through William McKinley in 1900 made the point about the benefits–economics, transportation, global reach, and security–of such a canal. Commercial groups in agriculture and manufacturing spoke of the international, or global, market for their goods. Cities like St. Louis, New Orleans, Des Moines, and Galveston espoused the local benefits that the proposed waterway would bring to it.

Central American governments sought to capitalize upon this in the 1880s; and when it came time for a decision in 1903, Costa Rica's intransience contributed to the selection of Panama. For example, Guatemalan President Justo Rufino Barrios sent a special envoy to Washington, D.C., in 1880 to sound out the proposal made by the U.S. Minister to Central America, Cornelius Logan, that the U.S. would provide a protectorate over a Central American Union in return for the right to build a canal. President Hayes was receptive to the canal idea but not to the proposed U.S. protectorate. In 1884, U.S. Secretary of State reached an agreement with Nicaraguan envoy to Washington, D.C., Joaquin Zelaya providing for a U.S. protectorate over Nicaragua in return for the right to construct a canal using the San Juan River. While the Nicaraguan Senate approved the treaty, U.S. President Grover Cleveland did not submit it for congressional consideration on the grounds that the treaty violated the long standing foreign policy principle of no entangling alliances. Finally, in 1903 when the United States determined to construct a canal using the San Juan River that bordered Costa Rica and Nicaragua in the canal project, the *Ticos* commenced an internal debate about who actually controlled the river, they or Nicaragua. The prolonged debate frustrated the North Americans, who shifted their attention to Panama and in 1903 secured the right to build a canal through that newly independent nation. For the most part the Honduran government stood on the sidelines of the canal debates. Frustrated that the nation never received a cross-isthmian railroad for its excessive international debt, Honduran political leaders in the late nineteenth century appeared more concerned with their survival than again pursuing a railroad route across the country. For sure, the Panama Canal would change the direction of Honduran global policy in the twentieth century.

§§§§§

Throughout the nineteenth century, Honduras appeared as a fringe participant in the international influences that impacted upon Central American development. This was evident in the 1840s and 1850s when the United States and Great Britain clashed over transisthmian canal interests and in the mid-1850s when William Walker desired to establish a Central American nation under his leadership. The same was true in the late nineteenth century as liberals across the isthmus opened the door to foreign investment. With little natural wealth to offer the foreign entrepreneurs, the Honduran economy never modernized, although mining companies made handsome profits. And, Honduras stood on the fringe at the end of the century as the United States determined that it would construct, operate, and own a cross-isthmian canal.

Honduras may have been a fringe participant from the international perspective, at the same time the Honduran political leadership viewed internationalism as an opportunity to strengthen its own position at. Except for the William Walker affair before 1860, British or United States presence on the isthmus, provided the new nation a sense of security against other foreigners, including its neighbors, from intervening in Honduran internal affairs. The same was true in the latter part of the century, particularly with the Central American unity efforts that were intended to secure the party in power.

A third observation about Honduran nineteenth century international affairs is the consistent increase in U.S. interests in the nation. Early political leadership saw the need to limit continental influences across all Central America, and it was the Hondurans who initially sought U.S. assistance to resist British advances at mid-century. Yet the perception of the United States became that of a foreign interloper beginning with the William Walker affair in the mid-1850s, followed by the Lincoln colonization scheme for black freedmen near the conclusion of the U.S. Civil War, and the economic activities of the foreign owned mining companies such as Washington S. Valentine's operations and of the numerous small banana companies late in the century.

It was the latter, the banana companies, and the United States desire for its control over a transisthmian canal that changed the relationship between the two nations in the twentieth century.

NOTE

1. John Quincy Adams to Thomas Mann in John Quincy Adams, *Memoirs of John Quincy Adams*, edited by Charles F. Adams, 12 vols. (Philadelphia: Lippincott, 1874-1877), 7, 325–326.

5

The Banana Republic or An American Colony: 1900–1933

Because the political parties in power controlled the elections in Central America, there was no opportunity for peaceful change in government. For those out of power for durations, revolution was the only means to gain control of the government.[1]

Stokeley W. Morgan
Assistant Chief, Latin American
Affairs Division
United States Department of State
January 29, 1926

The context of Honduran history significantly changed during the first three decades of the twentieth century for two reasons: (1) the internationalization of the banana industry; and (2) the United States construction of the Panama Canal. Some colonial Americans knew about bananas coming from the Caribbean region, and, in the early 1850s, clipper ships brought small bunches of the tropical fruit to U.S. east coast ports—Baltimore, New York, and Philadelphia—usually from Cuba and

Panama. At the U.S. 1876 World's Fair in Philadelphia, bananas, wrapped in tin foil and warmed over charcoal fires, became a steady fare. Of Far Eastern origin, banana cultivation spread first to Africa in the sixteenth century and then to the Caribbean by Canary islanders. From there, the banana industry soon spread to Central America and South America. The advent of steamships in the late nineteenth century made the export of this perishable fruit profitable and turned the banana industry into a worldwide business. In the 1870s, Italian immigrants ventured into Central America farming. Among them were the Machecca brothers and Santo Orteri who sent a schooner laden with bananas to New Orleans. They were so successful that in 1878, they agreed to divide and to monopolize the trade between them. Orteri purchased bananas from growers in the Bay Islands and the nearby Honduran coast, while the Machecca brothers concentrated upon the Honduran North Coast adjacent to Tela, British Honduras, and Guatemala.

The idea of a transisthmian canal can be traced to September 25, 1513, when Spanish conquistador Vasco Nuñez Balboa saw the Pacific Ocean as he stood at the heights of Panama. He quickly envisioned connecting the Caribbean Sea with the Pacific Ocean, a vision that the Spanish government finally took seriously in the late eighteenth century but could not take any concrete measures because Latin America erupted into revolution. Following independence, during the 1830s, other European powers, including the British, French, and Dutch, expressed interest in the construction of a transisthmian canal. So, too, did the Central Americans and the United States. While the 1850 Clayton-Bulwer Treaty prevented the United States and British from undertaking the canal project alone, it did not prevent other countries from so doing. From the 1850s through the 1880s, nearly 50 surveys of potential canal sites were made from Panama, north to Mexico's Isthmus of Tehuantepec. Nothing materialized until 1879 when Frenchman Ferdinand de Lesseps attempted to construct a sea level transisthmian canal at Panama. Although the project failed, it served to incite U.S. nationalism that demanded any canal across the Central American isthmus be U.S. built, owned, and operated. The Nicaraguan and Guatemalan efforts to lure the United States into constructing a transisthmian canal during the 1880s only contributed to the U.S. public jingoism.

The canal jingoism coincided with U.S. industrial growth that demanded external markets and resources in the vast trans-Pacific region, a region best reached from the U.S. industrial northeast and midwest via a tranisthmian canal. Agricultural interests across the plain states soon saw the same advantage. The large policy advocated by Naval Admiral Alfred T. Mahan, New York politico Theodore Roosevelt and Massachusetts Democratic Senator Henry Cabot Lodge, Sr. called for a two-ocean navy, a reality that, by itself, necessitated an isthmian canal. A fourth factor that helped direct U.S. policy in the late 1890s and after was the crusade to improve the quality of life for the world's backward and underdeveloped peoples. The movement grew out of the emerging U.S. domestic reform movements in the late nineteenth century that morphed into the progressive movement during the first generation of the twentieth century and whose spokesmen included Presidents Theodore Roosevelt, William Howard Taft, and Woodrow Wilson. In many ways, the new policy was a modern day reiteration of the Manifest Destiny that drove the United States to complete its expansion to the Pacific Ocean in the 1840s.

YELLOW GOLD: THE BANANA COMPANIES

The twentieth century brought significant changes in the banana industry, including the emergence in Honduras of three large companies in fierce competition with each other. Massachusetts fishing

Workers harvesting bananas along the Honduran North Coast circa 1910. (Thomas M. Leonard Collection.)

captain, Lorenzo Baker, and a Boston produce agent, Andrew Preston, along with other investors established the Boston Fruit Company in 1885, which merged with Minor Keith's Tropical Trading and Transport Company 14 years later, in 1899, to form the United Fruit Company (UFCO). UFCO then bought out seven smaller independent Honduran growers, including Santo Orteri. Immediately, UFCO controlled 75 percent of the U.S. market at the time. UFCO expanded again in 1913 with a Honduran government concession to build the Tela railroad to connect this port with the interior banana lands. It continually expanded until 1929 at which time it owned approximately 650,000 acres of Honduras's prime land.

In an effort to thwart UFCO's eastward expansion along the Caribbean coast, the Bluefield's Steamship Company signed a contract with 165 Honduran planters for a four-year supply of 130,000 bunches per month in the districts of La Ceiba, Puerto Cortés, and Trujillo, thus avoiding the North Coast. Bluefields survived until 1922 when the Vacarro brothers acquired it.

The second major producer of Honduran bananas also was founded in 1899. Sicilian immigrant brothers Joseph, Luca, and Felix Vaccaro, together with Salvador D'Antoni, from merchant families in southern Louisiana, began importing bananas and coconuts from the Bay Islands. A year later, in 1900, their Vaccaro Brothers Fruit Company brought 130,000 stems of bananas into New Orleans, the first non-UFCO firm to do so. Financial distress, however, forced the Vaccaros to sell 50 percent of their holdings to UFCO in 1905, only to have the deal overturned in 1909 by the U.S. Supreme Court as a restraint of trade. From then, until 1930, Vaccaro became one of two of UFCO's chief competitors.

The third important competitor was the Cuyamel Fruit Company founded by a Bessarabian Jew, Samuel Zemurray. With his family and without a formal education, he moved to the United States at age 14 and four years later, in 1895, entered the banana trade in Mobile, Alabama, and subsequently to New Orleans, Louisiana. There, the young Zemurray purchased ripened bananas from the delivery boats and sold them to local merchants, earning him the name Sam, the Banana Man, and by age 21, a $100,000 bank account. In 1910, with a $2,000 loan, Zemurray purchased 5,000 acres along the Cuyamel River to establish banana plantations; but soon after the purchase, Honduran President Miguel Dávila reneged on promises to grant him the tax, land, and transportation concessions Zemurray needed to make his investment productive and profitable. To gain his objectives, Zemurray organized and financed a military coup with support from former President Manuel Bonilla and two hired gunmen, Lee

Christmas and Guy "Machine Gun" Maloney. Following initial victories at Trujillo and Ironia, Christmas and Maloney turned their attention to La Ceiba on January 25, 1911. In what is believed to be the first use of machine guns on the battlefield, the rebels inflicted some 600 casualties upon the government troops defending the city. Professional army officers from throughout the Americas and Europe subsequently studied the use of machines guns in the Battle of La Ceiba. Tactical use of the machine gun became standard practice during World War I. Within weeks after Zemurray's hired guns arrived at Trujillo, Dávila resigned and was replaced by Manuel Bonilla, with Zemurray as his military commander-in-chief. Bonilla then awarded Zemurray the concessions he wanted, including the right for his Hubbard-Zemurray Company to incorporate under Honduran law as Cuyamel Banana Company. The firm owned the land near the small town of Omoa, where Zemurray built railroads to transport bananas to port, began extensive irrigation, pest control and agricultural research, as well as shops and a small, screened sanitary town. By 1916, Zemurray and his company were debt-free and prospering.

After World War I, the landscape of the Honduran banana industry appreciably altered in the decade prior the onset of the Great Depression. Most notable was transformation of the family owned and operated Vacarro Brothers into the publically traded Standard Fruit and Steamship Company in 1925 at a capitalization of $50 million. Among its most prized assets at the time were 262 miles of railroad track, 498,000 acres of land, the wharf at La Ceiba, and seven steamers. Its ancillary businesses included printing, ice making, and paper box manufacturing. In addition to ownership of two banks in Honduras, its most important legacies included the making of La Ceiba into a modern community, with supporting infrastructure and the building of Honduras's first hospital. The D'Antoni and Vacarro families continued to operate Standard Fruit and Steamship Company as it expanded its operations into Nicaragua, Panama, across the Caribbean, and eventually to Hawaii. In 1964, the company was sold to Castle and Cook, who placed the Dole label on its products.

By the 1920s, Samuel Zemurray turned his Cuyamel Fruit Company into a prosperous competitor to the United Fruit Company (UFCO), especially in the Montagua Valley along the disputed Honduran-Guatemalan boundary. Zemurray is credited with an excellent understanding of the relationship between local soil and climatic conditions with the growing of bananas, hence his extensive use of irrigation.

Always a shrewd businessman, Zemurray anticipated that UFCO would attempt to force him out of business or purchase his company.

Such instincts prompted Zemurray to begin secret purchases of UFCO stock in the mid-1920s and in 1929 he accepted UFCO's offer of $31.5 million to purchase Cuyamel. By terms of the UFCO agreement, Zemurray was required to retire from the banana industry, a requirement that sent him packing to New Orleans, where he bided his time for another opportunity. It came with the Great Depression that began in 1929 and by 1933 forced the value of UFCO's stock to plummet. In 1933, Zemurray returned to the company offices to assume control of its operations. Zemurray became company president in 1938 and remained active until his final retirement in 1951. Still, at the start of the Great Depression in 1930, UFCO stood as the most significant player in the banana industry and Honduras' primary economic pursuit, and it would remain so well past the end of World War II.

Consistent with the positivist philosophy at the time and recognizing the national inability to finance economic development, the Honduran government made generous concessions to the banana companies. For example, the 1910 grant to the Vacarro Brothersby President Miguel Dávila illustrates the point. The Vacarros were granted the right to construct, at their cost, a railroad from San Francisco toward Yoro, well into the Honduran interior, the precise location to be determined during construction. The rail bridges were to be constructed to specific standards, and all rivers were to remain navigation free. When complete, the line was to transport all government personal, public, and private mail without charge to Vacarro ships in harbor at La Ceiba for delivery to the United States. If in 14 years the rail line was not complete, the Vacarro company would pay the Honduran government 1,000 gold dollars for each unfinished mile. The company also needed to complete the wharf already under construction at La Ceiba.

In return for building the rail line and completing the La Ceiba wharf, the Vacarro Brothersreceived generous benefits, although less substantial than those who completed the first transcontinental railroad in the United States and their subsequent competitors. Among the most important concessions was the company's use of a strip of land, 50-meters wide, for the right of way; free use of coal and oil found in this strip; the right to cut timber on public lands for railroad ties, bridges, houses, warehouses, and stations; the duty free importation of all goods, materials, and tools needed for the route's construction; the right to import laborers of any nationality except Chinese and African Americans; the right to prevent another railroad from being built 20 kilometers on either side of the Vacarro rail line; and, probably most important, the company's right to use 250 hectares of public lands for each kilometer of line built. The Vacarro Brothers received the right to use the land immediately after signing the contract, but using an 1895 homesteading law, the Honduran government was required to assign the properties in checkerboard fashion. The Honduran homesteaders who moved into these checkered properties soon found themselves at the mercy of the Vacarros and, over time, were forced to sell their land to the fruit company. The company acquired nearly 63,000 acres of land through this method but received only the right to use it, not outright ownership of the property as Zemurray did.

In the rail lines terminal cities and at points along the rail route, companies built commissaries to sell food, clothing, medicines, household items, and other general merchandise to company workers. Those not employed by one of the fruit companies were not entitled to use the commissaries. In addition, the commissaries did not accept cash, only coupons issued to the workers as payment for their labor. Just as in Panama, where the canal administration run commissary system existed, it was most difficult for private Honduran businesses to compete with the company owned operation. The commissaries imported their wares duty-free; private businesses did not. Commissaries did not include shipping costs in their prices; private businesses did.

World War I adversely affected the Honduran economy, as its dependence upon the banana industry became glaringly evident. The war brought the European demand for Honduran bananas to a near halt; and at one point, the U.S. government considered embargoing the fruit from entering the United States as a nonessential food item. To avoid financial disaster, fruit company representatives appeared before the U.S. Congress to argue their own case and to correctly report the adverse impact such an embargo would have on the banana-producing Latin American countries, including the threat of violent upheavals. Still, shipping to and from Honduras was cut drastically, resulting in shortages of foodstuffs, textiles, and other consumer goods normally imported from abroad. Inflation quickly followed prompting most Hondurans to cease the purchase of flour because of its prohibitive cost. Other traditional Honduran exports such as coffee and cattle hides went begging for a market and when located, earned little income. Wages remained the same as the labor market became glutted with unemployed workers. In 1916, the Vacarro Brothers laid off about 400 employees in La Ceiba alone. In turn, the shortages contributed to inflation and the ever increasing demand for payment in silver coin (*pesos*), considered to be Central America's highest quality. By late 1917, little of the coin was in circulation, and, in fact, strong suspicions existed that the fruit companies assisted in smuggling coins out of Honduras for safe keeping in New York. At the same time because of the loss of customs duties, the Honduran government's revenues were down some 50 percent from prewar levels.

As the banana companies expanded prior to World War I, so too, did the need for labor. For the most part, uneducated and illiterate Honduran rural workers drifted towards the coast to fill employment needs, but as time passed, the U.S. banana companies preferred English-speaking workers, a preference that led to the importation of West Indian and North American blacks.

The development of the banana industry also contributed to the beginnings of organized labor movement in Honduras and to the first major strikes in the nation's history. The first of these occurred in late November 1917. Approximately 2,000 workers struck for higher wages against Cuyamel and smaller fruit company located in La Ceiba. The demonstrators soon rioted, raiding commissaries for food-stuffs, while others prepared to invade the company compound and subsequently loot the town itself. Met by armed guards and a group of Honduran troops, a skirmish followed that resulted in 40 civilians and 10 military being killed or wounded. Another skirmish at Balfate, 30 miles east of La Ceiba, ended without death. The Honduran government blamed German agents for leading the workers. Only a few U.S. officials agreed. Others focused upon the weakness of the Bertrand administration or upon the monetary crisis. Apparently no one attributed the uprisings to the plight of the people. Additional minor labor disturbances continued throughout World War I.

A most important incident occurred in 1920, when a general strike hit the Caribbean coast. In response a U.S. warship was dispatched to the area, and the Honduran government began arresting strike leaders, but an analysis of the strike at La Ceiba provided an excellent overview of the banana industry's impact upon Honduran social structure.

Initially, the strike was aimed at the Vacarro Brothers but evolved into an industry wide lockout when Cuyamel, United, and the Mexican Fruit Companies locked their doors in support of the Vacarro resistance. New Honduran President López Gutiérrez, who supported the laborers in previous strikes, contributed to the current confrontation when the government led propaganda campaign charged Vacarro with underpaying Honduran and West Indian black workers and further suppressing wages with the importation of American black employees. Allegedly the former group also monopolized the higher paying jobs. When the rioting turned violent in August 1920, the American blacks became victims of aggression instigated by local blacks, who sought to drive them not only from their jobs but also from Honduras. In addition to the apparent racism, U.S. Consul Parker W. Burhnam took note of class differences. A well known and respected planter and merchant, Jacobo P. Munguía, hijacked a Vacarro train engine and fruit cars to descend upon the company's compound at La Ceiba. En route, some 1,200 workers boarded the train. They destroyed company fruit, buildings, and bridges along the way; and upon their arrival at La Ceiba, officials there anticipated some rioting and some property destruction. Conflicting accounts explain that the striking workers then withdrew, either by order of the local governor or by gun-fire from government troops.

Consul Burham's report to the U.S. State Department on the 1920 Honduran crisis made several important observations about Honduran society that U.S. policymakers needed to be aware of: (a) racism existed between Honduran whites, *mestizos*, and blacks; (b) that racism existed between various black groups of laborers; (c) that an emerging middle sector, as represented by Jacobo Mungía in this instance, demonstrated its discontent with the foreign companies already linked to the ruling elite via and informal alliance.

CLASH OF INTERESTS: U.S. POLICY
AND HONDURAN POLITICS

The same concepts used to justify Manifest Destiny in the 1840s became applicable to U.S. policy towards the circum-Caribbean region in the early twentieth century. The Panama Canal, the approaches to it and the territory and seaports of the southeast United States needed to be secure from European intervention. A segment of that security policy involved overcoming the legacies of Spanish colonialism that left the regional governments unstable and irresponsible; factors that encouraged foreign intervention in their internal affairs. But once those deficiencies were corrected, the foreign threat would be removed, and, at the same time the door would be opened to U.S. investments that would help lead to modernization of society.

For the first 30 years of the twentieth century, the United States applied these new policies to the circum-Caribbean region that included Central America. The policy dictated that the United States uphold phold the Monroe Doctrine in order to secure the Panama Canal from foreign interlopers. It found expression in the U.S. man-dated Platt Amendment to the 1902 Cuban Constitution and the 1903 Hay-Bunau-Varilla Treaty with Panama. Each contained provisions that prevented Cuba and Panama from pursuing a foreign policy contrary to U.S. interests forbade the two nations from incurring foreign debt that was beyond their means to repay because it too, invited foreign intervention. The documents and the 1903 Roosevelt Corollary to the Monroe Doctrine addressed the habitual financial misbehavior of the circum-Caribbean nations that invited foreign intervention. Roosevelt promised U.S. interventions if such indebtedness invited the use of foreign force to collect the debt. Because the circum-Caribbean nations were plagued by the legacies of Spanish colonialism—undemocratic governments, malfunctioning judicial systems, and the lack of civil and human rights—modern political systems remained a vision in the early twentieth century. In the spirit of the progressivism that characterized the United States at the time, U.S. policymakers determined that the United States would bring political and judicial modernity to the circum-Caribbean region. President Theodore Roosevelt was determined to establish constitutional governments across the isthmus. If, in the resultant political tranquility, U.S. businesses came to the circum-Caribbean region, so be it. Economic development, coupled with the democratic governments would give the circum-Caribbean peoples a stake in the security of their government and concomitantly security for the Panama Canal or at least as the U.S. progressive Latin American policymakers thought at the time.

Honduras fell within the purview of the new U.S. policy starting with the 1907 Washington Conference sponsored and paid for by the United States government in an effort to settle all outstanding regional difficulties and to establish Central American relations on a permanently peaceful basis. The activities of Nicaraguan strongman José Santos Zelaya served as the conference catalyst. Smarting at the U.S. choice of Panama for a transisthmian canal, Zelaya set out on a separate course that eventually conflicted with U.S. interests. In 1902, he convened a conference at Corinto, Nicaragua, where all but Guatemala was represented. There, the other heads of state, including Honduran President Terencio Sierra, reached an agreement that called for the arbitration of all future disputes among themselves. In a move that enhanced his prestige across the isthmus, Zelaya promised not to aid revolutionaries anywhere. The Corinto Agreement came apart in 1906 when a combined force of Guatemalan exiles, with Salvadoran assistance, invaded their homeland to oust President Manuel Estrada Cabrerra. Recognizing that the political violence could spread across the isthmus and spill over into Panama, the Roosevelt administration arranged for a one day peace conference that convened on July 20, 1906. aboard the *USS Marblehead*, attended by all but Zelaya, an act that contributed to a further loss of his prestige in Central America and further tarnished his image in Washington. The loss of prestige did not deter Zelaya from ordering an invasion of Honduras on February 28, 1907. By the end of March, Nicaraguan troops reached Tegucigalpa, and Honduran President Manuel Bonilla fled into exile upon a U.S. warship.

Fearing that the conflict might engulf the region and still hopeful of establishing constitutional government in Honduras, the U.S. State Department sought out the mining tycoon Washington S. Valentine to assist diplomats in working out a Honduran-Nicaraguan agreement. Valentine's proposal that Nicaragua be allowed to establish a military government in Honduras as a means to bring it political stability and to prevent foreign intervention was a poorly disguised effort to protect his own Honduran economic interests. Almost immediately, El Salvador and Guatemala joined forces for a war with Nicaragua and Honduras, but cooler heads prevailed in Washington, D.C., and Mexico City where Roosevelt and Mexican President Porfirio Díaz called for another Central American conference that convened in Washington, D.C. on September 14 and concluded on December 20, 1907.

The United States delegation quickly brushed aside the Honduran - Nicaraguan proposal to discuss political union and instead focus its attention upon the completion of a 10-year General Treaty of Peace and Amity. The treaty provided for non-recognition of any Central American government that came to power via a *coup d' etat* or revolution. Furthermore, the five signatories agreed not to interfere in each other's internal affairs or in their presidential elections. The conferees also established the Central American Court of Justice, considered by many to the meeting's most important accomplishment. When called to order by a victimized state, the Court would convene to hear evidence and to present binding decisions. Each state was to send its most respected judge to the central court, where his rulings would not be based upon national interest. U.S. State Department officials appeared satisfied with these agreements as they addressed the immediate causes of Central American upheaval. The Central American elites currently in power were satisfied because the General Treaty promised nonrecognition to those seeking power through the most likely illegal means.

The Central American signatories and governments were also satisfied with other conference treaties that set a tone for a unity among them that dated to 1824. From this perspective, the most important act was the establishment of the Central American Bureau, commissioned to foster cooperation among the five nations for the introduction of modern education facilities; to develop agriculture and industry trade across the isthmus; and to reform legal institutions. Although the conference is credited with bringing momentary peace to the region, it also demonstrated the divergent objectives of the United States and Central America. The former was more interested in political stability, and the latter was concerned with a common path to modernity.

The Honduran legislature quickly ratified, and President Miguel Dávila quickly signed the 1907 agreements. Dávila, a member of the Liberal Party, came to power on April 18, 1907, thanks to coup d'état directed by Nicaragua's Zelaya as part of his ongoing feud with Guatemalan President Manuel Estrada Cabrera's ally, Miguel Bonilla. The 1907 Washington Treaty of Peace and Amity provided Dávila with a sense of international security because any government that succeeded him through a *coup d' etat* or revolution would be denied recognition by the other signatory powers. The Roosevelt administration extended diplomatic recognition to Dávila's administration. While Dávila's presidency clearly struck a blow at any future designs that Estrada Cabrera might harbor towards Honduras, the treaty did not prevent Honduran oppositionists and dissidents, some of them exiled in Guatemala, continuously plotted Dávila's ouster throughout his administration

When William Howard Taft moved into the U.S. White House on March 4,1909, his Secretary of State Philander C. Knox observed that the 1907 treaty system preserved political peace in Honduras, that the ongoing Charles Magoon 1906 Mission in Cuba was creating a constitutional political system, and that the 1905 financial treaty with the Dominican Republic rendered those governments stable and free from European intervention.

In contrast according to President Taft, Nicaragua's Zelaya's intrigues kept Central America in turmoil. Washington's distrust and dislike of Zelaya reached a high-water mark in 1909 when he challenged the Monroe Doctrine by allegedly making secret advances to the Japanese to build a canal through Nicaragua and by contracting a $US1.8 million loan from the British investment firm Ethelburga. Verbally encouraged by Secretary's Knox's call for Zelaya's ouster, the Nicaraguan conservatives rose in revolt and when the conflict threatened the American colony at Bluefields, Nicaragua, U.S. marines entered the conflict. They brought it to an end on May 27, 1912, and then supervised the November 2, 1912, presidential election won by conservative Adolfo Díaz, whose unpopularity in large part could be attributed to his affinity to the Americans. The introduction of the military option in Nicaragua became the third model of U.S. intervention throughout the circum-Caribbean, including Honduras, until 1930.

Honduras, Central America's most impoverished nation at the time, also was burdened by a massive national debt that dated to 1867 and, by 1909, accumulated to $120 million, an amount nearly triple the original obligation. Given the nearly $1.65 million in annual government revenues, the likelihood of full repayment of the obligation was impossible. For this, Honduras got approximately 60 miles of railroad track, most of which lay in the country's banana growing region on the North Coast and leased to U.S. businessman Washington S. Valentine. The U.S. government generally ignored the Honduran debt problem until 1908 when British Minister to Central America, Lionel Carden, proposed that the debt be restructured over a 40-year period with the railroad and the dock facilities at Puerto Cortés serving as collateral. Secretary of State Knox envisioned the loan as the first step towards a permanent British presence in Honduras at the expense of U.S. interests. In an effort to ward off the British, in 1909, Knox persuaded British creditors to accept a proposal put forth by J. P. Morgan that permitted Morgan's banking interests to purchase the outstanding British bonds at 15 percent of their face value. Encouraged by the U.S. proposal, President Dávila dispatched a mission to Washington, D.C., to discuss the matter. The resultant Knox-Parades Agreement on January 11, 1911, provided for the refinancing of the Honduran national debt, the establishment of a customs receivership administered by a U.S. appointed customs collector. President Taft justified the agreement on the grounds that it fell within the purview of U.S. security interests and its constitutional objective for Central America, but the U.S. Senate did not. It rejected the proposed treaty, and, for a time, U.S. bankers did not go further. In Tegucigalpa, both Zemurray and Bonilla campaigned against the treaty on the grounds that acceptance would turn Honduras into a U.S. colony. Added to the U.S. record of interference in its internal affairs, the Honduran legislature resoundingly defeated the treaty, but the debt problem did not go away.

The debt issue then became involved in Honduran politics and the intrigues of U.S. entrepreneurs. Anxious to return to the presidential palace, Miguel Bonilla teamed up with an American adventurer and soldier of fortune, Lee Christmas, equally anxious for military fame and reward. Together they found a financier, Samuel Zemurray, who arrived in 1905 at Puerto Cortés determined to build a successful banana company that later became Cuyamel Fruit Company. Zemurray correctly understood that any customs receivership would prevent him from bringing into Honduras, duty-free, any materials essential for the expansion of Cuyamel. Furthermore,

Located in Tegucigalpa, the Presidential Palace served as the working office for the President of Honduras from 1900 until shortly after World War II, when it was converted to the National Museum of Identity that opened in 1960. (United States National Archives, Still Photograph Division, College Park, Maryland.)

Zemurray also reasoned that Dávila's catering to the government in Washington, D.C., might result in favors for his chief competitor, the UFCO, including UFCO's proposal to make a loan for the repayment of the Honduran debt, provided that the Honduran government made further concessions on railroads and wharves. Acting President Francisco Bertrand was cool to this suggestion because, as his critics pointed out, UFCO would gain too much control over the nation's communications.

Despite the setback and their diverse interests, Bonilla, Christmas, and Zemurray had enough in common to continue working for Dávila's removal from the presidency. Finally, U.S. special agent Thomas Dawson worked out an agreement on March 28, 1911 which provided for the withdrawal of sitting President Dávila and for the elections in October that confirmed Bonilla as president. Once in office, Bonilla turned on Lee Christmas by appointing him chief commandant of Puerto Cortés, not something more prestigious as Christmas earlier envisioned. The ever suspicious Bonilla joined with a group of U.S Senators, all suspicious of the Knox-Paredes agreement, a suspicion that prompted J. P. Morgan to withdraw his proposed bond purchase and with it, Secretary Knox hopes for Honduran financial stability. Only the banana companies were left to pursue their own objectives.

Bonilla's presidency was short lived. He died while in office on March 21, 1913, but not before the granting of favors to the banana companies along the North Coast. His successor, Francisco Bertrand, confronted a barrage of personal threats for the six-years of his presidency from 1913 to 1919, State Department Latin American desk officer attributed Bertrand's political difficulties to the nation's chronic revolutions, lack of political leadership, and illiterate population that was easily swayed by political *caudillos*. Amidst the turmoil, three U.S private business groups headed by Minor C. Keith, Samuel Zemurray, and a New Orleans investment house offered to refund the national debt and refinance the country's international obligations in return for further railroad concessions that would only benefit the banana companies. Both the State Department and senate were reluctant to become involved in another Central American financial entanglement.

In addition, Bertrand mistrusted the United Fruit, Cuyamel, and the Vaccaro Brothers Fruit Companies, whose large tracts of land and generous railroad concessions enabled them to dominate the Honduran economy. Convinced that the fruit companies instigated at least two rebellions against him, Bertrand determined to secure his own position by allying himself with the Wilson administration. He therefore supported Wilson's call for Pan Americanism, signed one of Secretary of State William Jennings Bryan's cooling off treaties and, refrained from criticizing the 1914 Bryan-Chamorro Treaty that granted rights to the United States to construct a transisthmian canal through Nicaragua, although many prominent Hondurans saw it as another act of U.S. imperialism. In return, Bertrand found solace in the U.S. response to the violence that threatened to surface in 1915 after he announced his intention to stand for reelection despite a constitutional provision forbidding it. Secretary of State Robert Lansing pressured Guatemalan President Estrada Cabrera to guarantee that the neutrality provisions of the 1907 treaty would be upheld in order to prevent the crisis from escalating into an isthmian affair. Lansing also promised to prevent arms shipments to any Central American revolutionary and had the navy send two ships to cruise the Honduran coast. Following his re-election in 1915, Bertrand continued to applaud the United States. For example, despite the fact that Honduras shared the

Gulf of Fonseca with Nicaragua and El Salvador, he refused Honduran participation with Costa Rica and El Salvador in their 1916 appeal to the Central American Court of Justice regarding the 1914 Bryan-Chamorro Treaty. The Costa Ricans argued that the treaty violated the 1907 agreement guaranteeing the free use of each nation's territorial waters and Costa Ricans rights under the 1858 Cañaz-Jerez Treaty and the 1888 Cleveland Award, both of which prevented Nicaragua from making any canal concessions without consulting Costar Rica. The Salvadorans argued that the Bryan-Chamorro Treaty violated their rights in the Gulf of Fonseca and that a U.S. canal and naval station in the area would draw Central America into some unwanted future war. In 1917, when the Court ruled in favor of Costa Rica and El Salvador, Honduras voted with the majority, the first sign of a cooling relationship. Thanks to U.S. support, Nicaragua refused to implement the finding, meaning that the Court was no longer effective, prompting the press in Tegucigalpa to place responsibility upon the government in Washington, D.C.

When the European War erupted on August 1, 1914, President Bertrand declared his nation's neutrality, although in reality it was a pro-Allied neutrality that offered nothing but rhetoric to the Allied cause. Because only a few businessmen of German descent lived in Honduras at the time, the country was spared from being a focal point of the U.S. anti-German policies that followed. Those resident Germans were either small merchants selling predominately German made goods or worked as agents for or in the office of the banana companies.

Bertrand, however, fell victim to an intelligence plot organized by the U.S. Navy's Office of Intelligence (ONI). Sylvanus G. Morley, a archaeologist recognized for his work in Mexico and Guatemala, received the president's permission to survey the Honduran coast for any possible Mayan ruin sites. In reality, Morley was commissioned by ONI to identify any ports, bays or other posts that the German navy might use for supporting submarine operations in the Caribbean. While Morley did not find any such hideaways or German spies, he did provide the cartographic world with the first detailed maps the Honduran Caribbean coast.

Not directly confronted by the German menace, beleaguered by internal difficulties and, owing to U.S. intervention in its political affairs, the Honduran legislature delayed its declaration of war against the Central powers in World War I until July 19, 1918, a move designed by Bertrand to ferret out his political opponents not to demonstrate support for U.S. policy.

Central America's distrust of the United States prompted all the republics, except Costa Rica, to join the League of Nations as a means to curb Washington's meddling in their internal affairs. The Honduran representative to the Paris Peace Conference and long-time critic of U.S. interference in his country's affairs, Policarpo Bonilla, best stated the isthmian position when he asked for a clarification of the league's covenant regarding the Monroe Doctrine. Bonilla did not intend to internationalize the doctrine but rather weaken it in order to deny the United States a justification for future intervention in Central America. The issue became moot when the United States failed to join the league, an action that caused Honduras and its Central American neighbors to lose interest in the League of Nations by 1925.

In retrospect, Dana G. Munro of the State Department's Latin American Affairs Division naively noted in 1922 that the U.S. insistence on the implementation of the 1907 treaties and the Roosevelt Corollary to the Monroe Doctrine put an end to the wars that characterized Central America and resulted in political stability and financial responsibility. Apparently, Munro was blind to the trilateral relationship, both formal and informal, that linked the U.S. government with U.S. economic interests with selected political leaders, like Honduran Francisco Bertrand, in order to secure their diverse interests. In reality, Munro did not understand that the three models of U.S. intervention only served to escalate anti-Yankeeism throughout the region by 1920. Nor did U.S. policy makers or Central American political leadership understand the potential impact of the growing disparity of wealth and privilege and, the closed political system.

1920–1930

After World War I, the sense of regional unity that developed in response to U.S. policies from 1900 to 1917 was formalized by agreement between the Guatemalan, Honduran, and Salvadoran governments in 1920. Prodded by the United States, Nicaragua subsequently agreed to the pact. Only Costa Rica demurred, preferring to continue its independent course. Unfortunately, the effort at union soon collapsed and Central America returned to its historical patterns of state rivalries and cross border intrigues. The overthrow of Guatemalan President Carlos Herrera on December 10, 1921, served as the catalyst for the union's destruction and opened the door for another United States effort to bring constitutional government to the isthmus. Following Herrera's ouster border skirmishes between El Salvador, Honduras, and Nicaragua threatened to ignite a regional war and prompted the United

States to again intervene. In August 8, 1922, aboard the U.S. cruiser *Tacoma* in the Gulf of Fonseca, the presidents of El Salvador, Honduras, and Nicaragua agreed to terminate the conflict and to accept the U.S. call for another conference in Washington, D.C.

U.S. policymakers saw the conference as an opportunity to reinforce the 1907 treaties, to adopt an arms limitation agreement, and to create tribunals of inquiry to settle disputes not resolved through normal diplomatic channels. As before, the goal was to create political stability through the constitutional process and to discourage political change through revolution. For sure, the United States wanted to avoid all discussion of a Central American Union and to again avoid any treaty commitments. Despite the sense of unity that gripped the isthmian republics at the end of World War I, it disappeared with the events that led to the *Tacoma* conference and contributed to the lack of a common set of objectives when the conference commenced in Washington, D.C. on December 4, 1922, enabling the United States to dominate the conclave.

The conference ended on February 7, 1923, with the signing of twelve agreements, five of which met U.S. policy objectives. Article two of the General Treaty of Peace and Amity satisfied the U.S. goal for isthmian constitutional governments, as spelled out in the treaty's Article 2. It provided for the nonrecognition of governments that came to power by *coup d' etat* or revolution, even if subsequently legalized by free elections. Excluded from serving as heads of state were revolutionary leaders, their close relatives, and high-ranking civilian and military officials who had been in power six months before or after the event. The Central Americans further agreed not to interfere in each other's domestic affairs, assist exiles or contending parties, or harbor revolutionaries. The second agreement created international commissions of inquiry that could be activated by any party to a dispute and that possessed the authority o conduct impartial inquiries and issue nonbinding reports including recommendations for ending disputes. The third accord created a new Central American Tribunal. In an effort to eliminate the nationalistic politicking that marred the previous court, the justices would be selected from a list submitted by the five republics, plus the United States. Next, an electoral projects commission was established to codify voting procedures and verify election results in each nation. In effect, every threat to the established order that Central America experienced after 1907 was now declared illegal.

The final accord signed on February 4, 1923 reflected the global desire for disarmament and the United States success at the naval arms conference it hosted in 1922 that resulted in limitations on warships for the world's naval powers. In Central America, the United States wanted to remove armies as the final arbiter in politics and its role in serving the personal interests of political leaders, not the good of the nation. While each Central American nation agreed in principle to disarmament, each had concerns about internal security, border defense, and replacing standing armies with national guards with a formula that stipulated Honduras would have a standing army of 2,500 men. Although the United States was satisfied with the 1923 treaty system, the five Central American states ratified only the General and Arms Limitations Agreements. Still, Secretary of State Charles Evans Hughes was confident that the new treaty system set the foundations for greater isthmian political stability by correcting the weaknesses of the 1907 agreement. In contrast, the Assistant Chief of the State Department's Latin American Affairs Division, Stokeley W. Morgan, pointed out that, historically, every party in power in any Central American country always supported a treaty system, sought U.S. assistance to enforce the treaty system, but not election supervision; while the party out of power always sought exceptions to the provisions regarding government change and wanted U.S. election supervision.

The ink had barely dried on the 1923 treaties when a crisis developed in Honduras. President López Gutiérrez and the Liberal Party split over the issue of succession, an issue used by the exiled conservatives to threaten the national peace. With Nicaraguan assistance, the conservatives made several border incursions into Honduras. External efforts to find a solution to the problem failed. For example, the U.S. Minister Frank T. Morales could not get all sides to agree on a compromise presidential candidate. Secretary of State Hughes dismissed a Guatemalan suggestion that a conference be convened to settle the question because he knew that the Guatemalans would work on behalf of the liberals and Nicaragua and El Salvador for the conservatives. Hughes also warned that whoever gained power would have to satisfy Article 2 of the 1923 treaty. Subsequently, Tiburcio Carías Andino won the October 27–28, 1923 presidential election by a plurality but not a majority over his two liberal opponents, Policarpo Bonilla and Juan Angel Arias. When the Honduran Congress failed to come to grips with the issue, Carías took to the countryside with an armed force and declared himself president.

In the civil war that followed, American lives and property were threatened. The U.S. legation in Tegucigalpa was fired upon. Along the North Coast, from Puerto Cortés to La Ceiba, the property of the foreign fruit companies and American owned homes and shops were attacked and looted. Much of the anti-American sentiment could be traced to the Cuyamel Fruit, United Fruit, and Vacarro Brothers Fruit Companies, whose economic exploitation was made possible by generous central government concessions that they received. In face of the violence, the companies wanted to know which faction the U.S. government intended to support so that they could do the same in order to protect their own privileged positions in the Honduran economy. The U.S. government, through Frank T. Morales, informed the companies' executives that it supported neither side. The UFCO, which supported Carías in the 1923 election campaign, continued to do so when the war erupted. That declaration did not stop the Cuyamel Fruit Company from providing assistance to the opposition liberal faction, and a U.S. government embargo on arms shipments to Honduras did not prevent Cuyamel from shipping arms through Nicaragua. Shortly after the fighting broke out, U.S. naval ships patrolled the North Coast, but as the violence continued, the consuls at Puerto Cortés and La Ceiba asked for blue jackets to come ashore in order to protect fruit company properties that supported the warring factions. Meanwhile in Tegucigalpa, the inexperienced U.S. Minister to Honduras, Morales, requested the landing of marines to protect all foreign lives and property. The State Department filed the request.

Finally, in April 1924, Sumner Welles was dispatched to Honduras to bring the crisis to an end. He issued only a mild rebuke to the fruit companies for their political intrigue and proceeded to work out an agreement aboard the *USS Milwaukee* on April 28, 1924, that paved the way for the election of conservative Miguel Paz Barahona as President on December 28, 1924, but only because the liberals abstained from the election. Acceptable under the terms of the 1923 treaty, the United States and the other four isthmian nations extended recognition to Paz Barahona. During his four-year term (1925–1929), Paz Barahona persecuted all opposition to him, particularly journalists. On the positive side, he negotiated the cancellation of the nineteenth century debts for an international oceanic railway that was never built. In 1925, the debt with accumulated interest totaled nearly two million dollars.

The crisis passed and, despite two revolutionary threats, for the next eight years Honduras enjoyed relative political tranquility. After losing the 1928 election to Vicente Mejía Colindres, Carías did not seize power nor did he again take to the hills to lead a revolt against the government, knowing that U.S. nonrecognition would follow. Carías

Carias was first elected President of Honduras in 1932; and then twice, in 1936 and in 1939, manipulated the constitution to extend his term in office until 1949. (Reproduced with permission of the General Secretariat of the Organization of American States.)

won the 1932 election by a substantial margin and, subsequently, suppressed a revolt led by Ángel Zuñiga Huete. The United States extended recognition to Carías and also announced that should Zuñiga Huete seize power in violation of Article 2 of the 1923 Treaty, recognition would not be extended. Born in 1892, in the Yeguare Valley, Zuñiga Huete went on to a teaching position at the School of Law at the Honduran National University in Tegucigalpa where he began his political activism. By the mid-1920s, Zuñiga Huete emerged as a major figure in the Liberal Party and later served in the Tegucigalpa military command. Always a critic of Tiburcio Carías, Zuñiga Huete moved to Mexico after Carías won the 1932 election and from there for the next 16 years labored as Carías most vocal critic.

The second major U.S. objective at the 1923 Washington Conference was to end the use of the military as a national force to maintain political order, or vault someone to political power. U.S. policymakers concluded that this could be accomplished by limiting the size of standing armies to that needed only for national defense and creating national guards to serve as national police to maintain order in society. The anticipated revenue savings from the military makeover could then be redirected to social programs such as public health and sanitation, public education, and improved infrastructure. Toward that objective, the 1923 treaty stipulated that Honduras have an army of no more than 2,500 men for the next five years. From 1925 through 1929, the Honduran military strength remained constant, and that government military expenditures decreased slightly as a percentage of the annual budget, while there were equally small increases in health, education, and infrastructure, leaving the general impression that the treaty had a positive impact upon Honduras. Shortly after the Honduran legislature ratified the Arms Limitation Agreement in 1925, the government requested U.S. assistance in organizing and training a national guard or police force. In response, the State Department arranged for retired cavalry officer, Jean H. A. Day, accepts a three-year, $10,000 contract to develop a *Guardia*. The Honduran government never summoned Day to Tegucigalpa. Only as a result of diplomatic pressure did Day receive $7,500 for his unfulfilled services. In 1929, Honduras approached El Salvador regarding the development of a national guard but again let the issue drop, apparently awaiting the fate of a similar project in Nicaragua. In 1929 and 1930, the Honduran government approached the United States regarding the purchase of military air planes. In the latter year, 1930, army officers volunteered a portion of their salaries for the acquisition of the planes and a similar plan was soon extended to other government employees. Some Tegucigalpa newspapers suggested that the foreign companies who would benefit from any such purchase should have their employees contribute to the program Sufficient funds were never raised, and by 1930, the army remained the strongest force in Honduras, despite the fact it was ill-trained and ill-equipped.

The other Central American countries accepted the arms limitation agreement, and reduced the size of their militaries, at least in its annual reports to the League of Nations. With the exception of Costa Rica, each reported a large reserve force, although in practice, it meant little more than a count of villagers with personal rifles. They received no formal training. Nicaragua and El Salvador went on to form national guards, which in Nicaragua, quickly became a service tool for President Anastasio Somoza de Garcia in the 1930s.

Throughout the 1920s, the other Central American countries, notably Nicaragua, also experienced political turmoil, which prompted U.S. diplomatic and military interference; and by the end of the decade none of the countries, save Costa Rica, effectively reduced the size of the militaries, the essential element to maintaining or overthrowing a government. As State Department officer Stokeley W. Morgan observed in 1926, political revolutions seemed to be a way of life in Central America.

Other factors during the 1920s influenced a change in U.S. interventionist policy. The termination of World War I brought an end to the European threat. Latin America's larger countries such as Argentina, Chile, and Mexico used the 1923 and 1928 inter-American conferences to criticize the United States for its circum-Caribbean intervention. At home, Herbert Hoover as Secretary of Commerce, asserted that such criticisms created enough anti-American sentiment across the hemisphere to militate against the sale of U.S. goods and services throughout all Latin America. The Democratic Party publically and consistently criticized the Republican Party for continuing to interfere in Central America. Most damning was an article by Franklin D. Roosevelt that appeared in 1928 in the prestigious *Foreign Affairs Quarterly*. Finally, the public began to question the intervention policy as the body bags with dead marines arrived home from Nicaragua, where they were chasing the elusive bandit, turned guerrilla, Augusto César Sandino. Together, these events led to the "Clark Memorandum on the Monroe Doctrine," a State Department in-house study on the Roosevelt Corollary. Accordingly, the U.S. had no right to interfere in Latin America's internal affairs. The President-elect reiterated that pledge in his inaugural address on March 4, 1933, and eight months later at the Montevideo, Uruguay inter-American Conference, it was adopted as hemispheric policy.

§ § § § §

The three decades of U.S. involvement in Honduran affairs may have contributed to the security of the Panama Canal, but for sure it did not did not bring modernity to the country. In fact, the idealistic objectives of U.S. policy at the start of the century did not appreciably change the Honduran political landscape, enhance its economic development or provide for a more socially mobile society. By 1930, the Honduran political arena remained a battlefield for the elite only at the continued expense of rural workers and the newly emerging middle sector. Two entrenched political parties rivaled for government power, not for the nation's socio-economic development. Given Honduras' underdevelopment at the beginning of the twentieth century, supporters of the banana industry are quick to point out that they provided employment for thousands of workers at better wages than found elsewhere in the country and contributed to health and educational improvements. The companies greatly improved transportation systems and built communities with sanitary systems.

Critics, however, are equally quick to respond that the development of a monoeconomic culture deprived Honduras of developing its own economy; that the extensive fruit company land holdings prevented agricultural diversification; that small Honduran fruit growers were at the mercy of the banana companies for the transportation and the marketing of their produce, a fact that drove the small producer out of business; and that the fruit companies had unwieldy influence in national banking and politics. The fruit companies gave financial support to politicians who supported their cause; an informal relationship existed between them. Each had the same self-interest in maintaining the socioeconomic order, their own security and well being. To the critics, Honduras had become an American colony by 1930.

NOTE

1. Stokeley W. Morgan, "American Policy in Central America," Lecture at the U.S. Department of State, Foreign Service School, Washington, D.C. January 29, 1926.

6

The Era of Tiburcio Carías: 1932–1954

[Public] opinion and tradition support *continuismo*. As Roosevelt provided and excellent example in the United States, the extension of Carias's presidential term until 1949 gives expression to the Honduran peoples spontaneous desire to continue the nation's direction as provided by Carías.[1]

La Epoca, December 17, 1940

On October 28, 1932, 12 days before Franklin D. Roosevelt won the U.S. presidential election, Tiburcio Carías Andino defeated Angel Zúñiga Huete for the Honduran presidency. Like Roosevelt, Carías won an impressive victory. Carías garnered 81,211 populate votes compared to Zúñiga Huete's 61,643 and triumphed over his rival in 14 of the country's 17 departments. During his presidency, and especially during World War II, Carías often expressed public admiration for the great American democrat and often claimed to share FDR's passion for the common person. Hondurans did not share Carías's self description but instead saw him as a dictator, more concerned with his control over government and society than with the needs of the nation or its people.

Considered a *ladino* because of his Indian and black background, Tiburcio was born in 1876 in Tegucigalpa. The youngest son of General Calixto Carías, a leader in the Honduran Liberal Party (PLH) that dominated national politics in the late nineteenth and early twentieth centuries, the younger Carías enjoyed the privileges of an elite family. He did well in local schools and in 1898, received a doctoral law degree from the Central University of Honduras, after which he taught mathematics at the National Institute and night school classes for poor children and workers.

Tiburcio's political activity began with his campaigning for the PLH in the 1891 campaign, and subsequently, he engaged in guerrilla activities on behalf of the party. In 1903, Carías left the PLH to support Manuel Bonilla in founding the Honduran National Party (PNH), essentially a successor to the nineteenth century Conservative Party. Carías attained the rank of general during the 1907 Honduran civil war, which, when coupled with his doctor of jurisprudence degree bestowed the titles Doctor and General upon him. Carías also used the military as an important part of his political machine that helped to make him the most important National Party leader in the first half of the twentieth century. Carías served in the national congress and as governor of several departments (states) before standing as the PNH's presidential candidate in 1923. Carías won a plurality, but not the majority of the popular votes, in the election held October 27–29, 1923. Violence and property destruction followed the congressional failure to solve the problem and resulted in the United States mediation that led to the presidency of Miguel Paz Barahona. Carías again made an unsuccessful bid for the presidency in the 1928 election losing to Liberal Vicente Mejía Colindres by some 15,000 votes.

The campaign and election contrasted sharply with those of the Honduran past, where violence and voter intimidation was the norm. Of greater surprise was Carías's acceptance of the election results and the advice given to his supporters: work with the new government. Of greater surprise were Carías's acceptance of defeat and the urging of his supporters to accept the new government. Carías cast his attention to the 1932 presidential contest.

THE ROAD TO THE PRESIDENCY

As 1932 approached, three trends reached a maturation point that impacted upon the Carías administration. The first dealt with Honduran political dynamics. By 1930, two parties–the liberal and the national–dominated the Honduran political arena. Until the

1870s, only two issues separated the two distinct political groups in existence, so-called liberals and conservatives: the centrality of the Church to Honduran life and one's position on Honduras participating in a Central American Union.

The first serious attempt to organize a formal political party became the work of Céleo Arías from 1870 to 1890. Highly intelligent and well educated, Arías also well understood politics. His 1887 pamphlet, *My Ideas*, served as the basis of the Liberal Party's philosophy. It discussed the French rights of man and the Anglo-American doctrines of representative government. *My Ideas* earned Arías the title, "Father of the Liberal Party." Despite this rallying point, successive party leaders such as Dr. Marco Auerlio Soto, Louis Bográn, Policarpo Bonilla, and Miguel Dávila unsuccessfully attempted to impose party unity, but instead, the party continued to fracture. For nine years following the revolution of 1911, there was no Liberal Party in Honduras, and when the liberals tried to claim new President General Rafael López Gutiérrez as one of their own, one must remember that he never admitted membership in the party. The *personalismo*, individual rivalries and ambitions that historically plagued the party continued throughout the 1920s. In 1928 several *caudillos* sought the presidency under the Liberal Party banner. A year later, in 1929, the party was reconstituted and again recommitted to unity in anticipation of winning the 1932 presidential election. It did not remain unified, and it did not win the 1932 elections. Thereafter, the PLH became a negligible factor in Honduran political dynamics.

While the formal organization of the National Party was 1916, many Honduran historians point to President Trinidad Cabañas as the precursor to the party. In 1854, he charged that individualistic factions competing for power threatened orderly government and demoralized the people from supporting the government. He argued that national rather than personal and local issues should characterize all governments, one of the National Party's basic principles. Cabañas did not administer a cohesive government and not until 1874 was there another attempt to form a National Party, this time by General Ponciano Leiva. He, too, met with failure. During the 1890s, though politicians often discussed the need for a national government, not until 1911 were the first steps towards a party organization taken. By 1915, departmental clubs and committees existed in the name of the National Party. In February 1916, these groups joined together to become the Nationalist Party of Honduras (PNH) and campaigned on behalf of Francisco Bertrand's successful bid for the presidency. Bertrand's intention not to surrender the presidency led to

1920 manipulated election won by General Rafael López Gutiérrez, whose administration was mired by some 17 uprisings or attempted coup d'etats. In 1924, Honduran political history appeared to be repeating itself when López Gutiérrez announced his intention to remain in the presidential palace, a violation of the 1923 Central American Treaty system, and Tiburcio Carías arrived on the national political scene as the National Party's presidential candidate. Carías polled the most votes but failed to achieve the absolute majority required by the constitution. With escalating rhetoric each side charged that the election results were fraudulent until a civil war finally erupted in 1924. The violence between rebels and government troops, particularly along the Honduran North Coast affected U.S. lives and properties and prompted U.S. intervention and Carías's subsequent withdrawal from the presidential contest. The U.S. State Department dispatched Sumner Welles to Honduras, which resulted in a brokered deal that led to the unopposed presidential election of National Party candidate Miguel Paz Barahona, who served a full four-year term, 1925–1929. During that four-year period, Carías consolidated his power as PNH leader and exerted significant influence over the PNH dominated national congress. Despite his defeat, in the 1928 presidential election, Carías gained considerable prestige by peacefully accepting the electoral defeat, such behavior not constituting the norm in Honduran politics during the first half of the twentieth century. Undeterred, the Doctor and General set his site upon the 1932 presidential campaign.

Amidst the fluid political arena, a second trend developed: the foreign owned fruit companies, particularly the United Fruit Company, increased their presence and influence in Honduras. Lee Christmas's interference in the 1911 revolution, financed by banana entrepreneur Samuel Zemurray, served as a harbinger for future interference in Honduran internal affairs by the U.S. owned fruit companies. In the 1923–1924 fiasco, fruit company representatives visited Frank T. Morales, the U.S. Minister in Tegucigalpa to determine if the United States favored one of the candidates so that the companies would provide that person with financial support in return for a safety guarantee of the company's property. After Morales indicated that his government supported neither side, the fruit companies hedged their bets and funded both candidates Rafael López Gutiérrez and Tiburcio Carías; the latter received UFCO funds for his 1928 campaign.

Finally, in the mid-1920s, the U.S. government's policy of intervention in the internal affairs of the Central American nations underwent significant change. Honduras certainly stood as a prime example of the State Department's frustration when, in 1926, Stokeley W. Morgan's asserted that revolutions were simply a way of life throughout the region. In addition, the European threat that prompted U.S. concerns in 1900 disappeared in the 1920s, as Europe lay prostrate after World War I. Within the United States, the Democratic Party made a public issue of the Republican Party's failed interventionist policies, although it did not mention similar actions by Woodrow Wilson. Republican ranks were also split. Most important was Herbert Hoover, who as Secretary of Commerce (1921–1928) concluded that trade with the more modern and richer nations of Latin America's Southern Cone would increase if the United States withdrew from the circum-Caribbean region. In fact, the Southern Cone nations—Argentina, Brazil, and Chile—were the chief critics of U.S. policy at the 1923 Santiago and 1928 Havana inter-American conferences. After 1928, the U.S. public became increasingly critical of its government's pursuit of Nicaraguan rebel Augusto Cesar Sandino, a bandit who turned guerrilla fighter and then an alleged Communist, whose troops sent many Marines home in body bags.

As a result of these pressures, President-elect Herbert Hoover undertook a seven-week Goodwill tour of Latin America, promising a new policy once in the White House. As president, Hoover commissioned State Department officer J. Rueben Clark to reexamine the Roosevelt Corollary to the Monroe Doctrine that had provided the cover for the U.S. interventions throughout the Caribbean. Clark's *Memorandum on the Monroe Doctrine* concluded that the corollary overstepped the bounds of the original Monroe Doctrine. Misbehavior by a Latin American government did not justify U.S. intervention, only direct European involvement did. U.S. policy change was complete by the time of the Seventh International Conference of American States that met in Montevideo, Uruguay, from December 3 to 26, 1933. Here Secretary of State Cordell Hull promised that henceforth the United States would no longer interfere in the internal affairs of its Latin American neighbors; that it would be a good neighbor. To be sure, in 1934, the Central American governments abrogated the 1923 Treaty system and the U.S. pursuit of constitutionalism in Central America died with it, at least for the moment.

As the winds of change swept across Central America, Liberal Vicente Mejia Colindres assumed the Honduran presidency on February 1, 1929, 10 months before the onset of the Great Depression. Whatever plans he may have had for Honduras disappeared with the world's economic catastrophe that began later in October that same year. Banana exports reached a peak in 1930 and then drastically declined. In response to the lack of demand, the fruit companies dismissed thousands of workers, slashed wages for those who remained employed, and cut payments to the independent banana producers who supplied their entire crop to the companies. The workers economic plight led to many labor strikes and disturbances that the Honduran military quickly suppressed. And as the depression worsened, government tax revenues markedly dropped causing Mejía Colinas to borrow $250,000 from the fruit companies so that military salaries could be paid.

Amidst this economic plight, the Liberal Party held its nominating convention in May 1932 in Tegucigalpa, where they nominated long time Carías nemesis, Angel Zúñiga Huete, as its presidential candidate under suspicious conditions that led many to believe that his nomination was a foregone conclusion. Whatever the truth, the nomination rankled the party membership and split it into two factions, further weakening Zúñiga Huete's chance for victory in the November election. Zúñiga Huete's distaste, both personally and politically, for Carías dated to the 1923 disputed election that resulted in naming of Liberal Rafael López Gutiérrez as president and sent the enraged Carías into military action to oust the embattled president until the United States diplomatically intervened and negotiated an agreement between the feuding factions on May 3, 1924, that led to the 1925 presidential election of National Party candidate Miguel Paz Barahona. From his congressional leadership position, in 1926 Carías set out to gain his party's nomination for the 1928 election, which he did without much opposition. The liberals were not so fortunate. Still fractured internally, not until two weeks before the October 28 election date did it agree upon Mejía Colindres as a compromise candidate. With Carías, an imposing figure as its leader, the Nationals headed into the election confident of victory, only to be totally demoralized by Mejía Colindres resounding victory of Carías by more than 16,000 votes. Only more surprising at the time was Carías's acceptance of defeat.

Still undeterred, Carías anticipated the 1932 presidential contest. His prestige remained high, being elected as the deputy from Tegucigalpa to the national congress. Two years later, Carías again received the National Party's presidential nomination. Equally determined was Carías's perennial nemesis, Angel Zúñiga Huete. In 1930, he challenged the legality of Carías's electoral victory, but the congress refused his request to declare it invalid. Two years later, amid allegations that he manipulated the party convention, Zúñiga Huete became the Liberal Party presidential nominee. During the campaign, Carías and his National Party supporters focused upon the plight of the

Honduran economy and Mejía Colindres failure to do anything about it, not that he could because the global market place was beyond his control. But as often happens in such calamities, the party in power is held responsible for events at that time. And, as could be expected, the National Party spin doctors charged that Zúñiga Huete would pursue the do-nothing liberal policies. The National Party also charged Mejía Colindres with providing government funds to Zúñiga Huete's campaign, censoring opposition mail, and planning to use government employees to assist on election day. In response, Zúñiga Huete asserted that, in reality, the National Party was arming public employees to intimidate voters on election day. The Ministry of Government denounced all such accusations as preposterous and ridiculous.

The candidates attempted to remain above the rhetorical fracas, letting their minions do the work. On October 12, 15 days before the election, Carías declared his intention to abide by the election results no matter their outcome, and 12 days later, he called on all members of the National Party to do the same to avoid any post-election violence. On October 27, the day before the election, Zúñiga Huete asserted that he would abide by the will of the people. Carías won the election by a 20,000 vote margin, capturing the majority of votes in 14 of the country's seventeen departments.

Despite Zúñiga Huete's vigorous appeal to his followers, many liberals gathered around Generals José María Fonseca, José A. Sánchez, and Timoteo R. Borjas to charge Mejía Colindres with betraying the Liberal Party by permitting a Carías victory. In late November, they threatened to besiege the capital. The potential revolt fizzled when Carías took command of the army and secured arms in El Salvador; while the residents of Tegucigalpa took to the streets on behalf of Carías.

On November 16, 1932, Tiburcio Carías assumed office, beginning what was to become the longest period of continuous rule by an individual in Honduran history. However, Angel Zúñiga Huete did not disappear into political oblivion. He remained a critic of and political activist against Carías for his 16-year presidency, often from the distance of Mexico.

Along with contemporary Central American dictators—Maximiliano Hernández-Martínez (El Salvador), Anastasio Somoza García (Nicaragua), and Jorge Ubico (Guatemala)—Carías would be included among the last of the *liberal caudillos* that dated to the late nineteenth century. Each accepted a dominant government role in the economy and as strongmen did not tolerate political opposition. And for the duration of their administrations, each would be affected by U.S. policy. Only Costa Rica differed among the Central American republics. While liberal economic policies dictated its development from the mid-nineteenth century on, with the exception of 1917–1918, the country held regularly scheduled elections, followed by a peaceful transfer of power. Government administration, however, remained in the hands of the elite landowner coffee growers. Not until the mid-1940s did all Central America begin to experience the emergence of the generation of rising expectations that presented a challenge to their ruling governments.

THE CARÍAS PRESIDENCY

Throughout the 1930s Carías repeatedly preached that national peace and order provided the best opportunity for economic recovery from the Great Depression. What Carías meant by peace and order can be found in his frequent complimentary remarks about the liberal political leaders of the late nineteenth century, including Marco Aurelio Soto, Luis Bográn, and Policarpo Bonilla, who called for fiscal responsibility, economic development plans, road construction, and emphasis upon education. Carías explained that the government's abandonment of these principles during the so-called interregnum (1902–1933) prompted his resignation from the Liberal Party to become a founding member of the National Party. During that time period national budgets were not closely monitored. Not only were projected budgets usually 50 percent higher than actual income, there were no controls for containing over expenditures, hence constant government debt. To address the financial problem President Carías diligently labored to balance the national budget, achieved not only by reconciling government income with expenditures but also by cutting salaries of and dismissing government employees. Centralized control and monitoring of income and expenditures reigned in excessive federal and departmental expenditures. Despite the loss of income and the adverse impact upon government employment, Carías continued to meet the scheduled repayments of international debts, particularly to British bondholders.

Carías's centralized authority over government spending was mirrored elsewhere. Loyal followers became cabinet ministers charged with practicing fiscal responsibility; and department and local authorities became presidential appointees in order to circumvent local *caudillos* or the landed elite who treated their administrative units as personal fiefdoms. Carías also intimidated his political opponents by jailing and exiling them and through mail and press censorship. Angel Zúñiga Huete spent much time exiled in Mexico, from which he would send flysheets and newsletters attacking the Honduran president. At home, it became a common sight to see a Carías political opponent walking the streets of Tegucigalpa in a striped prison uniform with a heavily weighted ball and chain attached to his ankle. In effect, Carías became a dictator. The Communist Party of Honduras (PCH) was outlawed. The fear of personal reprisal meant that there was an absence of public dissent, congress became a rubber stamp, and the Supreme Court would not rule against the president.

Peace and order also meant a strengthening of the military. The historic role of the Honduran military differs from its Central American counterparts, save Costa Rica, which has no military tradition. It never developed a strong and overriding allegiance to a landowning oligarchy or to any other single economic interest group; it could thus play a mediating role between elite factions or between the elite and the lower classes.

For nearly a century following the collapse of the United Provinces of Central America in 1838 the Honduran military reflected the *caudillo* politics of the era. The military served the functions of government for the president, whomever it might be. Whether by an election, or by a *caudillo* revolt, whoever occupied the presidential palace appointed his own military officers who often returned to the countryside with political titles, such as governor of a regional department. The lines between political and military command became blurred. Each of the 17 departments had a command headquarters (*comandancias*), and a large number of subdepartmental (*subcomandancias*) units. For example, as late as 1914, Honduras had 80 *comandancias*, 183 *subcomandancias de pueblo* (town headquarters) or *subcomandancias de aldeas* (village headquarters). In addition to keeping local order, the military supervised elections; and often the local commanders assumed the role of politicians. The system was self-fulfilling but also significantly contributed to violence in the countryside. Occasionally, a foreign officer was hired to improve the military operations at the upper level only, such as President Miguel Davila in 1908. In the 1920s, politicians demonstrated a greater interest in the professionalization of the military but lacked the resources to carry out such programs, a reason to speculate on the size of the Honduran army as fixed by the 1923 Central American Arms Limitation Treaty and to explain the Honduran failure to follow through on the development of a national guard as the treaty required. Only the Honduran air force received new appropriations.

Carías inherited, continued to practice this system, and demonstrated his special interest in the fledgling air force with the establishment of the Military Aviation School, administered by a U.S. civilian director, Colonel William O. Brooks and assisted by six other Americans under private contract with the Honduran government. Brooks reported directly to Carías, but he resigned within a year because of a personal conflict with Carías. While they accomplished little with the Honduran pilots, the Americans did fly reconnaissance missions in search of alleged antigovernment guerrillas and reportedly engaged in bombing missions against their positions. A year later, in 1937, retired Marine Captain Walter C. Mayer, signed a seven-month contract as a fire arms instructor to the Honduran army. The contract was extended through 1942, although at the time, Carías made it clear that he wanted Mayer to remain on for the duration of his presidency in charge of the presidential honor guard. The guard consisted of a small group of young soldiers with unquestioned loyalty to the president. Stationed in the presidential palace and equipped with pistols and submachine guns, the guard accompanied Carías on all occasions. Also, in 1937 Carías purchased 5,000 rifles and five million cartridges from the H.M. Sedgley Company in the United States. The rifles proved ineffective because the parts were cobbled together from Springfield and Krag Jorgonsen rifles. Although the Sedgley Company repaired 50 percent of the equipment when Honduras complained, the Honduran government wanted the State Department to either repair the remainder or supply new rifles because it had issued the license approving the sale. The department refused, stating that it only issued a license and was not responsible for inspecting the equipment prior to delivery.

Carías moved into the presidential palace without plans to confront the impact of the Great Depression that only worsened with time's passage. In addition to the continuing drop in international demand for bananas, in 1935 the Panama disease (a debilitating fungus) and sigatoka (leaf blight) struck the Honduran banana producing areas. The Trujillo area was struck particularly hard. Thousands of workers were displaced and they did not regain employment two years later when chemicals successfully terminated the blight. By 1937, the world market adjusted to other sources of the banana trade lost with Honduras. Still, on average for the 1937 to 1939 period, bananas accounted for 62.5 percent of Honduran exports and employed an estimated 15,000–20,000, or 1.5 percent of the total population. Other exports included gold and silver, cattle hides, lumber, and coffee. Honduras remained a country of small self-sufficient farmers. Industrial development in Honduras lagged behind that of other the other Central

American republics and was limited to the making of shoes, soap, rope, candles, and cigarettes. A banana flour manufacturing plant went into operation on the eve of World War II in Puerto Cortés. While several small breweries dotted the nation's larger communities, the largest and most popular brand was the *Cervecería Hondureña*. For these reasons, at the start of World War II, the Carías administration successfully lobbied the U.S. Embassy in Tegucigalpa to remove the German brew master from the U.S. deportation list.

The corresponding loss of government income from the drop in banana exports meant that government workers received only 11 months pay from 1937 to 1939, and when paid in back wages, they received 70 percent of their salaries in certificates; while pensioners received only 20 percent of their anticipated income. Without a central bank, the government again relied on UFCO loans to meet its obligations, an estimated $540,000 in 1937 alone.

In 1935, the Honduran National Party commenced a propaganda campaign in the government's unofficial mouthpiece, *El Cronista*, stressing the need for Carias's continuance in office in order to maintain the national peace and order. The constitution, however, prohibited the immediate reelection of a president. To circumvent the problem, on January 6, 1936, Carías directed the national legislature to conduct an election for a constituent assembly. Members of the Liberal Party and dissident members of the National Party could not participate in the January 28 election. Although considered a foregone conclusion, the PNH captured 99.99 percent of the votes (132,194), while the banned PLH garnered .01 percent or 46 votes. The constituent assembly then appointed a subcommittee of jurists and lawyers to draft the new document. On March 8, the entire assembly began its debate on the new constitution and completed the discussions on March 28, 1936. The new constitution differed little from its 1924 predecessor. Of the 34 articles in the 1924 document, 30 were exactly the same in 1936. Most of the changes clarified and tightened ambiguous wording and phrases, including the definition of citizenship to encompass all those born within the country and by reason of blood relationship. Women, however, were denied citizenship and thus the right to vote. While individual rights and guarantees remained intact, the death penalty was restored for cases of parricide, assassination and treason. Based upon the need to strengthen national security, the 1936 constitution extended the territorial water line six miles to the 7.5 mile marker.

Regarding labor and capital, the eight-hour, six-day work week continued, and the employer remained responsible for injuries the

workers sustained on the job. Large companies needed to establish
hospitals for both workers and families, and child and women labor
restrictions established. The state became responsible for insuring that
needy families received economic assistance and that employers
guaranteed maternity leave to expectant mothers and care for minors
of working parents. The state was also assigned responsibility for a
national agricultural, industrial, and liberal arts education programs
to reach all children.

The final set of constitutional changes in 1936 further centralized
presidential authority. Congress lost its power to censure cabinet
ministers and to force their removal from office. Congress also lost its
power to approve diplomatic and consular appointees. By weakening
the requirements to be a supreme court justice, the president gained
greater control over these appointments. Two sections granted
overlapping power to the president and congress: (1) each had the
authority to raise revenue; and (2) both could declare war and make
peace. Finally, the vice-president received the same prerogatives
as the deputies, but the meaning and intention remained open to
question.

The most important change, however, extended the presidential
and vice-presidential terms from four to six years, and under the
terms of the new constitution the constituent assembly selected
Carías and his vice president, Abraham Williams to serve another
six-year term until 1943. Government forces quickly suppressed the
opposition protests that erupted immediately following the promul-
gation of the new constitution on March 28, 1936, but the military
did not snuff out the opposition as intrigue and threatened *coup
d'etats* continued against Carías until 1939. At the center of the
opposition was Angel Zúñiga Huete, who spent most of this time in
exile to avoid arrest and incarceration. Zúñiga Huete also appealed
for United States intervention on behalf of democracy, but the
appeals fell on deaf ears. Firmly in control of government, Carías
instructed the PNH controlled congress in 1939 to extend his
presidency another six years, until 1949.

In announcing the Good Neighbor policy in 1933, the United States
agreed to nonintervention in the domestic affairs of Latin American
states and abandons its use of nonrecognition of allegedly illegal or
defacto governments. Henceforth, or at least until the end of World
War II, the new Latin American government needed to (1) control the
nation's territory and administrative machinery, including maintenance of public order; (2) be able to meet its international obligations;
and (3) have the willing support of the populace. In the case of Carías,

there was little doubt that he controlled both Honduran territory and government machinery. His fiscal responsibility was laudatory. He regularly met obligations to foreign bondholders and, in fact, paid off two small international loans in 1935. The obviously rigged vote for the constituent assembly and the protestations that followed was alone sufficient evidence to challenge the suggestion that Carías had the willing support of the populace. That same year, on December 18, 1936, Carías solidified the legality of his government when signing a Reciprocal Trade Agreement with the United States. Designed by Secretary of State Cordell Hull and approved by the U.S. Congress in 1934, the trade agreements were designed to stimulate U.S. depression pressed industries. The agreements called for drastic tariff reductions on the importation of U.S. manufactured goods, while the United States agreed to lower its import duties on items from the foreign country. In application to Honduras, the agreement meant very little economically because Honduras already received most favored nation status in the United States for its primary exports of bananas, coffee, tobacco, and lumber; and its society had neither the demand nor the ability to pay for U.S. manufactured goods. But the treaty further legitimized the Carías regime. Other Central American dictators also benefitted from the Good Neighbor Policy and participated in the Reciprocal Trade Program for the same reasons as Carías: Maximiliano Hernandez-Martínez in El Salvador, Anastasio Somoza in Nicaragua, and Jorge Ubico in Guatemala. Also, given the history of U.S. intervention in their countries during the twentieth century and to obtain a reenforcement of their positions, the governments of El Salvador, Guatemala, Honduras, and Nicaragua supported resolutions that supported a continued U.S. pledge not interfere in the internal affairs of Latin American nations at the 1935 and 1938 Inter-American Conferences at Buenos Aires and Lima, respectively.

For its part, the United States, continuing to be plagued by the impact of the Great Depression at home, also became concerned with the rise of Nazi Germany and Fascist Italy in Europe, but the 1935 Buenos Aires meeting received little support in its call to consider hemispheric defense policy discussions. At Lima in 1938, however, the Guatemalan, Honduran, and Nicaraguan delegations supported the U.S. call for hemispheric defense planning, not so much because they understood the potential German threat to them, but because in such an emergency, U.S. largesse would assist with the modernization of their militaries. In other words, the Central American dictators, Carías included, sought to gain U.S. favoritism as a means to maintain their political position at home.

Throughout his reign, Carías maintained good relations with his fellow Central American dictators: Hernandez-Martínez, Somoza, and Ubico. Costa Rica continued to remain aloof from regional matters. The Ubico relationship was the closest because he helped Carías reorganize the Honduran secret police. Ubico and Hernandez-Martínez made serious efforts to keep the Honduran exiles from organizing military incursions into that country, and Carías reciprocated. the Honduran-Nicaraguan border dispute continued to inflame relations between Carías and Somoza, they also shared the common desire to prevent border incursions by exiles.

WORLD WAR II

Conventional wisdom suggests that the United States is responsible for the arming of the Central American dictators and that the origins of that policy can be traced to the 1920s, 1930s, and through World War II. Until the outbreak of the Second World War, with the exception of marine trainers for the National Guards in the Dominican Republic and Nicaragua, U.S. military officers were forbidden by law to undertake assignments for foreign governments unless they first resigned from the U.S. military. Private citizens were, of course, free to undertake private contracts and a few did, including in Central America. U.S. policy contributed to Latin American countries turning elsewhere during those early decades of the twentieth century. For that reason, one would find German, French, Italian, and Spanish military personnel across the hemisphere, which also exerted pressure upon the host governments to purchase their military hardware. Honduras fell within the purview of this experience and policy. One of the concerns Washington policymakers had during the 1930s was that Tiburcio Carías would turn to Germany for both advisors and military equipment. Some suggest that only the poor state of Honduran finances prevented him from so doing.

With the outbreak of the European War on September 1, 1939, Carías informed U.S. President Franklin D. Roosevelt that the resources of his country were available for U.S. use. Most important were the North Coast coastal ports at Cortés, Tela, La Ceiba, Trujillo, and Castilla, all of which could be used for refueling German ships in the Caribbean and for a possible, although remote, landing on Honduran soil. Otherwise, the U.S. Army officers who conducted bilateral military conversations with their Honduran counterparts in Tegucigalpa in September 1940, found little to encourage them in using Honduras in its Caribbean defense schemes, primarily aimed at securing the

Panama Canal from enemy attack. And once the war became global on December 7, 1941, Carías added Tigre Island in the Gulf of Fonseca for use by the U.S. Navy. An offer the navy dismissed out of hand.

Despite Carías's fascination with airpower, in September 1940, the Honduran air corps consisted of 25 planes of U.S. manufacture used primarily for the maintenance of internal order. At the moment, U.S. Army Reserve Officer, Captain Malcolm F. Stewart commanded the force and reported directly to Carías. And while there were numerous airfields throughout the country, only those at Tegucigalpa and San Lorenzo had runways from 2,400 to 3,000 feet in length, making them capable of handling U.S. military aircraft. On the ground, Carías boasted of any army of 3,000 officers and 53,000 men on the active list and 800 officers and 24,000 men in reserve. In reality, the army had only 322 officers and 1,981 men on active service. Like elsewhere in Central America, these troops were poorly educated and trained, using poor and outdated equipment and were ill-clothed and ill-housed. With an estimated 500 miles of paved roads and 816 miles of railroad track mostly serving the North Coast banana industry, the other major roads were found to be no better than mule paths. Only its 5,000 miles of telephone wire and 4,000 miles of telegraph lines that connected Honduras with the outside world through Panama had military value. In sum, Honduras offered little to the Caribbean defense plans. As a result of the bilateral military talks, like those conducted with the other Central American republics, the United States would determine wartime policy in Central America.

Given their inadequacies, the Central American republics, including Honduras, signed agreements in October 1940 whereby they would request U.S. assistance in case of an external attack or a Fifth Column internal uprising. They also granted the U.S. full use of railroads, roads, seaports, airports, and other facilities the United States might deem necessary for the war effort. The United States also obtained the right to surveillance of aliens and their sympathizers. In return the United States promised to provide assistance in acquiring U.S.-made armaments, to train Central American military, and to provide military advisors for that purpose.

The U.S. Navy moved into Puerto Castilla in June 1942 to assist with repelling the German submarine threat throughout the Caribbean. A former UFCO operation, the Navy inherited excellent housing facilities, two company owned radio stations, and several auxiliary buildings. In addition, the Navy personnel were permitted to import duty-free any items they wished and were connected with family at home through the postal service at Panama. After the German U-boat threat subsided in 1943, the Navy methodically withdrew from the base and returned it to Honduras in 1944. In addition to reconnaissance missions over the Caribbean Sea, seven Honduran pilots, armed with 30-caliber machine guns and 60-pound fragmentation bombs, logged 601 hours of antisubmarine patrol between La Ceiba and Trujillo in 1942 . Otherwise, the U.S.-Honduran military relationship was fraught with problems.

In January 1942, Carías requested that a U.S. air mission be sent to Honduras to train the nation's air force because the Aviation Academy's Director Lieutenant Colonel Harold White, an American civilian in charge of the Air Academy and not an aviator, had failed to properly develop the group of fliers into an effective unit. He also requested an infantry person to upgrade the Honduran Army. While the War Department was amenable to the suggestion, the military attaché assigned to the embassy in Tegucigalpa, Colonel Thomas A. Austin, demanded that White be dismissed as a precondition. At the insistence of the State Department, in February 1943, the Caribbean Defense Command (CDC) in Panama sent a study mission to Honduras to assess the situation. The commission concluded that the Austin-White feud was irreparable and that because of it, the Honduran pilots trained in the United States were being underutilized. Still, there was no need for an air mission at this time because the German U-boat threat had subsided, the Honduran government could not afford its cost-share of the project and the continued potential use of air power by Carías to punish his opponents.

In late 1942, Carías also requested the assignment of U.S. Army ground mission capable of instructing the Honduran Army in infantry, artillery, and mortar weapons. Again, the CDC refused to sanction one, an opinion shared by Ambassador John E. Erwin. They found the regular army a collection of uneducated and demoralized individuals whose training would take a significant amount of time and then would more likely serve the interests of President Carías against his political opponents. The Army and the State Department had no interest in or intention of getting involved in Honduran internal affairs. In 1943, CDC Commander Frank M. Andrews recognized the Honduran economic wartime economic problem and its potential for political violence. To help prevent it, Andrews suggested to his superiors in Washington that the United States construct an airfield along the North Coast even though it would now have minimal military value and a highway connecting the country's major cities. His suggestion was not considered in Washington.

Throughout the war, the U.S. military attaché in Tegucigalpa unsuccessfully pressured for both air and ground missions to contribute to the modernization of the Honduran military. Washington's negative response did not prevent him from continuing to serve as a private advisor to President Carías or prevent him from securing some ground and artillery equipment under the Lend-Lease Program for coastline defense purposes.

Finally, eight months after the European War ended on May 8, 1945, and four months following the Japanese surrender on September 2, 1945, the United States concluded a standard four-year military agreement with Honduras. It provided for both air and ground advisors and an engineer. It fell within the Army's postwar plans to have military missions in all Latin American countries in order to develop unified policies and strategies and to standardize equipment, presumably at first with U.S. surplus war material. But it came at a time when both the State Department and congress no longer favored supporting, in any manner, dictatorial regimes. Honduran Foreign Minister Julian Caceres argued that Carías governed as a constitutionally sanctioned president, that he had the support of the Honduran people, that he labored on behalf of his nation's development, and that he was much more lenient in his treatment of political opponents than Hernandez-Martínez, Somoza, or Ubico. It was wrong, Caceras concluded, to judge Carías on legal grounds, his taking advantage of a loophole in the Honduran Constitution. The U.S. State Department remained unimpressed. Although the military mission took its place in Tegucigalpa, its effectiveness was minimal until another U.S. policy change beginning in 1952.

Without a training mission in Honduras, the United States provided minimal equipment assistance to the country throughout World War II, and what did arrive should be credited to the endeavors of Colonel Thomas A. Austin, the U.S. military attaché assigned to the embassy in Tegucigalpa. Honduras was eligible for military assistance under the March 11, 1941, Lend-Lease Act that empowered the president to loan, give, lease or any other means provide the allies with military supplies in fighting the Axis during World War II; and the details were spelled out in a February 28, 1942, U.S.-Honduran agreement. According to this pact, Honduras would receive $1.3 million in military assistance but would only have to pay 9.23 percent of that amount.

A month prior to the completion of the February agreement, the Honduran government presented a $2 million request that included two twin-engine long range bombers that its airports could not handle and 10,000 rifles that its 1,400 active military servicemen could not absorb. Throughout the war, the Honduran government continued its request for military assistance, but without a U.S. mission in the country and the concern that Carías would use the arms to maintain internal order, the requests were denied in Washington. Only in 1946, with an air mission present, did the Honduran Air Force receive six AT-6 trainers, whose bomb racks were removed and placed inside the plane's cabin, then delivered to Honduras where the bomb racks were remounted. Carías finally got his bombers.

For several reasons, all Latin America received minimal Lend-Lease military assistance and the Central American nations even less. When the United States concluded Lend-Lease treaties with Latin American governments in 1942, its industrial capacity to immediately produce the equipment was, at best, minimal. Because the war focused primarily upon the defeat of Germany, most of the military production made its way to Britain's storage facilities for the anticipated cross-channel invasion. After the decision for D-Day was made in November 1943, the Americans began to ship excess equipment to the Asian theater. Throughout 1942 and into early 1943, when the German U-boat threat to the Caribbean drastically subsided, military assistance to Central America was largely confined to items necessary for coastal defense. The amount of Lend-Lease military equipment Colonel Austin obtained through June 1944 totaled $172,440.77; including $58,963.83 for its air force, $71,992.05 for ordnance, $35,061.34 in quartermaster supplies, $1,210.77 for transportation, and $162.75 in medical supplies. By the terms of the February 28, 1942, Lend-Lease Treaty, Honduras was responsible for only $16,778.44.

Throughout the war, Carías rejected outright any plan to build up a professionally trained army. He did not want to build an institution of this kind, particularly if segments of anew military force were to be deployed anywhere outside Tegucigalpa.

Yet, in fact, Carías changed the structure of his military forces during World War II via the U.S. military group in Tegucigalpa. Local militias were merged, trained, and directed from the national level, but Carías insisted they remain as before in departments and municipalities. Officer training emphasized command structure, obedience, and loyalty to the state as a professional institution. The aviation school headed by a North American gave the air force a new mission. It would operate outside Honduran territory with antisubmarine reconnaissance training flights with U.S. Army Air Force in the Caribbean.

Honduran Air Force pilots assisted the United States Army Air Force during World War II in combating the German submarine threat in the Caribbean Sea. (United States National Archives, Still Photograph Division, College Park, Maryland.)

The number of army recruits increased in 1942 and 1943, and departmental militias received infantry training assisted by U.S. military personnel. In fact, Carías's personally loyal Special Expeditionary Force that dated to his revolutionary days was enlarged and transformed into a professional group that eventually served as the core of the national army. As the war drew to a close in 1945, Carías established The Day of the Soldier in an effort to instill a sense of loyalty to the nation. By war's end Carías pointed to a U.S. trained Light Regimental Combat Team with 122 officers, 3 warrant officers, and 2,588 enlisted men. In addition, it had one light infantry regiment, a field artillery battalion, and engineer and quartermaster company.

U.S. wartime planners also were concerned with Latin America's enemy alien communities, and in Central America, they were primarily concerned with the German nationals and their descendents. Guatemala housed the largest number of Germans, followed by Costa Rica, Nicaragua, El Salvador, and Honduras and in each country, for the most part, remained cultural communities unto themselves. A large number of Italian descendents resided throughout the region with Costa Rica having the greatest number, but they were considered less of a threat because of their assimilation into the host country's society. The number of Japanese nationals residing in Central America was minimal at best. The families of the two Japanese shipping companies who resided in Honduras on the eve of war disappeared shortly after the German invasion of Poland on September 1, 1939. Only the Japanese community at Puntarenas, Costa Rica, was considered a threat to U.S. interests as part of a potential larger Japanese plot to sabotage the Panama Canal.

The United States military attaché and political consul at the U.S. Embassy in Tegucigalpa first began to shadow and report on the German community. Immediately following the outbreak of war on December 7, 1941, the U.S. Embassy reported to Washington that of the 26,076 foreigners residing in Honduras, including 510 Germans and 231 Italians. In late January 1941, the State Department's Office of Intelligence Research reported that there were 443 German-born people, another 200 Germans born in Honduras, 199 native Italians, and another 300 Italians born in Honduras. The always unreliable Honduran government statistics counted 319 and 185 Italians living in the country. Whatever the correct number, enemy aliens accounted for less than 1 percent of the total 1940 Honduran population, estimated to be 1.7 million.

The U.S. concern with these communities throughout Central America was two-fold: (1) sabotage and (2) propaganda. In addition to plotting against the Panama Canal, the Germans were suspected of potentially destroying a nation's infrastructure: roads, electricity, urban water supplies, port wharves, roads, and railroads. Germany's embassy in Guatemala City served as the nerve center of Nazi propaganda throughout Central America. Prior to the war's outbreak in 1939, the propaganda focused upon the superiority of German manufactured and consumer goods and claimed that Germany was the center of scientific research because it had the world's most advanced educational system. From September 1939 through late 1943, the propaganda focused upon German military victories in the field and its air and ground equipment superiority. From Guatemala City, the propaganda made its way to other capitals, often as packages on the Salvadoran *Transportes Aereos Centro-Américanos* TACA airlines. Once in Honduras, the German Embassy further distributed the materials. The U.S. policymakers feared that the Germans just might convince the Central Americans to turn against it, or worse, be neutral in the war.

To combat the German presence and its potential sabotage and propaganda impact upon the United States initiated a number of measures in cooperation with the local governments. Carías proved a willing participant. Two of the U.S. policies had most tragic consequences upon Honduras as they focused upon its German communities in Amapala, San Pedro Sula, and Tegucigalpa.

In October 1940 Rockefeller and a supporting team from his Office of Inter-American Affairs (OIAA) visited Latin America to determine the extent of German economic influence in each country. His group identified 39 German owned and operated business In Honduras that were placed on the initial list of Proclaimed List of Blocked Neutrals that could no longer do business in the United States. Companies could be removed or added to the list, and it reached its high point in 1943. At the insistence of the United States, a Honduran government administrator monitored the business expenses to insure there was no direct or indirect contact with Germany and that all bills, including property taxes, were paid. The families were ostracized for being German and for real or alleged Nazi activities. As could be expected, under such conditions, many businesses floundered or went bankrupt because the individuals could not meet their tax assessments. In the end, the Carías administration confiscated the German properties, homes included, and gave or sold them to his friends and political allies.

Next, the United States determined to control hard-core German and Italian nationals in Honduras. The primary policy was the deportation of Nazi-influenced Honduran citizens. Following the outbreak of war, the German diplomatic corps returned home in accordance with international law, the United States ordered the deportation to the United States of 695 Germans and their descendents, including 118 from Honduras, for real or imagined Nazi activities, where they would be interned awaiting to be exchanged for Americans caught behind German lines.

The Germans who remained in Honduras endured severe restrictions on their civil liberties. Mail was censored, group meetings prohibited, travel outside one's native town or city restricted and closely monitored, and they faced the constant threat of being charged as Axis sympathizers, a crime that led to incarceration in local internment centers.

The loss of German business caused by blacklisting and subsequent confiscation proved to be a less significant consequence to the Honduran economy than the loss of the international trade for the country's primary products. Still, in the 1930s, the United States was the most important trading partner of Honduras, accounting for 86 percent of the total Honduran trade, and the largest importer of Honduran bananas, 68 percent.

At the time World War II erupted, the United States considered Honduras a poor credit risk because of its unbalanced budget, unpaid current bills, and its unwillingness to admit just how bad its financial position was. Corrupt government officials pocketed a good portion of any funds that came into the government coffers. Given the anticipated international shipping problems, the Honduran economy did not have an immediate bright future. For this reason, U.S. State Department official John M. Cabot recommended that any loans be as minimal as possible and primarily directed at completing the Inter-American Highway through Honduras as a way to insure that the United States received something for its investment. Cabot would be disappointed. Despite its previous record, the Carías administration had little interest in completing the Inter-American Highway through Honduras, only a hard surface, 100-mile road connecting Tegucigalpa with San Lorenzo on the Gulf of Fonseca. In 1943 the Export-Import Bank (EXIM) advanced a $1.7 million loan to the Honduran government for that purpose. Rather than using the funds as appropriated, the monies went towards the establishment of a national bank.

As Cabot expected, the Honduran economy worsened. In August 1942, the War Production Board (WPB) determined that the U.S. would import 20,000 tons of bananas a month, with 15,000 coming from Guatemala. Also, UFCO's refrigerated ships made irregular visits to the banana ports but did not give advance notice of their arrivals owing to the German submarine threat in the Caribbean. Then, for nearly 18 months in 1942 and 1943, no commercial ships landed at Central America's Caribbean ports because of the U-boat operations. As unemployment increased in the banana regions of Honduras, Nelson Rockefeller's Office for Inter-American Affairs pumped more than $1 million into road and rail construction and in the cities sanitation facilities. The U.S. government also invested in the planting of rubber trees, abaca plants (cordage), and increased its purchase of hardwoods to be used in ship construction. Because the self-sufficient nature of the farming system, its primitive methods, and the country's poor transportation system, Honduran cities began to endure food shortages in the summer of 1942. Despite the OIAA's construction of a 6,000-acre farm in the centrally located Comayagua Valley, food shortages persisted throughout the war. There were other wartime shortages: gasoline and rubber tires for automobiles, newsprint, and copper were among other essentials not readily available. Scarcity contributed to inflation, which reached a 200 percent annual rate in 1943.

At the end of World War II, the Honduran economy was in a most precarious position. Production of its primary products came to a near standstill during the war because its primary market, Europe, closed. In 1945 no one could anticipate when the European market would open again. At the same time, Honduras was in no position to finance its own industrialization program, and the prospects for outside financial assistance were dim, at best.

THE END OF AN ERA

On the eve of World War II, with his political opposition effectively silenced at home or exiled abroad, Tiburcio Carías appeared secure in the Honduran presidential palace. In 1940, spokesmen for political change were more evident in the city of San Pedro Sula, 110 miles northwest of Tegucigalpa. Since the beginning of the twentieth century, San Pedro Sula developed into the country's most vibrant commercial center with its merchant houses engaged in international trade. Poor transportation connections with the capital of Tegucigalpa, however, meant that the city had little influence in national politics. In October 1940, the city's Liberal Party leaders joined General Salvador Cisneros in a failed coup attempt that surprised the Carías administration, but it did not produce a national consequence. Over the next four years, the political atmosphere appreciably changed.

Carías, like his fellow dictators across the isthmus—Maximiliano Hernandez-Martínez in El Salvador, Anastasio Somoza in Nicaragua, and Jorge Ubico in Guatemala—publicly emphasized their commitment to the Allied cause to defeat the dictatorial military regimes in Germany, Italy, and Japan. In their annual messages to congress, each extolled the virtues of the Atlantic Charter, the Four Freedoms, and the virtues of western democracies. Each Central American dictator identified personally with U.S. President Franklin D. Roosevelt. Newspapers, such as Tegucigalpa's *La Epoca*, the government mouthpiece, and San Pedro Sula's *Diario Comercial*, printed by the United Fruit Company, portrayed Allied military successes on the battlefield and reprinted editorials prepared by Nelson Rockefeller's Office of Inter-American Affairs about a more prosperous and socially fluid postwar world. Such exhortations did not impact all Hondurans, as evidenced by its 48 percent literacy rate, but the U.S. sponsored propaganda did influence the traditional liberal opposition and the generation of rising expectations, a middle sector group that included professionals, small merchants and businessmen, and intellectuals and students who experienced the limitations of a political dictatorship.

The idealistic principles of World War II clashed with Central America's historic closed political systems in the spring and summer of 1944. Violence in San Salvador led to the ouster of Hernandez-Martínez on May 9, and the Army escorted Ubico out of Guatemala on July 4. In Nicaragua, Somoza promised to step away from the presidency at the end of his term in November 1947, a promise he failed to keep. In Honduras, Carías survived the "threat" against him.

The origins of the 1944 political crisis in Honduras can are found in the November, 16, 1943, municipal elections in which his National Party swept to complete victory with 88,725 votes to 1,228 for all opponents. Carías used this electoral victory to arrange for a congressional extension of his presidency until 1949, naming him the Founder of Honduran Peace and Benefactor of the Country (Fundador de la Paz de Honduras y Benemérito de Patría). The rigged municipal elections and subsequent congressional action triggered a coup attempt to start on November 21. Honor Guard Captain Jorge Ribas Montes, a 23-year-old graduate of Guatemala's military academy led the charge and was joined by an estimated 80 conspirators, including members of the presidential honor guard, members of the army general staff with training in Guatemala, Mexico, and the United States, members of the Liberal Party and National Party dissidents. The plan was doomed before it began. It lacked coordination between the various groups, nor did it have a plan for governing if the coup succeeded. The conspiring leaders served two-year terms before going into exile. While Carías emerged as confident as ever, regarding his political security, he failed to take serious note that the conspirators included military officers frustrated with his failure to establish a professional army and that this was the first time that the military acted in concert with civilian political interests. The protests, however, did not stop.

With the overthrow of Hernandez-Martínez on May 9, 1944, and the following demonstrations against Ubico in mid-May, Honduran university students in Tegucigalpa took to the streets demanding freedom of the press, freedom of elections, and removal of the president. Students in the National University's School of Medicine and Engineering quit classes and refused to sign a declaration of allegiance to Carías as demanded by their deans. Store owners called for a general strike but failed to gain widespread support. On May 28, an estimated 300 women, led by Carlota de Vallardes, the widow of a prominent newspaperman, a teacher Visitación Padilla, and prize winning novelist Argentina Díaz Lorenzo, marched on the presidential palace demanding the release of political prisoners and the holding of free elections. Carías promised only to review the matter and subsequently explained the reason for holding political prisoners. On July 4, 1944, a well-organized group of some 200 students and women, including was Emma Bonilla de Larios, daughter of Liberal Party leader Policarpo Bonilla, marched through the capital to the presidential palace asking for Carías's resignation, free elections, the release of political prisoners, open frontiers for the return of exiles, a free press, and a revision of the 1936 constitution. Later that same day a more rowdy group, estimated at 2,500, demanded that Carías resign when it made an attempt to enter the presidential palace grounds. Carías ignored a petition presented to him on the evening of July 4 signed by some 200 professionals (lawyers, physicians, dentists, and engineers) to save the country from bloodshed. Throughout the day, Carías ordered the troops to disperse in order to avoid violence. In the North Coast towns of San Pedro Sula and La Ceiba, marchers taunted workers in the offices of the United and Standard Fruit Companies. On July 4, marches against the Carías regime served as reminders of U.S. support for the dictator. In La Ceiba, Carías permitted an estimated 600 people to protest in front of UFCO's office complex in order to avoid violence.

A July 6 demonstration in San Pedro Sula, however, turned violent. An estimated 1,000 people paraded down the city's main thoroughfare (*Avenida Comercio*) calling for the release of political prisoners, freedom of the press, implementation of the constitutionally mandated civil rights, and an end to dictatorial rule. By previous agreement, there would be no speeches during or at the conclusion of the demonstration, and government troops were to step aside for the marchers. As the march proceeded, the atmosphere became increasingly tense, until some unknown person fired a shot that erupted into general shooting among and between civilians, police, and the military. Estimates of casualties vary between 20 and 144 deaths. The San Pedro Massacre, as the incident became known, caused hemispheric-wide protests against Carías, who until now cultivated the opinion that he was a different kind of dictator.

The protest, signs, and banners against the four dictators bore great resemblance to the democratic ideals put forward by President Roosevelt, the OIAA, and the dictators themselves in the battle against Germany, Italy, and Japan. For example, the women of Honduras were exalted to unite in order overthrow the tyrant of tyrants, Tiburcio Carías Andino. One student held a placard reading, "The Students of Nicaragua are With the Democratic Students of Honduras." Another read, "We Shall Sustain Democracy in Central America."[2]

Carías's opponents appealed directly to Ambassador John D. Erwin in Tegucigalpa and to the State Department in Washington, D.C. for U.S. intervention to move Carías out of the presidency. The U.S. refused, citing its promise of the Good Neighbor Policy in 1933 to no longer interfere in the internal affairs of Latin American nations. The U.S. rejection only prompted the opposition to charge the United States with aiding Carías to remain in power.

In response to the protests, the administration took several actions. Carías's supporters organized a demonstration on his behalf on July 10 in Tegucigalpa. Utilizing the usual measures to provide good attendance, some 8,000 people, mostly women and students, carried placards honoring Presidents Carías and Franklin D. Roosevelt. Carías and Vice President Abraham Williams addressed the marchers, asking them to maintain order. Congressional President Plutarco Muñoz was dispatched to the North Coast to lead proadministration demonstrations, which were highly exaggerated in the progovernment newspaper, La Epoca. For example it claimed that 16,000 turned out in Puerto Cortés, where the area population was estimated to be 10,000. Government officials used such claims to point out that the protesters were only a small minority of the population. The administration also released propaganda pointing to its progress with new schools, hospitals, roads, and 11 years of continued peace. Subsequently, the dissidents were confined to their homes and denied public services. On the surface, the crisis passed because the opposition needed better organization. Finally, the November 1944 reelection of U.S. President Franklin D. Roosevelt further strengthened the Carías regime because it meant no change in the U.S. policy of nonintervention.

Unlike his colleagues elsewhere in Central America, Carías survived the protests against his dictatorship. Honduran geography and communications played a role. Tegucigalpa and San Pedro Sula were unconnected, and communications between the cities controlled by the government. The dissident liberals and nationals remained unorganized, disparate groups without a clear plan of action. While some officers within the military shared the middle sector's goal for political participation, their relationship was immature and tenuous at best.

Isolated protests against Carías and border incursions from exiles based in El Salvador and Guatemala continued throughout 1945 and 1946. Exiles, particularly Liberal Angel Zuñiga Huete, continually appealed for U.S. assistance in gaining the release of political prisoners and insuring that Carías would not attempt to again extend his presidency. In 1947, at age 71, Carías made it clear that he would not remain in power beyond January 1, 1949. To insure his legacy, Carías labored on behalf of his War Minister Juan Manuel Gálvez to be the National Party's presidential nominee in the 1948 election. The opposition Liberal Party remained disorganized and discouraged when it again nominated Zuñiga Huete for president and Francisco Paredes Fajardo of San Pedro Sula for vice president at its May 16, 1948, convention, the same individuals that the party put forth in the 1932 election. And to the new U.S. Ambassador in Tegucigalpa, Herbert Bursely, the Liberal Party's platform was nothing more "than a warmed over 16 year-old dish."[3]

The disheartened liberals recognized that they could not win a free election, and on September 22, 1948, the party's supreme council announced its abstention from the polls because of the atmosphere of oppression that permeated the country. On election eve, October 9, 1948, Zuñiga Huete and eight other Liberal Party leaders became guests in the Chilean, Guatemalan, and Mexican legations, a move thought by some to be a cover for a liberal revolt on election day. The revolt never materialized. Official election results gave Gálvez 254,802 of the 300,000 votes cast, and his transition to the presidency on January 1, 1949, went smoothly.

THE GÁLVEZ ADMINISTRATION

Following the passing of the presidential sash on January 1, 1949, Juan Manuel Gálvez departed the National Theater and walked to the Hotel Sótano in downtown Tegucigalpa. In the hotel lobby, Gálvez held an impromptu press conference and announced that he was *"un presidente en camisa"* (a president in shirt sleeves). The walk with no guards and the press conference signaled a break with the past, that Gálvez would be more comfortable with the people than Carías had been. Gálvez did not move into the presidential palace, instead he lived in his home in Tegucigalpa from which he walked to work every day, stopping at his favorite barbershop for a morning shave. In fact, over the course of his presidency, Gálvez regularly met and conversed with the people by attending agricultural fairs, school and sporting events, and visiting outlying communities often accomplished by flying only with the plane's pilot. Gálvez's unassuming style made him comfortable with the people, and they responded in kind. The change in style and subsequent change in substance from his predecessor was done without criticizing Carías. Once in office, however, Gálvez demonstrated greater independence from Carías than contemporary observers anticipated, an independence that caused the mentor to become irritated with his protégé.

During Gálvez's tenure, Honduras experienced a period of relative peace and order. He continued some of Carías's programs such as road building and the development of coffee as an export commodity. By 1953, nearly one-quarter of the government budget was directed to road construction. In 1949, Gálvez concluded a new 25- year contract with the UFCO that was very favorable to the latter. Gálvez also continued Carías's austere fiscal policies including regular payments on the government debt.

Gálvez's independent policy initiatives included an increased share of the national budget for education. Although the Honduran congress completed action on a national income tax, government enforcement of the code was lax and sporadic. Labor also benefitted because congress approved and Gálvez signed laws providing for a minimum wage, eight-hour workdays, worker's paid holidays, limited employer responsibility for work-related injuries, and women and children work regulations. Like the tax code, however, the labor legislation proved difficult to implement, owing to business resistance particularly by the banana Companies.

During the Gálvez administration, large-scale commercial agriculture expanded its holdings in response to increased world market prices for meat, cotton, and coffee. The expansion of production also led to foreign investment in ancillary industries, such as food processing, chemical production, and clothing manufacturing.

Gálvez implemented a 1950 International Monetary Fund (,) recommendation and assistance to establish the Central Bank of Honduras (BANTRAL) the country's first such institution, and the National Development Bank (BANADESA). The IMF also assisted in establishing the Faculty of Economies (School of Business) at the National University and the Supreme Council of Economic Planning (CONSUPLANE) and Ministry of Economics and Commerce. The United Nations Food and Agricultural Organization (FAO) provided guidance on forestry and agricultural extension programs. Although the future awaited the impact of these programs, the totality of Gálvez's initiatives moved Honduras towards the modern world and away from its image as a banana republic.

In the political arena, a large amount of press freedom was permitted that led to the publication of three new newspapers in Tegucigalpa that offered different opinions than the government spokesman, *La Epoca*. Political tensions were further eased with the release of political prisoners, the return of political exiles, and allowing parties to again function. The latter decision resulted in the revival of the PLH under the leadership of Dr. José Ramón Villeda Morales.

§ § § § §

Carías received a warm reception as he walked among the people on the day of Gálvez's inauguration. To Ambassador Bursely and many other observers this was a most interesting incident when one considered that Carías was widely known as a dictator, who stifled political opposition, suppressed political rights, controlled government machinery, and balanced the federal budget with draconian austerity measures. Carías also left behind a country that had not appreciably changed since he came to power in 1932. Postwar economic recovery had yet to arrive in Honduras, although an infantile coffee market appeared to be in the making. Banana and cotton exports remained below prewar levels. The Honduran manufacturing sector was the smallest among the five Central American countries. In 1948, Honduras remained a nation of poor, rural farmers. Only 10 percent of the 1.4 million Hondurans lived in cities over 10,000 people: Tegucigalpa with 72,000 and San Pedro Sula with 21,000 were the largest cities and were yet to be connected by a hard surface road. In fact, Honduras had only 268 miles of paved roads and 1541 miles of unpaved roadways. Once out of office, Carías failed in his attempt to remain a vital force in the National Party. He parted ways with his hand chosen successor, Juan Manuel Gálvez, and failed in his 1954 presidential bid. A new and younger generation of political leadership came to the forefront.

After 1954, Carías remained at his home in central Tegucigalpa where he daily greeted visitors that included political friends and foes alike. In 1963, the National Party made him its honorary chief. Accolades and honors continued until his death on December 23, 1969. Carías also spent a good deal of time overseeing the management of his haciendas outside the capital. *El Berrinche*, a 200-acre experimental farm, exported fruit and *El Espinal* produced cattle and sugar cane. And, at *Villa Elena*, coffee beans and assortment of flowers were produced for local markets.

Assessing the Carías administration remains a challenging and conflicting task. He provided the nation with a period of relative political peace. The nation's fiscal stability made constant progress, and given the limited amount of funds he had to work with, Carías can be credited with some improvements in education and expanding the network of roads to connect the larger towns with each other.

However, as a dictator, the political opposition and labor groups were silenced, the nascent democratic institutions revised to serve Carías's intentions, and oftentimes national interests were sacrificed in favor of nepotism.

Still, as Carías prepared to leave office in 1949, the portents of change bubbled below the public surface; and when they came to forefront in the next decade, one must ask whether or not these movements were internal national movements responding to the adverse conditions that the masses endured since independence, if not before, or whether these were part of an international Communist conspiracy. Honduras would become locked into the Cold War.

NOTES

1. "Prolongaciono Continuismo en el Poder Supremo de las Democracias," *La Epoca*, December 17, 1940, 4. Author's translation.

2. United States National Arhives (USNA), College Park, Md., Record Group 59 General Records of the Department of State, Record Group 59 (RG59), File 815.00/7-0444; 815.006/7-0644; and 815.00B/7-2644.

3. USNA, RG 59, 815.00/5-2148, Herbert S. Bursley to State Department, May 21, 1948.

7

The Cold War Comes to Honduras

Distinctions between extreme leftist parties and the communists are often fluid. [Therefore,] we should caution against [labeling] leaders as communists. Henry F. Holland Assistant Secretary of State for Latin American Affairs.[1]

April 15, 1955

The economic and political changes that took place in the 10 years following the 1944 summer protests were accompanied by demographic changes that had long-term influence upon the country. The commercialization of the expanded agricultural sector led to technological unemployment among the traditional agricultural workers, many of whom made their way to urban centers, where, as unskilled workers, they faced limited economic opportunities and blighted living conditions. The expanding export based economy also contributed to a growing middle sector that included government and business technocrats, professionals such as lawyers, doctors, dentists, engineers, accountants, journalists, educators, small merchants, and businessmen. Like the rural *compesinos*, these urban middle-sector groups formed their own popular organizations and found their way into the National and Liberal political parties, where the younger generations were discontented with the old guard's leadership. The discontentment was more than generational; it drew attention to the changing global sociopolitical dynamics.

As World War II drew to its conclusion in 1945, and for the next two years, the United States envisioned a more democratic world held together by the United Nations, but the idealism gave way to the to the Soviet Union's consolidation of power in eastern and central Europe and its intentions in western Europe. Doubtful that it could gain U.S. public support and active cooperation from European allies for the immediate military containment of perceived Soviet expansion, the Truman administration chose a policy of economic recovery. In doing so, it recognized that socioeconomic disparities served as a breeding ground for political change, specifically meaning the appeal of communism.

In 1947, United States put its containment policy in place with the Truman Doctrine and its call for an economic plan, subsequently known as the Marshall Plan. Two years later, in April 1949 the establishment of the North Atlantic Treaty Organization (NATO) militarized the containment policy. Over the next 12 months, U.S. policymakers concluded that the Soviet Union intended to reach beyond western Europe. The National Security Council (NSC) concluded on April 14, 1950, that the Soviet Union had global ambitions and in the underdeveloped Third World local communist organizations, quietly linked to Moscow, capitalized upon local issues as a means to gain popular support that legitimized their cause and organization. The latter had already taken place in China, where on October 1, 1949, Mao Zse-dong declared the establishment of the communist People's Republic of China (PRC) and further verified on June 25, 1950, following North Korea's invasion of South Korea. The NSC also concluded that the United States must assume free world leadership in combating communism's global threat. Finally, Secretary of State George C. Marshall's 1947 reorganization of the State Department only reaffirmed the NSC's observation that Communists used local discontentment as a vehicle to strengthen their political position. In these early Cold War years, U.S. policy toward Central America, in general, and Honduras, in particular, fell within these broad policy parameters.

As World War II drew to its close in 1945, United States interest in Central America focused upon the transition to civilian democracy, save Costa Rica, which long enjoyed regularly scheduled elections and peaceful transfer of the presidency. To avoid any impression of linkage to dictators, the State Department and the congress refused to approve the sale of excess military equipment and supplies to Central America. State Department representatives clearly indicated the U.S. preference to work directly with democratic governments to U.S. diplomats in the Central American capitals and directly to the isthmian officials in Washington, D.C., Central America's need for economic assistance at the war's end was obvious, but the United States could afford only one economic recovery program at that time; and because of Europe's strategic priority, it took precedence. The Central Americans were advised to be patient and to understand that as the European economy recovered from the ravages of war; prewar trade patterns would be reestablished.

In the Central American political arena, the NSC concluded in 1950 that local communist organizations had become a legitimate spokesman for the needs of the disenfranchised masses. At the end of World War II, in-field diplomats and State Department analysts including Ellis O. Briggs, John. M. Cabot, Andrew Donovan, Laurrence Duggan, John D. Erwin, Edwin Kyle, Robert Newbegin, Murray Wise, and Robert Woodward, had long records of Central and South American experience. They understood the middle sector's desire for greater political participation, and that like the elite, the middle class lacked interest in social and economic reform for the masses; but they did not interpret the latter's demands as part of a larger communist plot to overtake any particular Central American country. Rather, they understood the masses demands to be the reality of their lives. Beginning in late 1947, the newer officers in the field and in Washington, D.C., did not have extensive Latin American experience and were also influenced by the increased tempo of the United States – Soviet rivalry. Included in this group were William Tapley Bennett, Edward Cale, Raymond Oakley, Richard Patterson, Herbert Bursely, and Harold Montamat. To these foreign service officers, the world had been divided into two camps by 1947 in which there was no room for middle ground. Like communist efforts in eastern and western Europe and in the United States, the communists sought to infiltrate education, government, and labor institutions for their own objectives. To these analysts, a communist was anyone challenging the established order and/or expressing sympathy for the Soviet position in world affairs, even if no direct link to Moscow could be established. The demands for correcting the legitimate socioeconomic grievances of the downtrodden masses were viewed as tools for bringing communists to political power.

The policy debate permeated the State Department's Central American desk in 1950 and 1951. Clearly, U.S. officials failed to sort out the differences between Nationalism and Communism, much less anything resembling revolutionary Nationalism during the Truman administration. The debate was finally resolved in 1952 with the incoming administration of Dwight D. Eisenhower. The new U.S. president and his secretary of State, John Foster Dulles viewed the world only in black and white terms, Communist or anti-Communist. There was no gray matter. The Cold War arrived in Central America.

HONDURAS: TWO NEW POLITICAL ACTORS, LABOR AND THE MILITARY, 1954–1963

On April 10, 1954, UFCO dockworkers at the Tela railroad complex refused to load a company ship with bananas destined for market in the United States unless paid double time for work on Sunday. The workers based their pay demand upon a 1948 law, approved by then President Tiburcio Carías, which provided for a 12-hour workday and overtime pay for extra hours; but like other Carías sponsored populist legislation, the law was never enforced. To achieve their objective the worker's filed suit only to be rebuffed by the state judicial system. As a result of the court's decision, UFCO workers struck on May 1, 1954, at Puerto Cortés, El Progreso, La Lima, and Bataan to demand back overtime pay and double time for such endeavors, an 8-hour workday, improved health care services for workers, health care protection while working, and abolition of the obligation to eat in company run eateries on workdays. By May 4, an estimated 25,000 United and Standard Fruit Company workers were on strike, and by May 15, the strike reached to San Pedro Sula and Tegucigalpa where workers in the industrial and commercial sector–textile and match manufacturers, mining, and retail–joined those in agriculture. The number of striking workers was estimated to be between 40,000 and 50,000. The government of dismayed President Juan Manuel Gálvez confronted the country's first general strike.

Labor unions were an anomaly in Honduras. Although workers possessed the legal right to organize unions, strikes were frowned upon by both the government and the fruit companies. The first strike of significance occurred in 1917 in response to war-inspired inflation, but like those that followed in the 1920s, it was confined to singular plantations or company branch operations. President Carías gave lip service to labor's demands, as illustrated by the 1948 labor law. While labor unions evolved largely into mutual aid societies by the mid-1940s, they also became a component of the generation of rising expectations after World War II when fruit company workers' demands expanded beyond increased wages. Already among the highest paid laborers in Honduras, wage increase demands varied in 1954 among the striking groups, ranging from 50 to 72 percent in addition to demands for overtime pay, paid vacations, and severance pay. The striking workers also sought better housing, health care, worker's compensation, and education for their children. In this regard, Honduran labor leaders were influenced by events in Guatemala, where after 1945 Presidents Juan José Areválo and Jacobo Arbenz implemented *socioeconomic* programs that benefitted labor at the expense of the traditional landowning elite and foreign owned companies. The traditional ruling elites and foreign owned companies in Guatemala and in Honduras described this attack upon their privileged position as Communist inspired. One, of those companies, UFCO, conducted its own anti-Communist campaign in the United States that alleged a link between the local communists and Moscow, an allegation never factually proven.

Communism in Honduras dated to a 1927 organizational meeting in La Ceiba. Two years later, at Tela, one of the La Ceiba leaders, Manuel Calix Herrera, assisted in the establishment of the Honduran Syndicate Federation (FSH; *Federación Sindical Hondureña*) to distinguish itself from the Honduran Worker's Organization (FOA; *Federación Obrerra Hondureña*) in Tegucigalpa. The difference between the two organizations rested with the socioeconomic structures of the North Coast and the capital city. The North Coast did not have a large local landowning elite, only the fruit companies for whom the overwhelming majority of the population worked. The Arab-dominated middle sector in San Pedro Sula, not only cared little about peasant labor, but lived a life apart from the entire banana industry. In Tegucigalpa, a large landowning elite combined with the local commercial elite to dominate the economy, politics, and society at the expense of the emerging middle sector and the dormant rural and urban working class. In 1937, following Carías's illegal *continuismo*, leaders of the worker's groups went into exile in El Salvador and Guatemala where, with political exiles, they formed anti-Carías groups that frequently contained the word "revolutionary" or a derivative thereof. At the end of World War II many of the exiles, including Communist labor leaders returned to Honduras and contributed to the administration's charges that Communists were rampant in the country, a charge not substantiated by the Honduran government or the U.S. embassy in Tegucigalpa. In 1947 the two groups merged to form the Democratic Revolutionary Party of Honduras (PDRH; *Partido Revolucionarío Democratico de Hondureño*) with directorates in San Pedro Sula and Tegucigalpa. Generally, membership consisted of those people who fell within the definition of the generation of rising expectations: lawyers, doctors, schoolteachers, merchants, engineers, and students who opposed the exile leader Ángel Zúñige Huete. At best, the U.S. Embassy identified 20 PRDH members as communists on lists that included socialists, liberals, and other radicals. PRDH leadership, however, consistently denied they were influenced by communists inside or outside of the party, although they put forth an economic and political philosophy that mimicked some of the ideas espoused by Guatemala's Juan José Arévalo, Peru's Victor Raúl Haya de la Torre, and Costa Rica's José Figueres.

A series of interrelated events followed the presidential election of Jacobo Arbenz in Guatemala on November 12, 1950 that led to the settlement of the general strike in Honduras and also altered the course of its political dynamics. In Guatemala, President Arbenz trekked a path that led first, to the distribution of German owned properties that were seized by the Ubico government during World War II, and then to his own government-directed land confiscation program that eventually struck at the UFCO holdings. As early as 1951 and 1952, the Truman administration sounded out Anastasio Somoza in Nicaragua, Óscar Osorio in El Salvador, and Gálvez in Honduras about possible intervention in Guatemalan internal affairs. All but Gálvez were amenable. Shortly after the Eisenhower administration took office on January 20, 1953, it gave special attention to matters in Guatemala, and by the late summer of 1953, the Central Intelligence Agency (CIA) began planning for the removal of Arbenz. At home, the administration pursued a public relations campaign against international Communism that was reenforced by UFCO's own campaign against Communism in Guatemala and to a lesser degree in Honduras. To sanctify its forthcoming invasion of Guatemala, on March 28, 1954, the delegates at the Tenth Conference of American States met in Caracas, Venezuela, from March 3 to 28. U.S. Secretary of State John Foster Dulles obtained a resolution reaffirming the western hemisphere's commitment to state sovereignty and freedom from direct or indirect intervention in the domestic affairs on the part of any singular or combination of states that sought to impose totalitarianism. Everyone in attendance understood that Dulles and the United States directed the resolution at Guatemala. It cleared the way for the subsequent CIA sponsored invasion of Guatemala. This time, Gálvez was a willing participant. His delegation at Caracas approved the resolution, and he permitted Honduras to serve as the training and staging area for the rag-tag 480 man army of General Miguel Ydígoras Fuentes that became a mere sideshow in the overthrow of Arbenz. The CIA sponsored invasion of Guatemala began on June 18, 1954; and nine days later on June 27, Arbenz resigned the presidency and was militarily escorted out of the country. The United States selected General Ydígoras Fuentes to restore Guatemala's old order.

In Honduras, President Juan Gálvez wanted to extend his presidency beyond his current term that expired on January 1, 1955. To do so, Gálvez reasoned that he needed to balance the conflicting interests of the landowners, including the fruit companies, and labor's rising demands. Gálvez was motivated to act quickly when he learned the contents of a May 16 telegram from the embassy to the State Department, asserting that the U.S. should encourage a strike settlement that excluded the Communists, by force, if necessary. Gálvez then prodded the fruit companies into agreeing that they would make some concessions to the workers. Gálvez appointed a new and more worker-friendly government negotiating committee to mediate the labor crisis.

In San Pedro Sula, Honduras, on July 6, 1954, the general strike ended with a labor agreement that provided for a $20 bonus for all workers who immediately returned to work, 10 to 15 percent wage increases, promises of paid vacations, and medical treatment for their families. The settlement differed greatly from the original set of worker's demands, but it was concluded under the threat of foreign intervention and negotiated by a government committee that favored the fruit companies not the Honduran workers. With the specter of foreign intervention removed, labor leaders accused of having ties with Arbenz in Guatemala were jailed or exiled.

Despite the limited gains, the 1954 strike marked a major turning point in the growing strength of the Honduran labor movement and the decline of the fruit companies over state affairs. Coupled with the 1949 labor law, the settlement of the1954 labor strike paved the path for the full unionization of Honduran labor in 1955, when the state legalized 50 unions, including the North Coast banana workers. Over time, some of the unions would disappear or merge with others; but in the late 1960s, Honduras led all Central American nations in the unionization of workers.

The political fallout that followed the 1954 labor strike, however, momentarily continued to reflect the course of Honduran history. Unhappy with Gálvez's advances to labor, former President Carías decided to compete for the presidency in the scheduled October 1954 elections. He received the National Party's nomination and in so doing split the organization. The party's splinter group, the National

Reformist Movement (MNR; *Movimiento Reformista Nacional*), as the dissidents were called, nominated former vice-president and Carías confidante Abraham Williams Calderón. Exiled Liberal Party leader and medical doctor Ramón Villeda Morales returned home to become the party's standard bearer. He appeared out of character for a Honduran politician. An eloquent speaker and highly cultured, Villeda Morales was a stranger to the violence that permeated Honduran politics. Always concerned with the plight of the poor, Villeda Morales founded the Liberal Party newspaper *El Pueblo* that espoused his thoughts about government responsibility for them. Villeda Morales also had successfully managed the campaigns of several reform-minded liberals in municipal elections, tasks that enhanced his public image.

The formation of the MNR served as the death-knell for the PHRD that previously embraced the dissident liberals, including the Communists who now banded together to form their own party, the Communist Party of Honduras (PCH; *Partido Communista de Honduras*) came into being on election day, October 10, 1954. Its program called for the liquidation of large land holdings; the revision of all contracts and prohibition of new contracts with foreign companies; and the nationalization of all lands, minerals, and public services. Such a program drew the ire of the Honduran and foreign elites and the middle sector. Because of this opposition, interim-President Julio Lozano Díaz outlawed the party on December 5, 1954.

Given Honduran electoral history, the campaign and October 10 election itself were remarkably free and honest. Nearly 260,000 of the 400,000 eligible voters went to the polls and provided Villeda Morales with a clear margin of victory. He won 121,213 votes, Carías received 77,041, and Williams 53,041, but the constitution provided that a majority of the total votes was required to be elected president. With 48 percent of the vote and some 8,000 ballots short of a statistical majority, Villeda Morales would have to await a congressional decision. It never came, despite the fact that PLH won a majority of the congressional delegates but not enough to insure the placing of Villeda Morales in the presidential palace.

The October 1954 scenario reminded observers of the 1924 presidential quagmire because of the constitutional requirement that two-thirds of the members of the new legislature must be present and vote to choose a president and that the victor must receive two-thirds of the legislatures vote in order to take office. To further complicate the situation, President-elect Gálvez left for Miami, presumably for medical treatment, although some think that he fled to country to avoid arrest. With his departure, the government fell into the hands of lesser known Vice President Julio Lozano Díaz.

The MNR refused to accept Villeda Morales as president, making a compromise with the PNH impossible. Without any agreement, the delegates to the new congress failed to take their seats, resulting in a national crisis. Under such conditions, the constitution provided that the supreme court determine the president. Because the court was dominated by Carías appointees, the PLH refused to accede to this course of action. Loranzo Díaz seized the initiative on December 5, 1954. He suspended the legislature and announced that he would serve as president until new elections could be held. With support from the three candidates in the 1954 presidential election, Loranzo Díaz formed a cabinet that included representatives of the three major political parties. He also appointed a council of state, comprised of representatives of the three political parties, to replace the suspended congress until a constituent assembly was chosen to write yet another constitution.

Loranzo Díaz's broad base of support rapidly dwindled. His ambitious development plan to be financed by international loans and increased taxes also included a labor code. The PHN quickly objected to the proposed international loans on the grounds that it would result in new foreign companies to exploit the country. And, as could be expected, the elite opposed any tax increase that impinged upon its wealth. The proposed labor code guaranteed workers the right to organize and to strike (except in the public sector) but also gave employers the right to lockout workers. The proposed code also contained minimum wage provisions and regulated hours and working conditions. While this proposal gained Loranzo Díaz momentary labor support, over time workers cooled to the new president because of the Council of State's failure to implement the program and because of the government's failure to prod the fruit companies to fully implement the agreement that ended the 1954 strike.

As time passed, it became clear that Loranzo Díaz wanted to replace the traditional political parties with one of his own that would insure the continuation of his presidency. Toward that goal, Loranzo Díaz converted the council of state into a consultative body, postponed elections, and formed his own party, the National Union Party (PUN; *Partido de Unidad Nacional*). After limiting the activities of other political parties, in August 1956, Loranzo Díaz directed the arrest and exiling of Villeda Morales and other PLH leaders after the army crushed an uprising in Tegucigalpa. Loranzo Díaz served only to increase opposition protests and contribute to rumors about a *coup d'etat* against him.

The catalyst for change came with the October 7, 1956, congressional elections that were boycotted by most opposition candidates because of anticipated fraud, an allegation confirmed by the elections results. PUN candidates were declared winners of all 56 congressional seats. PUN's joy of victory, however, was short-lived. On October 21, 1956, the commanders of the army and the air force academies along with the son of former president Major Roberto Gálvez ousted Loranzo Díaz and set up a military junta to govern Honduras. What President Tiburcio Carías feared when refusing a U.S. military mission during World War II became a reality: the military became an institution unto itself.

MILITARY GOVERNMENTS: 1956–1982

The October 21 coup proved to be a high water mark in Honduran political history. For the first time in the nation's history, the military acted as an institution, not on behalf of a political party or leader. The coup leaders and their supporters represented a new generation of military men: younger, more nationalistic, and reform minded. They benefited from the changed U.S. foreign policy that viewed communism as a global threat that led to the post World War II training by U.S. military personnel and lifting of the congressional ban arm sales to Latin America in 1952, and in 1954 U.S.-Honduran military agreement finally provided for the direct U.S. military training for Honduran troops. Over time, the military would become the final arbiter of Honduran politics.

The junta governed for a year until elections for a congressional assembly were held on October 7, 1957. Under a system of proportional representation, the PLH won a majority and in November voted 37 to 20 in selecting Villeda Morales as President of Honduras. He embarked upon a six-year term beginning December 21, 1957.

Villeda Morales initiated a program that, in theory, appealed to all political sectors. Utilizing support from the International Monetary Fund (IMF), he is credited with stabilizing the national currency, the *lempira* and World Bank funds were used to pave the highway from the Caribbean coast to Tegucigalpa via San Pedro Sula. The 1958 Development Law provided tax relief and investment guarantees to domestic and foreign capital. On June 1, 1959, Villeda Morales signed into law a new national labor code that guaranteed workers rights in the areas of wages, hours, working conditions, vacations, workmen's compensation, severance pay, and maternity leave. It also provided a mechanism for settling labor disputes. A new insurance law in

July 1959 dealt with unemployment, health, old age, maternity, accidents, disability, and death benefits. Despite Villeda Morales's intention of satisfying the demands of the country's two most prominent interest groups, labor and the military, his programs exacerbated their conflictive relationship, particularly the elite's angst towards labor and contributed to a series of political crises.

Questions about Villeda Morales's commitment to social reform surfaced shortly after his December 21, 1957, inauguration, as henceforth he put forward conflicting signals about his political leanings. According unsubstantiated reports he met with UFCO officials and the U.S. Ambassador to Honduras, William Willauer at UFCO's Caribbean compound where Villeda Morales promised not to introduce radical labor and agricultural reforms in exchange for substantial loans and support for the Honduran military. Whether the meeting ever took place remains publicly unknown, but for sure, U.S. assistance to Honduras increased throughout the Villeda Morales administration.

Villeda Morales supported labors' demands for increased pay during a 1958 banana workers strike yet traveled to Choluteca to resolve a land occupation by peasant groups in favor of the landowners. The 1962 Agrarian Reform Law further infuriated elite landowners even though it shifted emphasis from expropriation of unused lands to resettlement of peasants on to public lands. The newly created Agrarian Institute was to supervise the relocation and development programs, such as the 175,000 acres in the Aguan Valley for 6,000 families. The 1962 law also established a tax on uncultivated land. Villeda Morales's cordial relations with Fidel Castro and his revolution before April 1961 served to bolster the assertion that Villeda Morales himself was leaning towards Communism. After the failed U.S.-sponsored Bay of Pigs invasion, designed to overthrow Cuba's Castro regime, for the remainder his presidency Villeda Morales allied itself with the U.S. camp against the Cuban dictator. In addition to warning his people about the dangers of Communism, Villeda Morales increased coastal defenses against alleged incursions from Cuban sponsored revolutionaries.

In addition to the large landowners and fruit companies, Villeda Morales came under attack from other conservative factions. It was assumed that the Caribbean's remaining dictators, Nicaragua's Anastasio Somoza and the Dominican Republic's Rafael Trujillo, plotted to oust Villeda Morales because of his reform programs. At home, the National Party constantly sniped at the president and often was the center of plots, real or imagined, to oust Villeda Morales. Their opposition finally coalesced around Colonel Armando Velásquez, a

1956 presidential aspirant. A leader in the National Police, Velásquez was linked to several revolt plots in 1959. The culmination came in July 1959 when National Police units attacked the presidential palace, only to be fended off by the presidential guard and armed civilians supportive of the administration. Only at the insistence of the armed forces did Velásquez receive permission to leave the country.

The 1959 assault on the presidential palace convinced Villeda Morales that he needed to reorganize the nation's security forces, which were controlled by the Minister of Defense, Colonel Osvaldo López Arellano. Both he and the national police had close linkage to the National Party, Villeda Morales's political rival. For his own security, Villeda Morales dissolved the national police force and replaced it with a 2,000 man civil guard under the authority of the ministry of government and justice. The military reacted negatively as it perceived the guard as a potential challenge to the military's institutional autonomy. The guard's creation also caused increased criticism of Villeda Morales from the right for not being tough on Communism and from the left for not doing enough for the workers. The conflict increased tensions as the 1963 presidential elections approached.

Villeda Morales was unable to persuade the Liberal Party to choose a presidential candidate to his liking, instead settling upon Modesto Rodas Alvarado, a fire-brand who campaigned throughout the country calling for more social reforms and the termination of the military's autonomous status. The National Party put forth a compromise candidate, Dr. Ramón Ernesto Cruz Uclés, a supreme court justice, but a colorless campaigner. On October 3, 1963, 10 days before the scheduled presidential election, López Arellano seized all powers of the state in a *coup d' etat* that resulted in the deaths of hundreds of citizens. He appointed his confidante, Ricardo Zúñiga Augustinius, as secretary of the presidency. Together, they centralized authority through patronage, careful delegation of powers and control of the national budget. While the arrangement provided for a high degree of partisanship, it also made López Arellano the focal point of criticism for the government's failure to stimulate an already slow economy.

López Arellano set out to silence the so-called radical political elements, a factor he used to justify the *coup d'etat*. The government quickly disbanded alleged Communist, pro-Castro organizations, and other leftist groups. By its refusal to appropriate money for the National Agrarian Institute (INA; *Instituto Nacional Agrario*), the 1962 Agrarian Reform Law lay dormant. Land distribution to the peasants came to a momentary halt. And while the military constantly harassed existing peasant unions, a new one, the National Union of peasants (UNC; *Unión Nacional de Campensinos*) with the help of the Christian Democratic Party (PDC; *Partido Democratico Christian*) actually grew in membership during the López Arellano years.

To legitimize his presidency, López Arellano arranged for congressional elections that were held on February 16, 1965. The PNH won 35 seats in the unicameral congress, and the PLH won 29. Amidst charges of electoral fraud, the PLH leadership attempted to boycott the congress when it convened on March 15. The attempt failed and with the required quorum present, the congress elected López Arellano president for the 1965–1973 period. The anti-Reformist nature of the López Arellano administration was reaffirmed with the March 1968 municipal elections. Using coercion and other illegal means, the PNH gained control of 90 percent of the municipal governments.

Shortly after the February congressional elections, Honduras joined the Central American Defense Council (CONDECA) that included El Salvador, Guatemala, and Nicaragua. Absent of its own military, Costa Rica did not join. Publicly envisioned to be another step toward Central American integration, in reality CONDECA conducted coordinated military action against guerrilla groups, but national rivalries led to its collapse in 1975. U.S. President Ronald Regan revived the organization in the 1980s to help combat the FSLN in Nicaragua and the Farabundo Martí National Liberation Front (FMLN) in El Salvador. In effect, it tightened the relationship between the Central American militaries and the Pentagon in the United States.

Opposition to the López Arellano regime came largely from North Coast business and labor leaders. In April and May 1968, they met with the president, his cabinet, and military commanders where they criticized government inertia regarding socioeconomic development and bureaucratic corruption. The group also pressed for participation of all social sectors in discussions and in planning the nation's development. For a time, the López Arellano administration took the suggestions under advisement. The government's deferral did not dissuade north coast interest groups from continuing their meetings and sending missives to the central government at Tegucigalpa.

López Arellano tightened his grip upon the government and society during the 1960s, at a time when Central America, in general, and Honduras, in particular, fell under the influence of U.S. policy. As early as March 1958, Brazilian President Juscelino Kubitschek advised U.S. Treasury Secretary C. Douglas Dillon that the United States needed to develop a long-term program designed to address the human needs of Latin America's poor or at some point in the near future confront a revolutionary continent. The point was driven home by Fidel Castro on January 7, 1959, when he marched triumphantly into Havana to mark the beginning of the Cuban Revolution. Over the next two years, Castro eliminated from Cuba almost every vestige of the old order: the landowning and business elite including the U.S. presence on the island and in place of the dictator Fulgencio Batista and his henchmen, Castro and his group of intimate advisors comprised the government. Cuba's middle sector, which had supported Castro because of his promises for democracy, now began to leave the country. The message was clear to the Honduran upper and middle sectors; Communism stood as a threat to the existing order and to the promises of a democratic government. López Arellano would now have every reason to justify his crackdown on leftists.

President Dwight D. Eisenhower responded to Latin America's growing socioeconomic crisis with the Social Progress Trust Fund, established on September 18, 1960, but it did not focus upon social issues. Instead, it emphasized expanded agricultural production for export and construction of the necessary infrastructure to get the products into the world market. Apparently, the increased agricultural wealth would, in part, pass down to the workers for their personal use and then recycle through the economy. President John F. Kennedy went far beyond Eisenhower when he proposed the Alliance for Progress on March 13, 1961. The proposed $100 billion, 10-year, ambitious program was to bring social and economic progress to all Latin America. The United States would make a $20 billion commitment, while the remainder was to come from other global sources, including the recipient countries themselves on a cost share basis. The objective was to produce a bloodless social revolution, obviating a Communist revolution.

Over the course of the 10-year program, Central America received $644 billion, including assistance for the Central American Common Market (CACM). National Planning Agencies were established to guide the development and implementation in six categories of assistance: industry, agriculture, infrastructure, taxation, health and sanitation, and housing and education. The industrial program was designed to improve banking, management, commodity marketing, and training in technical skills. Other funds included small business finance and training in the United States for training labor leaders and public administrators. Agricultural programs supported by the Alliance included crop diversification, agricultural research, and land distribution programs for the poor. Supporting infrastructure, particularly roads and projects like the Rio Lino electric plant in Honduras, were also included. To improve government income, U.S. advisors assisted locals with tax collection and the training of tax technicians. Health projects ranged from hospital construction to water sanitation. Housing projects improved the quality of living conditions for the poor but often were influenced by local politics, such as at La Lima and El Progreso in Honduras where the banana workers were strongly pro-American. Rural health clinics and prenatal care also reached out to the poor. Two areas of educational emphasis in Honduras were upon primary school curriculums and teaching methods and the development of MBA programs at the university level.

As the Alliance got underway, the United States clearly preferred to deal with democratic governments. Thus, President Kennedy warmly greeted Honduran President Villeda Morales when the two met at the Central American Conference that convened in San José, Costa Rica from March 18 to 20, 1963. Villeda Morales, a staunch anti-Communist, was also firmly committed to the Alliance objectives. The Honduran president promised to clarify the vague 1962 Agrarian Reform Law that prompted UFCO to cancel development plans and lay off 600 workers. The vague law implied that all privately owned land could be confiscated by the government for redistribution to the peasants. Whatever understanding Kennedy and Villeda Morales may have had was cancelled on October 3, 1963, when López Arellano seized power.

The Alliance for Progress did not meet its lofty objectives. Contemporary analysts placed primary responsibility upon the United States for attempting to force its ideas for development upon Latin America's traditional societies. Others quickly pointed out that Lyndon Johnson, who succeeded Kennedy in the presidency, lost interest in socioeconomic reforms and his successor, Richard M. Nixon had even less interest in Latin America. The Vietnam War took precedence in the Johnson and Nixon administrations, and with the latter also consumed by the Watergate scandals, Latin America became a distant spot on the U.S. policy radar screen.

But, the United States alone is not responsible for the failure of the Alliance for Progress. Latin Americans generously share in the blame, and Honduras serves as an excellent microcosm of the total picture. López Arellano, the Nationalist party, the large fruit companies, and the landowning Honduran elite all opposed any land reform program that included land redistribution to the peasants. They also resisted a primary requirement of all Alliance recipients: further democratization of the political arena. If anything, López Arellano moved in the opposite direction as he centralized government and rigged elections. Supported by the military, the Honduran old order wanted to preserve its own existence.

Within weeks after winning the presidency in his own right on November 3, 1964, Lyndon B. Johnson completely altered the course of U.S. policy towards Latin America. In December 1963, he replaced Kennedy's Latin American appointments and shortly thereafter appointed Thomas C. Mann as the lone voice on Latin American affairs. Mann, a cold warrior who served under John Foster Dulles in the State Department, implemented Johnson's deemphasis on economic and social programs and instead promoted the military suppression of Communism. Subsequent promises to promote constitutional government became empty rhetoric. Johnson continued Kennedy's military assistance program that emphasized the purchase of small, lightweight weapons and mobile equipment, and the U.S. supervision of military training in counterinsurgency techniques that focused upon internal security. Military governments were now acceptable. In February 1964, Johnson extended recognition to the López Arellano administration in Honduras.

Counterinsurgency included a wide range of economic, political, social, psychological, and military activities utilizing several U.S. government agencies. For example, the Agency of International Development (AID) was charged with the responsibility for economic programs and its office of public safety, for the training of police forces in interrogation and riot control methods. The U.S. Information Agency (USIA) worked to improve the U.S. image in each country. The military missions provided training and support to local armed forces. Under the commander in chief of the Southern Command (SOUTHCOM), headquartered in the Panama Canal zone, counterinsurgency training included the construction of schools, hospitals, and bridges; serving as medics in rural areas; and clearing jungle areas for rural farmers. By 1965, however, evidence began to mount that the counterinsurgency program was not meeting Kennedy's stated goals but rather became an instrument to secure the traditional power structure. López Arellano found another instrument to maintain order. The importance of counterinsurgency to U.S. policy in combating insurgency in Honduras can be measured in dollars. During the Kennedy-Johnson years, $5.9 million in military aid was extended to Honduras, $4.8 million increase over the preceding five-year period (1953–1961).

As time passed, charges of human rights violations against citizens increased. In the process, the people of Honduras further mistrusted the United States.

By 1968, López Arellano faced several obstacles that raised questions about his continuance in office. The economy sagged. While the foreign owned banana companies continued to fare well, whose tax exceptions deprived the Honduran government of income; world prices for the nation's other primary products—cotton, coffee, and timber—markedly dropped, further eroding the economy. The PLH and the PNH, the country's traditional political parties were in disarray, its unimaginative leadership incapable of new ideas to meet the current challenge. Labor and business groups, particularly on the North Coast, demanded a national dialogue that would include all sectors of society to discuss national problems and suggest possible solutions. The López Arellano administration brushed the suggestion aside. In 1969, Honduras appeared paralyzed and on the verge of collapse. In the midst of this economic stagnation and political tension, a four-day war (July 14 to 18, 1969) erupted between Honduras and neighboring El Salvador.

The immediate cause of the war resulted from riots that erupted at the Tegucigalpa soccer (football) stadium where the two national teams were to compete for a place in an international soccer tournament, the World Cup. The historic origins of the conflict, however, date to the 1920s, when Salvadoran peasants began migrating into Honduras because of the unavailability of land in El Salvador. The initial Salvadoran immigrants settled along the country's common border. With time's passage, the number increased through continued migration and propagation of those already residing in Honduras. The newer groups moved deeper into the Honduran interior. The Salvadorans remained on these lands, in some cases for two generations but never made any attempt to obtain clear title to the land or apply for Honduran citizenship. Over time, conflicts between the foreign and the native settlers became violent.

The situation worsened in the 1960s, first because of Honduras' 1962 Agrarian Reform Law, which provided that only native-born Hondurans could receive land under the law administered by the National Agrarian Institute (INA). In the mid-1960s, the Villeda Morales administration began to evict the Salvadorans from the land that they had occupied for up to two generations and, in turn, assign the lands to the Honduran peasants. For the time, the Honduran estates and UFCO's holdings in the far western sector of the country were able to absorb the displaced Salvadorans to work in the export-based agribusiness at wages lower than Honduran workers accepted. This arrangement changed in the latter part of the decade as the economy slowed and demand for Honduran primary exports decreased. This occured at a time when Honduran peasants increased their demand and their pressure upon the López Arellano administration to deliver on the promises of the 1962 Agrarian Reform Law. Furthermore, Honduras still lacked an industrial base to absorb either its own rural poor or the Salvadoran migrants. By the late 1960s, the Honduran government forced the repatriation of Salvadoran workers. Publicly, the Salvadoran elite resisted the peasants forced removal and return on moral grounds, but in reality, because the repatriation of these peasants to El Salvador would have significantly increased pressure upon scarce lands in that country.

The forced removal of the Salvadoran peasants from Honduras exacerbated the tense relations between the two countries because of the CACM that was established by an agreement between El Salvador, Guatemala, Honduras, and Nicaragua. A year later, Costa Rica joined on December 13, 1960. At that time, Latin American nations accepted the precepts of Raúl Prebisch and the Economic Commission for Latin America (ECLAC) that emphasized increased private and public investment in manufacturing and infrastructure to overcome the dependence on the exportation of primary products. ECLAC also encouraged the establishment of common markets and Common External Tariffs (CETs). The 1960 Central American treaty reflected these thoughts as it provided for intraregional free trade on specified items to be implemented over a 10-year period.

During the 1960s, CACM recorded significant gains in intraregional trade, with its total value rising from US $33 million in 1960 to just under US $1 billion in 1970. Urban industrial growth averaged 5.8 percent a year under CET protection. These figures, however, conceal some major difficulties. The bulk of the intraregional trade consisted of consumer goods, mostly processed foods. By the late 1960s, food processing accounted for 50 percent of CACM's industrial activities. In the agricultural sector, U.S. assistance provided for increased production per acreage and also introduced mechanization that displaced unknown numbers of farm workers who made their way to cities in search of jobs that did not exist because industrial development was capital, not labor intensive and centered in El Salvador and Guatemala, CACM's most developed countries. The displacement of rural labor not only strained the urban sector's infrastructure but also prompted some, like the Salvadorans, to seek economic opportunity in Honduras. Already the region's poorest and most underdeveloped country, Honduras received little, if any, benefit from CACM. In fact, Honduras found itself with an ever increasing trade deficit to the more industrious El Salvador.

The tense relations between Honduras and El Salvador over the economic and migration issues worsened when Honduras closed the escape valve for Salvadoran peasants in January 1969. The atmosphere was further exacerbated on June 27, 1969, when El Salvador severed diplomatic relations with Honduras. The intergovernmental tense relations were transferred to the crowds of people attending the qualifying games for the World Cup that were played in San Salvador and Tegucigalpa from July 14 to 18, 1969. Suddenly, on July 14 Salvadoran troops invaded western and southern Honduras with the objective of quickly occupying territory to be used as a bargaining chip over the migration issue. The Salvadoran troops rapidly advanced to Nueva Ocotepeque and Santa Rosa de Copán, leaving the impression of a forthcoming attack upon the capital of Tegulcigalpa. Initially caught off guard by the ground assault, the Honduran army still was no match for its Salvadoran counterpart. With its ground troops in retreat, the Honduran government turned to its superior air power to rout the Salvadorans. The conflict, dubbed the "Soccer War" by the international press, lasted only four days. The Organization of American States (OAS) negotiated a cease fire that went into effect on July 20, 1969, but not until October 30, 1980, did U.S. President Jimmy Carter orchestrate an agreement that sent the dispute to the International Court of Justice at The Hague. In 1992, the Court awarded the disputed border territory to Honduras, but not until 1999 did El Salvador accept the decision.

The war also prompted Honduras to withdraw from CACM and to suspend economic relations with El Salvador. The Central American wars of the 1980s further impinged upon intraregional economic development. Under these circumstances, CACM fell into disarray, only to be revived with the changing global economy in the 1990s. Personal costs were higher. An estimated 2,000 people, most of them Hondurans, were killed in the conflict. Estimates range from 60,000 to 130,000 peasants who returned to El Salvador where their presence complicated an already tenuous land tenure system that contributed to the Salvadoran civil war that erupted in 1979.

On the positive side for Honduras, a greater sense of nationalism emerged from the Soccer War. During the conflict, many Honduran peasants living and working in the battle zones provided the sustenance and medical care for the battered Honduran troops, which, in turn contributed to the military's better understanding of the peasant's plight. Subsequently, the enlisted men and younger officers led the military's reexamination of its policies of resistance to socioeconomic reforms.

The internal political struggle, suspended by the Soccer War and its immediate aftermath, again came to the forefront in 1970 when various Honduran interest groups pressured the government to hold free and open elections, reorganize the military, and adopt new economic programs. Labor, peasant, and business representatives held a series of meetings known as *fuerzas vivas* (living forces) to produce a Plan of National Unity that was presented to President López Arellano. The plan called for free elections, a coalition cabinet, and a division of government posts and congressional seats. The plan also led to an agreement between the Liberal and National parties on January 7, 1971, by which they agreed to form a national unity government following the March 19, 1971, elections. In the January 1971 meeting, the party leaders also agreed to pursue an agrarian reform program, to increase spending on technical education, to pass a civil service law, and to reform government administration. The party agreements gave false hope to the beginning of political stability and the addressing of national issues. Unfortunately, Honduras soon returned to its game of political musical chairs.

The PLH nominated a 52-year-old respected businessman Jorge Bueso Arias, and the PNH named 68-year-old university professor Ramón Ernesto Cruz as its standard bearer. Cruz ran a more aggressive campaign, utilizing the mass media and modern campaign techniques for the first time in Honduran political history. Cruz won the March 18 relatively unfettered elections by a 299,807 to 269,989 vote count over Bueso Arias. Despite that fact that the constitution made voting obligatory, only two-thirds of the eligible Honduran voters went to the polls, an indication that the masses of people had lost confidence in its governing system. That confidence was further weakened in late 1972 when the military sanctioned discussions to revise the January 7, 1971, pact. Public opposition against President Cruz mounted as agrarian reform came to a halt; labor and business expressed their dissatisfaction with the government's failure to revitalize the economy. When peasant and labor organizations announced their intentions to orchestrate a 20,000-person hunger strike on Tegucigalpa, the military acted. In a bloodless *coup d' etat* on December 4, 1972, the military ousted Cruz and replaced him with former President López Arellano.

On the surface, López Arellano appeared to have abandoned the conservative ways of his previous presidency. Economic growth and land distribution, however, remained evasive. Part of the problem lay beyond López Arellano's doing. Hurricane Fifi, the most devastating natural disaster in Honduran history, hit in September 1974, causing immense damage along the Caribbean coast and destroying a vast number of banana plantations, homes, and infrastructure essential to the export of commodities. An estimated 10,000 people died.

Against the backdrop of Hurricane Fifi's devastation to the banana industry, in April 1974, a number of press reports indicated that President López Arellano accepted a $1.25 million cash bribe, with a promise of another $1.25 million future payment, to void an increase in the Honduran export tax on bananas. Responding to the charges, the military replaced López Arellano as commander of the armed forces on March 31, 1975. Three weeks later, April 22, 1975, he was replaced as president by 45-year-old career officer, Colonel Juan Alberto Melgar Castro. Although he gave lip service to agrarian reform, he did little to distribute land among the peasants. Still, he drew the wrath of the large landowners and from the broad based middle sector for not moving rapidly toward the holding of elections, raising suspicions that he intended to remain in office.

Melgar also was accused of being in the pay drug traffickers who used Honduras as a safe haven for their product en route from South America to the United States, which led to demonstrations in Tegucigalpa for and against him throughout the summer of 1978. The turmoil prompted the military to remove Melgar from office on August 7. General Policarpo Paz García headed a three-man military junta that replaced him. His administration was characterized by administration and a high level of military repression. He established a right-wing paramilitary death squad, trained by the CIA that was later used by the Reagan administration to support the *Contras* during the 1980s. His was the last military coup d'etat in Honduras until June 28, 2009.

From the start of his administration, Paz García promised elections and a return to civilian government. The first step in that direction came with the election of a congress on April 20, 1980, in which 81 percent of the 1.2 million registered voters cast their ballots. The PLH won 49 percent of the vote, and under a complex apportionment system, won 35 seats in the congress. The PHN received 33 seats and the newly formed independent Innovation and Unity Party (PINU) received 3 seats. An interim coalition government was formed, representing the three political parties. Over the next year, the congress completed a new constitution and provided for new elections on November 27, 1981. Liberal Party candidate, 57-year-old medical doctor Roberto Suazo Córdova, campaigned on a sweeping program of economic and social development. He captured 53 percent of the popular vote. The PLH also won narrow control of the congress: 44 seats to 34 for the PNH. The PLN also won 61 percent of the municipal elections.

HONDURAS AND THE END OF THE
COLD WAR (1980–1991)

Roberto Suazo Córdova took over the Honduran presidency on January 27, 1982, a time when the country's neighbors were engaged in civil conflict, such as El Salvador and Guatemala, or experienced leftist governments that were under foreign attack like Nicaragua. The crisis of the old order that had been smoldering since the end of World War II came to the forefront of isthmian life in the 1950s and 1960s, and a decade later produced repressive military regimes. The fundamental historic factors that produced conflict elsewhere existed in Honduras but never rose to the level of national rebellion, yet the country would be drawn into the conflict that marred the isthmus for a decade after the overthrow of Nicaraguan dictator Anastasio Somoza De Bayle on July 19, 1979, and the election of Ronald Reagan as U.S. President on November 4, 1980. Reagan came to the presidency as a cold warrior, meaning that he interpreted international affairs within the context of east-west relations. To him and his administration, the struggles in Central America were not local legitimate nationalist movements to correct historic socioeconomic differences but rather the Soviet-Cuban use of local proxies capitalizing upon those historic grievances to establish communist governments throughout the region. The Central American elites and military shared the latter perception. The Reagan administration came to office determined to oust the Sandinistas from power in Nicaragua, to assist the Salvadoran military to thwart the FMLN, and to turn a blind eye to the horrific human rights violations committed by the Guatemalan military to suppress alleged Communism in that country.

U.S. concern with possible Sandinista expansion into Honduras surfaced in 1980, the final year of the Jimmy Carter administration, when he added $59 million to the Honduran economic assistance package and another $4 million in military assistance to tighten its border security against guerrilla activities and alleged Cuban arms shipments through Honduras to the Salvadoran rebels. Reagan came to office determined that only a military solution could halt the spread of communism on the isthmus. Toward that end, he approved the use of clandestine CIA activities to destroy oil facilities at Corinto on Nicaragua's Pacific coast and port facilities at Puerto Cabezas on its Caribbean coast and to cut power grids, blow up bridges, and burn crops in the fields, all in an effort to undermine the Sandinista government in Nicaragua. In each instance, unoccupied Honduran coastal lands or interior jungles were used as staging areas. By the time some of these events became public in 1982, Reagan already had contracted with the Argentine military to train the *Contras* in Honduras. While Reagan referred to the *Contras* as "freedom fighters," the term is a contraction for the Spanish word equivalency of counter-revolutionaries.

Honduras was in a precarious position. As host to CIA-supported Contras, it was constantly threatened with retaliation by Nicaragua. Its Salvadoran and Guatemalan border areas were considered havens for rebels operating in those countries, a fact that contributed to the fear of intervention. Guerrilla groups also operated with the country. The most notable was the Chinchineros\Populist Liberation Movement, considered by Honduran authorities to be an arm of the Salvadoran-FMLN. By late 1982, the Chinchineros were credited with over $2 million in ransoms and robberies. The group's most publicized affair occurred in September 1982 when it seized the Chamber of Commerce Building in San Pedro Sula and held more than 100 hostages. Their demand for the release of an estimated 80 political prisoners failed, but the government granted the 12 rebels who seized the building with safe conduct out of the country.

President Suazo Córdova came to the presidency unprepared to deal with such an international challenge. His initial approach in dealing with Honduras's role in the regional crisis stressed coexistent rather than confrontation, but it could lead to a balance of power not in Honduras's favor. In his inaugural address, Suazo Córdova stressed his country's neutrality in face of the regional crisis. In following the conciliatory attitude, he dispatched Foreign Minister Edgardo Paz Barnica to the Organization of American States (OAS) with a proposed peace plan. It called for general disarmament in Central America, withdrawal of foreign military advisors, international enforcement of any final agreement, an end to regional arms traffic, respect for delineated borders, and the establishment of a permanent multilateral dialogue. The other Central American governments, particularly Nicaragau, showed little interest in a Honduran proposal. Gradually, Suazo Córdova became convinced, as did his military officer corps, that the Sandinistas not only were an obstacle to regional peace, but also that they intended to undermine Honduran political stability through intimidation, propaganda, and military aid to dissident groups. This attitude change coincided with the Reagan administration policies.

The commander-in-chief of the Honduran armed forces, General Gustavo Álvarez Martínez, himself a hardliner, wanted the war against the Sandinistas to be an allied affair that included El Salvador,

Guatemala, and Honduras, but President Suazo Córdova refused to pursue the matter. Álvarez, who trained in Argentina during its "Dirty War" to rid the country of Communists, also used the Central American war as a reason to ferret out all left leaning, real or imagined, individuals and groups in Honduras. Over time, the Honduran and other international human rights organizations linked Álvarez to the disappearance, torture, and death of hundreds of Honduran leftists. The perception of a genuine leftist threat to Honduran stability enhanced Álvarez's political image at home and with U.S. policymakers but also raised questions about the nascent democracy under Suazo Córdova. Álvarez, not the president, appeared to be in control of the civilian government. Coupled with his close association to the business elite and the PNH leadership, he served as an ever present reminder of a possible military *coup d'etat*. Some argued that Suazo Córdova permitted a free hand to Álvarez so that he could pursue his own domestic policies. Others argued that Suazo Córdova actual did control the general, as evidenced by the president's refusal to increase the military budget. That argument is dismissed by the fact that the United States provided over $174 million in military aid to Honduras between 1981 and 1985.

In June 1983, Suazo Cordova traveled to Washington, D.C., where he agreed to the U.S. construction of a $250,000 training facility at Puerto Castilla on the Caribbean Coast. Named the Regional Center for Military Training (CREM; *Centro Regional de Entrenamiento Militar*), the facility was primarily used for the training of Salvadoran ground forces, although some Hondurans took part. And on May 21, 1985, an agreement was concluded that provided for the U.S. to construct a sprawling military base, including an airfield at Palmerola near Comayagua. By that time the number of *Contras* training and residing in Honduras was estimated to be between 15,000 and 17,000.

Álvarez fully cooperated with the United States in its proxy struggle with the Sandinistas. In 1983, 1,600 U.S. and 4,000 Honduran troops conducted a joint exercise named "Big Pine" designed to improve the deployment techniques and logistical support in the field. U.S. naval and air forces also participated with their Honduran counterparts. Once the exercise ended, a number of U.S. training personnel remained in the country to train the Honduran army in infantry techniques, and the air force technical personnel constructed and operated a large radar installation south of Tegucigalpa. Such exercises were expanded to include some 5,000 U.S. ground troops and air and naval operations when repeated in Big Pine II exercises between August 1983 and February 1984. The purpose of the exercise was to send a message to the Sandinistas to desist from stirring insurrection in Central America. Big Pine II and Universal Trek were joint U.S- Honduran exercises in February and May 1985 that included 39 U.S. warships to defend Honduras from a mock Nicaraguan invasion. An even bigger operation, Solid Shield in May 1987, was designed for the implementation of U.S. assistance to Honduras in resisting a Nicaraguan invasion.

A combination of factors between 1984 and 1986 resulted in a moderated Honduran policy, U.S. withdrawal from the region, and finally a Central American peace in August 1989. Opposition to Álvarez's growing power came from the military's officer corps who concluded in 1982 that Álvarez reached an agreement with President Suazo Córdova whereby the former would conduct foreign policy, and the latter focused upon domestic issues. In 1983, these officers fretted over Álvarez's changes to military command structure in such a way that gave him more power. Álvarez could dismiss officers who appeared as a threat to his position and with it the officers would lose their legal and illegal financial rewards.

On the broader policy scale, most Honduran military officers held isolationist tendencies. They believed that Álvarez sacrificed too much national sovereignty in becoming subservient to U.S. policy in Central America. They also opposed becoming involved in any war with Nicaragua should the United States invade that country as most people believed it intended to do. From this perspective, the October 1983 Operation Urgent Fury, the code word for the U.S. invasion of Grenada, was seen as a forerunner to an invasion of Nicaragua.

In sum, Álvarez appeared to be consolidating his control over the military in order to claim the presidential palace for himself. In addition, his pro-U.S. leanings could lead to Honduran involvement in regional affairs beyond the nation's fundamental interests. Given these potential scenarios, on March 31, 1984, a group of senior military officers ousted Álvarez and sent him off to Miami, Florida. The overthrow of Álvarez produced serious consequences for Honduran-U.S. relations.

New Commander in Chief, Air Force Brigadier General Walter López Reyes demanded increased U.S. military assistance for further Honduran cooperation in the Central American crisis, a challenge given the changing mood in the United States towards the regional conflict. Arguing that the training of Salvadoran soldiers on Honduran soil might serve as a pretext for dragging Honduras into that conflict, López ordered the closing CREM. A new Military Assistance Agreement in 1984 expanded the U.S. base and its operations at Palmerola, but it curtailed Honduran cooperation in troop training, as would be evident in the subsequent joint military exercises.

Increasingly, the Honduran leadership expressed its frustration with the *Contra* troops and supporters based in southern departments of El Paraíso and Olancho. In what many considered an act of bravado and frustration, on January 22, 1985, Foreign Minister Barnica announced that the *Contras* would be expelled from the country once the conflict ended. During the two following months, the Honduran government directed the *Contras* to shut down their hospital outside of Tegucigalpa, and their office in the capital used for receiving foreign visitors and as a propaganda distribution center. Many Honduran leaders believed, as most analysts did, that the Sandinistas would eventually defeat the *Contras* and that the remains of the rebellious army would not assimilate into Honduran life and culture. Furthermore, these people reasoned that the United States would depart Honduras once the war was terminated and offer no assistance with the *Contras* assimilation.

The change of direction in Honduran policy was influenced by the growing U.S. public and congressional opposition to the Reagan policies in Central America. Reagan's critics argued that the movements across Central America were indigenous to the region and not some part of a Communist global conspiracy. They pointed to the long history of oligarchic rule across the region, the mistreatment of peasants, and the failure of the middle sector to achieve its political ambitions. These critics accepted the Marxist orientation of the indigenous groups as a natural response to an economic political system that served only the elite. They further argued that Reagan's determination for a military solution prompted the rebel groups to look to Cuba and beyond, to the Soviet Union, for support. By 1985, the U.S. domestic opposition became nationwide with public forums on university and college campuses, church halls, and in public buildings.

The first congressional restriction came in the form of the 1983 Boland amendment that forbade the administration from providing military equipment, training, advice or other support for military activities designed to overthrow the government of Nicaragua. With its bank closed between then until June 1985, the *Contras* found military assistance elsewhere: Argentina, Taiwan, and some private groups in the United States. In 1985 and 1986, in light of Soviet-bloc military assistance to Nicaragua, the U.S. Congress appropriated $125 million for the *Contras*. During the same time period, the Iran-*Contra* Affair spilled over into the public arena. In the absence of congressional funds, National Security Council officer Marine Colonel Oliver North devised a plan to have some oil-rich nations purchase arms for the *Contras*. The congressional investigation that followed lasted for nearly a year, and its impact on U.S. and Central American policies was significant.

Among other things, Iran-*Contra* contributed to an acceleration of the peace process. The initial effort to mediate the conflict came from Colombia, Mexico, Panama, and Venezuela, known as the Contadora group, the name of the island off Panama's Pacific coast where the initial meetings were held in January 1983. Subsequently, a support group—Argentina, Brazil, Peru, and Uruguay—joined the process. Still confident of victory, the Reagan administration initially resisted the peace process, although the Sandinistas wanted to be part of a negotiated settlement. Finally, in mid-summer 1987, Regan succumbed to the domestic pressure and offered his own six-point peace plan. Like Contadora, the proposal received little consideration. Critics pointed out that it was ploy to force Nicaraguan rejection, which in turn would prompt congress to vote for pending legislation that provided the *Contras* with another $140 million in military aid.

Where the outsiders failed to bring peace, the Central Americans did. Led by Costa Rican President Oscar Arias, the process began in February 1987 and terminated on August 7, 1989, at Tela, Honduras, where the five Central American Presidents (Oscar Arias, Costa Rica; Alfredo Cristiani, El Salvador; Vinicio Cerezo, Guatemala; José Azcona, Honduras; and Daniel Ortega, Nicaragua) gathered in a seaside compound once owned by the UFCO to reach an agreement for the disbandonment of the *Contras* by the year's end. Just as UFCO represented the long standing arrogance of U.S. economic imperialism in the region and, particularly in Honduras, the *Contras* represented the last U.S. effort to dominate the region's political affairs. The symbolism escaped no one.

Ironically, as the Central American peace initiative took root, USAID began a classroom program deep inside the mountains of southern Honduras to teach the rudiments of democracy to the freedom fighters that chose to return home to Nicaragua to participate in the political process. Shortly thereafter, the exodus south began.

By the mid-1980s, international opposition, including U.S. public opinion, to the Central American Wars was matched by the Central American leadership to end the conflict. For the Nicaraguans and El Salvador, the war's two focal points, and end to the war would bring an end to economic disruptions, the destruction of internal infrastructure, and the waste of human lives. An end of the war would stem the tide of refugees from the war torn countries into Costa Rica, where its welfare system strained under the influx of the war related migrants. The persistence of Costa Rican President Oscar Arias paved the way to the Central American peace treaty agreed to at the old UFCO compound at Tesoro Beach in Tela, Honduras on April 7, 1989.

The peace, however, did not address the historic roots of the region's conflicts: oligarchic rule and serious socioeconomic disparities.

§§§§

Throughout the twentieth century Latin America's ruling elites resisted any communist penetration, real or imagined, into their countries. Communism was viewed as a threat to the existing socio-political and economic orders, and as it had done in Russia, would destroy the elites privileges. In the early part of the century, the Southern Cone nations Argentina and Brazil brutally attacked and deported communist labor leaders. In the mid-1920s Central American leaders quietly applauded the Mexican Revolution's successful challenge to United States economic presence in that country but feared the same thing happening in their region. Thus, leaders like Nicaraguan Augusto César Sandino and Salvadoran Augustín Farabundo Martí were challenged and labeled communists. Immediately after World War II, labor leaders who demanded increased wages and improved quality of life for the workers were rejected as communists just as Sandino and Martí before them. In fact communist parties and organization were outlawed. They threatened the established order, meaning the privileges of the ruling elites. Central American leaders found a kindred spirit in the U.S. policymakers who concluded that Communist groups capitalized upon local socioeconomic disparities and political exclusion to gain support of the masses and eventually control of the government. This association reached its high-watermark in Honduras in the 1980s when the Reagan administration in Washington, D.C., determined to topple the Sandinista (FSLN) regime in Nicaragua and prevent the FMLN from coming to power in El Salvador. As it had so many times throughout its history, Honduras became the U.S. staging area from which it conducted the fight.

NOTE

1. Henry F. Holland, "U.S. Relations with the American Republics," *Bulletin of the Department of State*, 41:4 (April 11, 1955), 598–604.

8

Honduras Today: The More Things Change, the More they Stay the Same

There has never been real democracy in Honduras. All we have is an electoral system where the people get to choose [from] candidates . . . chosen by the rich . . . we can't talk about real democracy because the people don't participate in the decisions.[1]

Bishop Luis Santos Villeda
Santa Rosa de Copán
July 30, 2009

In the early 1980s, the northern industrial nations, particularly the United States, Great Britain, and Germany, advocated that the developing world adopt the economic principles of neoliberalism, also identified as the Washington Consensus or globalization. In practice neoliberalism called for the implementation of several measures, including disciplined fiscal policy, moderate interest rates, trade liberalization, openness to direct foreign investment, privatization

Taken in the morning, before the shops opened for business, this scene illustrates typical shopping areas in downtown Tegucigalpa. (Thomas M. Leonard Collection.)

of state owned enterprises, deregulation, legal security for intellectual property rights, tax reform, and the redirection of public expenditures toward education, health, and infrastructure investment. To some, it was simply supply side economics. In other words, Latin America needed to open its doors to foreign investment, encourage domestic investment by lowering taxes on the upper class, strip away protections from domestic industries, and protect the new investments from legal challenges. Effectively, neoliberalism promised expanded economic activity, which in turn would produce increased government revenues that could be spent on roads to reach the ports and education and health care, two of the most important concerns held by the masses of people across Latin America. Many analysts drew parallels between twentieth century neoliberalism and late nineteenth century Liberalism. Both opened the door to foreign investment and the exportation of primary products, but neoliberalism came at a time when democratic governments permitted the participation of the lower socioeconomic groups participation in the political arena.

NEOLIBERALISM AND HONDURAS SINCE THE 1980S

Similar to other Latin American countries in the early 1980s, Honduras experienced a return to democracy, (and neoliberalism) a term that has different applications across the southern part of the western hemisphere. In Honduras, Roberto Suazo Córdova survived the infighting of the National Party (PLH) to be its presidential candidate in the November 27, 1981. Like presidential candidates before him, Roberto Suazo Córdova campaigned in 1981 on promises to implement a program of sweeping economic and social development. Suazo Córdova captured 52 percent of the popular vote, 4 percent more than National Party candidate Ricardo Zuñiga. The PLH also gained control of congress: 44 seats to 34 for the PNH, and the PLN won 61 percent of the municipal elections. When Suazo Córdova took the presidential sash on January 27, 1982, he was the first Honduran civilian president in 10 years.

The dominance of the Central American wars during the early 1980s led most observers of Honduran politics to conclude that the armed forces Commander-in-Chief, Colonel Gustavo Álvarez Martínez, prevented Suazo Córdova from acting as an independent president. In March 31, 1984, Suazo Córdova appeared to seize control of the situation when he replaced Álvarez with Air Force Brigadier General Walter López Reyes. Suazo Córdova went on to manipulate the PLH into nominating Oscar Mejía Arellano as its candidate for the 1985 presidential election. Recognizing that Supreme Court held the key to the presidency should no candidate capture a firm majority of the popular vote, congress acted on March 29, 1985, by dismissing five of the court's nine justices for alleged corruption. Their replacements quickly took the oath of office. Suazo Córdova reacted quickly. He directed the military to arrest the new justices and the 53 legislators who voted for them. They were charged with treason. The rump congress then voted on April 3, 1985, for the replacements of the five displaced court justices, not all *Córdovistas*. The crisis continued until the military emerged as the final arbiter. On April 21, it brokered an agreement that all parties publically claimed satisfaction with. In a most complicated settlement, the agreement provided that the faction receiving the most votes within the party that received the most total votes could claim the presidency for its nominee. This method paved the way for José Azcona Hoyo to win the November 22, 1984, presidential elections, not only over the PHN candidate Rafael Leonardo Callejas Romero, but also four other PLH candidates. Because the five PHN candidates gathered 51.5 percent of the popular vote between them, and because Azcona gained the highest between them (27.5 percent), he was declared president over Callejas who gained 42.6 percent of the vote.

Arguably, the 1981 Suazo Córdova presidential victory followed by that of José Azcona Hoyo in 1984 fell within the traditions of Honduran electoral politics, a contest among the elites for self-serving reasons and between two political parties with only small ideological differences. From this perspective, the meaning of Honduran democracy rang as shallow as the U.S. administration's public justification for its military buildup during the 1980s in that Central American country: "We are fighting to preserve Honduran democracy."

In addition to the beginnings of the Central American wars, Suazo Córdova inherited a national economic crisis of epidemic proportions. It had been building since the late1960s. Despite annual growth rates approximating five percent, Honduras also experienced a great amount of flight capital, a decline in trade induced by a drop in global demand for its primary products, a growing national and foreign debt, and unchecked and unbalanced government budgets.

To deal with the crisis, Suazo Córdova pursued two sets of policies, both tied to the neoliberal economic policies advocated by the northern hemisphere's industrialized countries. In addition to a return to democracy, Honduras, like all Latin American countries, accepted the neoliberal economic principles espoused by the northern hemisphere's leading industrial nations at the time: the United States, Great Britain and Germany, all of which had conservative governments at the time.

Assessments of neoliberalism began to appear a decade into the program. At best, they were mixed. The macro instability caused by the debt crisis of the 1980s was corrected. Markets were opened to the world and tariff barriers reduced from a continent wide average of 41.6 percent to 13.7 percent. Also, structural reforms in banking and commerce made it easier for Latin America to participate in the global market that led to a significant amount of foreign direct investment in the region. The Latin American governments also carried out a substantial proportion of the total amount of global privatization during the 1980s. The changes in economic policies, however, did not trickle down to the masses. While there was economic recovery, annual growth rates did not match the 5–6% rates of the 1960s and 1970s. This translated into limited job growth. Although unemployment rates were lower by the end of the 1980s, they did not continue into the 1990s, in part because of the increase in population across Latin America. In 1996, 8 of every 100 Latin Americans willing to work had no job. In fact, when Vicente Fox assumed Mexico's presidency, he faced the improbable task of creating one million jobs per year over the 6 years of his presidential term to meet the needs of 16-year-olds entering the labor market. The number of people living in poverty did not decline from the approximately 150 million people in 1980. Latin America remained the region of the world with the widest disparities in income distribution.[2]

The frustration of the masses soon found expression in the democratic electoral politics. When Latin America returned to democracy in the early 1980s, a plethora of political parties emerged, the majority of which appealed to the lower classes. These parties were labeled leftist because of their emphasis upon government sponsored programs to assist the downtrodden. They stood in sharp contrast to the rightist political parties that accepted the neoliberal/free market economic principles.

In the late 1990s, Latin America began its left turn with the election of Hugo Chavez to the Venezuelan presidency in 1998. At midpoint in the first decade of the twenty-first century analysts have identified other heads of state or potential heads of state to accompany Chavez in the left turn: Argentina's Nestor Kirchner (2003), Bolivia's Evo Morales (2006), Brazil's Luis Inacio Lula da Silva (2003), Chile's Ricardo Lagos and Michelle Bachelet (2005), Costa Rica's Oscar Arias (2006), Peru's Alan García (2006), Uruguay's Tabare Vazquez (2005), and Nicaragua's Daniel Ortega (November 2006). Some of these leaders like Chávez and Morales outright rejected capitalism in favor of socialism; others like Lagos and Bachelet and Kirchner did not but directed significant reform programs in their in Chile and Argentina, respectively.

Did Honduras follow the same pattern? Within this context, Suazo Córdova quickly opened the Honduran door to foreign investment. Over the next decade the United States government provided Honduras with $274 million for economic development. The most effective use of this foreign aid was in the health area. There was a drastic drop in infant mortality rates from 119 per 1,000 in 1970 to 43 per 1,000 births in 1990. From 1987 to 1994 a 6 percent rate drop in the rate of malnourished children under the age of 2 was recorded. The most visible health improvements could be seen in rural areas: additional health clinics, water purification, sanitation systems, and immunization programs implemented. Literacy rates also expanded from 57 to 72 percent from 1960 to 1990; and thanks to an AID contraceptive program, the birth rate also dropped dramatically.

Agricultural assistance, particularly the P.L.(Public Law) 480 programs proved controversial. The focus of agricultural assistance was to make the small farmer self-sufficient and able to sell surplus crops in local markets at competitive prices. That did not happen because the P.L. 480 program made U.S. imported foodstuffs cheaper than home grown agricultural products. Critics, however, fail to point out that the international market price for Honduran agricultural products also dropped markedly during the 1980s, thus cutting demand that resulted in production cutbacks and with it local availability.

The Honduran manufacturing sector remained small throughout the 1980s, except for the expansion of the *maquiladora* or assembly industry along the country's North Coast. The country's first free-trade zone opened at Puerto Cortés in 1976 under government sponsorship, and 14 years later, 5 additional free-trade zones were in operation at Omoa, Coloma, Tela, La Ceiba, and Amapala. A series of privately operated free-trade zones also appeared in the same geographic area and offered the same benefits as the government zones. Together these assembly industries employed about 16,000 workers, but the operation was free of local taxes, thus providing little tangible benefit to the government.

For several reasons, the export-based textile industry adversely affected all other Honduran manufacturing sectors whose products were directed primarily at the domestic market. The foreign-owned *maquildora* plants paid an average of U.S. $4 per day, double the Honduran mandated minimum wage paid by local manufacturers. Honduran law also permitted the *maquiladoras* to import, duty-free, all components essential to complete its final product and received exemptions from corporate taxation, provided it exported 100 percent of its finished products. Such privileges contributed to higher production costs for Honduran manufacturers and made their products noncompetitive, even on a regional basis. Well into the 1990s, analysts continued to debate the actual benefits of the shift away from the import-substitution industrialization (ISI) policies of the 1960s and 1970s toward a new focus on free zones and assembly industries in the 1980s. Critics pointed to the apparent lack of commitment by foreign manufactures to any one country site or to the creation of permanent infrastructure and employment. The critics also questioned whether new employment in the *maquiladoras* would offset the loss of jobs in the more traditional manufacturing sector.

Whatever opinion one drew, in 1990, Honduras remained one of the poorest countries in the western hemisphere, with agriculture remaining the most important economic sector. It accounted for 30 percent of the Gross Domestic Product (GDP), employed 62 percent of the workforce, and produced two-thirds of Honduran exports. Still, productivity remained low. Industry employed nearly 15 percent of the work force and accounted for 23 percent of the GDP but generated 20 percent of the nation's exports. Finally, the service sectors, including public administration, accounted for 48 percent of the GDP but employed nearly 20 percent of the labor force. The major problems confronting Honduras at that time included an export sector dependent mostly upon bananas and coffee, whose value on the world market fluctuates widely. Government offices remained inefficient operations and could not meet the demand for basic services. A high unemployment rate (12 percent unemployed and 30 to 40 percent underemployed) continued to plague the nation.

Beginning with 1989, the next four presidential elections were characterized by the continuance of intraparty conflicts but also the emergence of a new generation of political leaders influenced by domestic affairs after 1954 and not always part of the Honduran upper class. In 1989, the PLH candidate Carlos Flores Facusse survived a brutal four-way battle for the party's nomination by capturing the December 1988 primary election, only to lose the general election on to the unified PNH nominee Rafael Leonardo Callejas, who gathered 51 percent of the vote. A long-time party activist, Callejas had strong ties to the Honduran industrial leaders. The 1993 Liberal Party candidate, Carlos Roberto Reina, proved victorious in the November 22, 1993, elections with 53 percent of the popular vote. He came to office as a long-standing human rights advocate, owing to his treatment by the earlier Honduran military regimes, and with sympathy towards the social programs pursued by Cuba's Fidel Castro. His successor in 1998, Carlos Roberto Flores was a businessman, journalist, and politician prior to his presidential inauguration on January 27, 1998. The PHN finally returned to the presidential palace when Ricardo Maduro won the 2001 presidential election in spite of a constitutional ban on those not born in Honduras from becoming president.

Particular challenges confronted each of the presidents, while collectively they continued to confront broader issues that affected Honduras over their collective 16 years (1990–2006) of administration. For example, with the wind down and withdrawal of the U.S. military from Honduras in the 1990s, Callejas faced a drastic drop in U.S. military and economic assistance from a total of $1.6 billion in the 1980s to less than $200 million during the 1990s. The economic ripple effect significantly contributed to a recession. Reina came to office determined to correct human rights abuses that he personally experienced. Immediately after his inauguration, Maduro, who lost his son Ricardo to gang violence, brought out the military to patrol the streets of large cities with the local police, and the PHN-led congress enacted legislation that made illicit association a crime that resulted in the jailing of hundreds of gang members. During the first year of his administration, he stripped the military of oversight authority of human rights abuses and placed it in civilian hands. He also ended the compulsory military draft that often resulted in the military roundup of young men. While Reina's policies are credited with a lessening of human rights violations, it also opened the door to charges that it contributed to growth of urban gangs in the country. Corruption and crime became the major characteristics of the Flores administration, U.S. President Bill Clinton halted a $5 million aid package to Honduras for its government's failure to halt violations of international copyright laws that adversely impacted U.S. printing, recording, and movie industries but also upon products ranging from pharmaceuticals to clothing.

On the broader issues such as economic development and lifting people out of poverty, there was little progress. Economic growth declined by 3.7 percent in 1997 following five years of solid growth. Throughout the generation 1980 to 2000, agriculture accounted for employing 62 percent of the labor force and two-thirds of the national exports. Coffee replaced bananas as the country's chief export. The manufacturing sector employed 20 percent of the work force and accounted for about 28 percent of all exports. The United States supplied Honduras with 50 percent of its imports and took in 65 percent of its exports.

While the Honduran government reported only a 3.8 percent unemployment rate for 2000, other international organizations report it to be much higher: 16 percent and another 290 percent underemployed. For sure, 59 percent of the population lived below the poverty line in a country where the lowest 10 percent of the households receive 0.7 percent of the national income, while the highest 10 percent received 42 percent of the national income.

Underdevelopment and poverty remained, with its commitment deficiencies in education, health and housing. The situation was exacerbated by Hurricane Mitch that swept across Central America from October 30 to November 1, 1998. Honduras was the hardest hit. The hurricane caused 5,657 deaths, left another 8,058 missing, injured 12,272, and displaced another 1.4 million people. Some 60,000 homes were destroyed; and six weeks after the storm's floods receded, there were 20,000 cases of cholera, 30,000 cases of malaria, and 208,000 serious cases of diarrhea reported in Honduras alone. With crops destroyed and fields flooded and littered with debris, the North Coast banana companies laid off their entire work forces, estimated at 20,000 laborers. The country's infrastructure, roads, railroads, water, and sewerage systems were in disarray, if not destroyed. Foreign relief dollars quickly flowed into Honduras and when coupled with debt forgiveness, the government of Honduras did not go bankrupt. Reconstruction efforts moved forward in 1999, and in the year 2000, recovery began to take root.

In 2003, Honduran political leadership viewed the Dominican Republic-Central American Free Trade Agreement (DR-CAFTA) as another opportunity to improve its economy and, in turn, the quality of life for its people. The DR-CAFTA agreement had its origins in events beyond the government in Tegucigalpa. The origins of DR-CAFTA can be traced to the collapse of the September 2003 World Trade Organization, meeting in Cancun, Mexico, where a group of 21 developing nations walked out in protest over U.S. and European agricultural subsidies and to the November 21, 2003, ministerial meeting in Miami, Florida, at which the Bush administration faced strong opposition, led by Brazil and Venezuela, to a Free Trade Association of the Americas. In March 2004, the Bush administration pursued a new strategy to reach free-trade agreements with single nations or with clusters of nations. The DR-CAFTA pact fell within the purview of this strategy, and in fact, negotiations were already underway resulting in the Central America treaty signing on December 17, 2003 in the main hall of the Organization of American States (OAS). The Dominican Republic joined on October 4, 2004.

The agreement provided for the immediate elimination of import duties on about 90 percent of U.S. exports to the region and the elimination of tariffs on industrial goods over a 10-year period and, on most agricultural goods, services, and investments over an 18-year period. There would be immediate intellectual property right protections for films and other recordings and medicines and greater transparency in order to fight corruption.

The Honduran unicameral legislature narrowly approved the DR-CAFTA Treaty, 65–62. Many groups, including small businessmen (particularly shop owners), labor, and small farmers, viewed the agreement as a threat to their existence. Others made comparisons to the banana companies that historically dominated the Honduran economy, causing them to wonder aloud if this new agreement only opened the door to a new form of U.S economic dominance.

THE HONDURAN MILITARY STRIKES—AGAIN

Shortly before the polling stations were scheduled to open in the morning hours of June 28, 2009, members of the Honduran military stormed into the home of President Manual Zelaya and whisked him off to Toncontín Airport in Tegucigalpa for a flight to and exile in Costa Rica. Later that day, the National Congress appointed its president, Roberto Micheletti, as President of Honduras. Zelaya's ouster ended 27 consecutive years of democratically elected governments and the peaceful transfer of political power between them.

Zelaya, a prominent businessman from Olancho Department and long-time Liberal Party activist served two congressional terms and held several appointed government posts prior to his presidency. He was considered a moderate conservative when narrowly elected president on November 27, 2005, over National party candidate Porfirio Lobo Sosa.

Zelaya's administration was anything but successful. He lacked a clear program to deal with long-standing socioeconomic problems, which led to the rise in economic populism. While his distribution of government funds directly to political leaders at local levels resulted

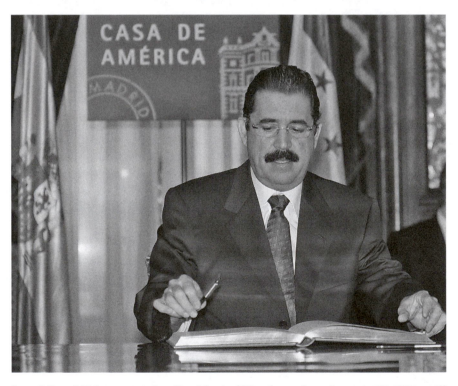

Juan Miguel Zelaya served as President of Honduras from January 27, 2006 until his ouster by the military on June 28, 2009 that led to a constitutional crisis. Several western governments refused to extend diplomatic of the interim-government led by Roberto Micheletti. Zelaya now lives in exile in the Dominican Republic. (AP Photo/Paul White.)

in increased spending by the poor, it also opened the door to corruption. Zelaya increased the minimum wage and expanded the number of hours for telephone and electricity to operate in rural villages. But corruption went beyond monetary distribution into the highest reaches of government that led to the dismissal of several of Zelaya's appointees. For example, in 2007, *Hondutel*, the government-run national telephone service was exposed for receiving bribe money from the U.S. based international telephone carrier, Latin Node, Inc., for distribution to company officers in exchange for control of international telephone calls. Because the vast majority of the nation's radio and TV stations were controlled by six families, which along with the major newspapers turned reporting into highly bipartisan platforms, opposition journalists left the country to escape government harassment, if not jail. Zelaya found himself under constant criticism and spending too much time defending his administration. On May 24, 2007, he ordered 10 two-hour broadcasts on all TV and radio stations to counterattack the media attacks. Zelaya also abandoned his predecessor's (Ricardo Maduro) tough stance against street crime and gang violence to one of rehabilitation. It did not work. Street violence increased during Zelaya's term in office.

The Honduran economy was deteriorating before Zelaya came to office and only worsened with the global recession that began in late 2006, dimming the prospects for implementing reform packages and stimulus programs, that is, if the national congress would approve such actions. Gaining legislative approval for Zeyala's economic initiatives was near impossible, given that his Liberal Party split among itself and had only a seven-seat majority in the unicameral national legislature. Zelaya alienated middle and upper class sectors by showing great sympathy for Fidel Castro's Cuba and joining with Venezuela's Hugo Chávez in placing responsibility for Latin America's poverty at the U.S. doorstep. On July 28, 2008, Zelaya announced that for several months Honduras had been a member of The Bolivarian Alliance for the Peoples of Our America (ALBA; *Alianza Bolivariana para los Pueblos de Nuestra América*). Venezuela's Chávez declared the establishment of ALBA to integrate the economies of the socialist and social democratic governments based on a vision of social welfare and bartering mutual economic aid rather than trade liberalization as advocated by free trade agreements. Chávez also made oil available to Honduras at discounted prices. Zelaya's public standing plummeted in September 2008 when he refused to submit an annual budget to congress, as required by the constitution. Zelaya defended his decision on the grounds that government income could not be determined in light of the global recession.

As the opposition and discontent with the president grew during the winter of 2008–2009, Zelaya decreed on March 23, 2009, that a fourth ballot be added to the scheduled November elections. The ballot would ask the Honduran people if a constituent assembly should be convened to approve a new national constitution. Although the assembly would not meet until after Zelaya completed his presidential term in January 2010, his critics interpreted the proposal as the first step towards the extension of his presidency. The controversy escalated from mid-May until the ouster of Zelaya on June 28. The national congress legislated that referendums could not be held within 180 days of a general election. The opposition also used the court system to declare the decree, which was never published, null and void. The supreme court also invalidated Zelaya's directive that the armed forces deliver the ballots to polling stations or resign. In response the Zelaya's maneuverings, the Honduran Attorney General's Office charged Manuel Zelaya with violations of the constitution, laws, and court orders. The supreme court issued an arrest warrant that was executed on the morning of June 28 and resulted in Zelaya's expatriation to Costa Rica. In accordance with the constitution, congress appointed Roberto Micheletti provisional head of state until the legal end of Zelaya's term in office, January 27, 2010.

Born in El Progresso, Micheletti's only notable activity was as member of the honor guard of President Ramón Villeda when he was toppled on October 3, 1963. Ten years later, in 1973, Micheletti moved to Tampa, Florida, and then New Orleans. Little is known of his activities in either city. He returned to Honduras in 1976 and six years later became an elected member of the national congress. He twice sought the Liberal Party's presidential nomination, the last being in 2009 when he lost out to the eventual winner Elvin Santos.

The Micheletti government received very little international support because global leaders condemned the overthrow of a constitutionally elected president. Several leaders called for his reinstatement. The United States rejected the overthrow of Zelaya, refused to recognize the Micheletti government, and suspended all economic and military assistance. The United States found itself a strange bedfellow with the Cuban and Venezuelan governments that also called for Zelaya's return to the presidency. Eventually, all Latin American governments withdrew official recognition from Honduras. The OAS said that it would not recognize any government other than that of Manuel

Zelaya, and on July 4, 2009, suspended Honduras from the organization. The European Union did the same, and like the United States, suspended economic assistance.

Throughout the summer and fall of 2009, violence continued to escalate, and it prompted Micheleti to declare a 45-day state-of-siege on September 26, 2009. The government shut down radio and TV stations opposed to the Michelleti administration and its violations of civil and human rights that were confirmed by the Inter-American Commission on Human Rights. OAS, U.S., and Costa Rican efforts to mediate a solution to the crisis all met with failure. The blocking point to any agreement dealt with Zelaya's fate. He insisted upon returning to the presidency, an event the opposition would not tolerate under any conditions.

Finally, on November 29, 2009, National Party candidate Porfirio Lobo was elected President of Honduras with 58.6 percent of the vote. His opponent, Elvin Santos of the Liberal Party received 38.1 percent. For good measure, the newly elected national congress voted against restoring Zelaya to the presidency, 111 to 17.

Lobo promised to create a unified government cabinet, including individuals from the Zelaya and Micheletti camps and that there would be no new taxes on the middle and lower income families. Lobo also promised a government austerity program, and his first directive grounded the use of government vehicles for private use. Henceforth, government subsidies will be scrutinized so as not to repeat the habits of the past, where allegedly 8 percent of government subsidies went to 20 percent of the people who did not qualify for them. In addition, Lobo repeated the traditional call for improved education and health care and for national security.

Honduras presents many challenges to President-elect Lobo. It is the second poorest country in Central America, behind Nicaragua. In a country in which the median age is 21, an estimated 60 percent of the workforce is unemployed or underemployed. The government claims that 80 percent of the population is literate, meaning that they are able to read a book and write, but external investors fret over the quality and skill level of their workforce. The national government spends only 3.7 percent of its Gross National Product (GNP) on education. Today, approximately 48 percent of the population lives in urban areas, and this growth has contributed to the further degradation of forest land that is also depleted by poor use of land and the logging industry. Internal transportation systems include 468 miles of rail track, 9,112 miles of roadway of which 1,859 are paved, and 94 airports, three of which are capable of handling large aircraft used in international flights.

§ § § § §

Since the mid-1980s, the Honduran experience paralleled that of many other Latin American countries. The promises of the neoliberal economic model failed to materialize for the masses of people. In fact, the percentage of Latin American people living in poverty in 2000 was slightly over 50 percent, the same percentage as the early 1980s when the neoliberal economic model was adopted. As the percentage of national wealth continued upwards for the landowning and commercial elites, concomitantly, the percentage of people living under the poverty level expanded. The size of the middle sector also diminished. Given these realities, many Latin Americans moved leftward on the political scale, meaning that they were voting for an end to the neoliberal economic model and for a greater state role in economic development and social reforms. The Honduran hesitation about DR-CAFTA illustrates the dichotomy of interest between the political elite and masses of people. From this perspective, President Zelaya stood as a threat to Honduras's existing order of elite domination of the government, economy, and society. If this is correct, so too is Bishop Luis Santos Villeda who described the June 28, 2009, coup d'etat as a preemptive strike to maintain Honduras's historical order. On the other hand, the Zelaya's ouster might well represent the Honduran people's frustration with the neoliberal economic model and serve as an indication that we on the verge of witnessing the emergence of a new economic model that entails greater government involvement in society. Or, as State Department official Stokeley W. Morgan observed in 1926, Zelaya's ouster was just another coup d'état common to Honduran political life. As it is important to ask about Honduras's future, it is equally important to examine its historical experience to determine how it arrived at its position in the contemporary world.

NOTES

1. Paul Jeffrey, "Honduran Bishop: Wealthy Elite Behind Ouster of President," *Catholic News Service, August 06, 2009* (American Catholic.org)

2. Inter American Development Bank, *Economic and Social Progress in Latin America: 1997 Report "Latin America After a Decade of Reforms,"* (Washington, DC: Inter American Development Bank, 1998); and Economic Commission for Latin America, *Social Panorama of Latin America, 2004,* (Santiago, Chile: United Nations, 2005).

Notable People in the History of Honduras

Álvarez Martínez, Gustavo Adolfo (1937–1989) Born in Tegucigalpa, Álvarez studied military affairs in Argentina, Guatemala, and the United States before graduating from Peru's Military Academy in 1972. Six years later, he rose to the rank of commander of an infantry battalion. Strongly anti-Communist, Álvarez and his close circle of advisors tightly controlled the military in the 1980s. From 1982 to 1984, he served as head of the Honduran armed forces and exercised great influence over the civilian government. A rabid anti-Communist, he conducted a violent repression campaign against leftists, real or perceived. A staunch supporter of U.S. Central American policies in the 1980s, Álvarez permitted Salvadoran armed forces and Nicaraguan *contras* to train in Honduras. After losing a power struggle with his successor, Walter López Reyes in March 1984, Alvarez was exiled to Costa Rica. He returned to Honduras only to be assassinated, reputedly by the leftist Chincerono Group on January 25, 1989.

Callejas Romero, Rafael Leonardo (1943–). Active in affairs of the Honduran National Party (PNH) in the 1970s and 1980s, Callejas captured the presidency in 1990 for a four-year term. His administration is noted for challenge the military's government influence and for implementing the unpopular neoliberal economic reforms. He also initiated a land reform program that some claim led to the further concentration of holdings by foreign companies. He also ended the long established fixed exchange rate for the lempira of two for one U.S. dollar, a move that resulted in immediate inflation. His administration by the rapid withdrawal of U.S. money following an end to the Central American Wars of the 1980s that further contributed to economic instability. After a Human Rights Commission reported that the military was responsible for the illegal capture, detention, torture, and death of political leaders in the 1980s, Callejas commenced court proceedings against military officers. A broad range of opponents surfaced in 1992, largely because of the poor state of the Honduran economy, which led to the election of Liberal Party candidates in the next two presidential elections, 1993 and 1997.

Carías Andino, Tiburcio (1878–1969) Under the façade of constitutional government, Carías ruled Honduras as a dictator from 1933 until 1948. Born in Tegucigalpa, Carías became active in politics just prior to the turn of the twentieth century. He was forced to leave Honduras in 1904 after opposing a coup against President Manuel Bonilla and returned in time for the 1915 elections. Unable to advance in status, Carías left the Conservative Party for the National Party (PNH) and twice stood as its presidential candidate: 1924 and 1928, before winning the prize in the 1932 contest. Carías consolidated his control over the PNH by intimidation of opponents, constitutional manipulation, close association with the military, and by courting the international banana companies. He supported U.S. policies during World War II, except for preventing the training of his military officers. He feared that such training would encourage the military to act independent of the president. After surviving a brief protest against his rule in 1944, Carías stepped away from the presidency in 1948 in favor of his hand chosen successor, Juan Manuel Gálvez.

Ferrera, Francisco (1794–1851) Served as the first constitutional President of Honduras from January 1,1841 to January 1,1843; from February 1843 to October 1844; and again from November 1844 to January 1845. Subsequently, as Minister of War and Chief of the Armed Forces, he acted as a strongman in putting down rebellions in the new nation.

Lindo Zelaya, Juan (1770–1853) Born into a landowning family, Lindo earned a law degree from Guatemala's University of San Carlos. After independence in 1821, he favored annexation to Iturbide's

Mexican Empire over linkage to Guatemala. He served in the Honduran legislature as a member of the Conservative Party. In 1838, he promoted Honduras's separation from the UPCA. In 1840, Lindo moved to El Salvador and immediately became active in state politics, serving as head of state in 1841 and 1842, after which he returned to Honduras. The Honduran assembly elected Lindo to serve as the nation's president on February 12, 1847, and under the terms of a new constitution he was elected to serve until 1852, becoming the first Honduran president to complete his constitutional term. He is credited with establishing the University of Honduras. He also survived several attempts to remove him from office after 1850 After his presidency, Lindo retired to private life in the city of Gracías.

López Arellano, Oswaldo (1921–2010) A native of the southern town of Danlí. López Arellano joined the Honduran Air Force, eventually rising to the rank of brigadier general. In 1963, concerned about the leftist drift of the Ramón Villeda Morales administration, the military engineered a coup, after which López Arellano directed a ruling junta one then president until 1971 and again as junta leader from 1973 to 1975. Linked to the conservative PHN, the López Arellano administration crippled the National Agrarian Institute (INA), effectively ending land reform programs. The adverse effects of the 1969 Soccer War with El Salvador, combined with the military's human rights violations, significantly contributed to López Arellano losing the 1971 presidential election to PNH candidate Ramón Ernesto Cruz, who served only one year. Following another military *coup d' etat*, López Arellano served as head of state for another three years before a secret deal with UFCO was exposed and forced him from office. Thereafter, López Arellano remained in private life and engaged in several successful business ventures until his death in 2010.

Medina, José María (1826–1878) Medina was temporary president of Honduras in 1863 and again from 1864 to 1872. Medina received his primary education in his birth province, Gracías a Díos, joined the army at age 18, and subsequently earned a fine reputation in the wars against William Walker in the mid-1850s. As president, Medina oversaw the implementation of two constitutions, 1865 and 1873, which further narrowed political participation by implementing land qualifications as a perquisite for voting rights and strengthening the president's hand in politics at the expense of the legislature. As a result, Medina endured several *coup d'etat* attempts, a major characteristic of Honduran politics.

Morazán, Francisco (1799–1842) Most remembered for his leadership of the United Provinces of Central America throughout the 1830s, Morazán also served as president of Honduras (1827-1829). As head of the UPCA, Morazán confronted a bitter liberal-conservative rivalry over the power of the central government. Both liberal and conservative state leaders, free from the central authority of Spanish rule, refused to give their loyalty or to submit to the authority of a centralized government. Dissension was so great, the UPCA congress removed Morazán from power in 1838. After failing to depose of Guatemala strongman Rafael Carrera a year later, Morazán went into exile in Costa Rica where he again attempted to restore Central American unity, only to betrayed by some of his own followers and subsequently executed. Today, he is hailed as a hero throughout Central America for his unity efforts.

Suazo Córdova, Roberto (1927–) A member of the PLH's conservative wing, Suazo Córdova's administration, 1982–1986), is best noted for its links to the armed forces and as a defender of U.S. policy regarding the Central American wars of that time period. A trained medical doctor, Suazo Córdova served several congressional terms between the 1950s and 1980s.He captured the 1981 presidential election with 54 percent of the vote. His administration became known for its nepotism, corruption, and reversal of several progressive reform measures. In return for badly needed financial aid, Suazo Córdova implemented neoliberal conservative economic reform measures that added hardship to the living standards of most Honduran people. Suazo Córdova permitted the military excessive influence in government foreign policy, supporting the U.S. efforts against the FMLN in Nicaragua and FSLN in El Salvador. He turned a blind eye to the military's violations of human rights. The PLH rejected his efforts to continue in office beyond 1988.

Soto, Marcos Aurellio (1846–1908) Soto received his early education in his home town of Tegucigalpa and went on to study at the University of San Carlos in Guatemala. Known as a Liberal, Soto was one of Honduras's most popular nineteenth century presidents, holding the office from 1876 to 1883. His contributions to Honduras included the establishment of a national mint, a government budget department and spending accountability, and a postal and telegraph service that linked the rural towns with the capital. He directed the construction of a national library and free primary education. He attempted to affirm civilian control over the military. Most of his reforms were incorporated into the 1880 constitution. The new constitution also enhanced congressional powers at the expense of the executive. His liberal economic policies paved the way for generous concessions to foreign, mostly U.S., mining interests. Soto was forced to resign in 1883 because of pressure from Guatemalan strongman Justo Rufino Barrios.

Vaccaro Brothers–Joseph, Luca, Felix, and their brother, Salvadore D'Antonini, all Sicilian Americans engaged in the sale of produce in New Orleans in the late 1890s. In 1899, a severe freeze of their orange groves prompted them to begin the importation of bananas from Honduras. Their investments in banana properties, railroads, and wharves contributed to their company—the Vaccaro Brothers—to rank second behind UFCO in the exportation of the fruit from Honduras. The company also constructed Honduras's first bank and hospital. The need for capital to continue the company's expansion forced the brothers to go public in 1925, and the company became known as the Standard Fruit and Steamship Company. The Vaccaro and D'Antoni families continued to administer the company until 1964 and always maintained their home in La Ceiba, Honduras.

Valle, José Cecilio del (1776–1834) Born in Chuloteca, Valle went on to become one of Central America's most important statesmen. Considered an outstanding intellect of his time, Valle graduated from the University of San Carlos in Guatemala. He served as Mayor of Guatemala City in 1821 when he played a major role in guiding Central America into the newly formed Mexican Empire. For two years he served as secretary of foreign affairs and represented the province of Tegucigalpa in the Empire's national congress. Following the collapse of the Mexican Empire, Valle unsuccessfully sought the presidency of the newly formed United Provinces of Central America (UPCA) in 1823. A decade later, he was named the confederation's President but died before taking office.

Walker, William (1824–1860) Probably the most famous U.S. filibuster of the midnineteenth century, who led expeditions into Mexico and Central America. Walker conquered and controlled Nicaragua from 1856 to 1858 and had visions of establishing a Central American empire under his control but drew the wrath of the local leaders, who came together twice to drive him from the isthmus. On Walker's third attempt, he landed first at Roatán off the Honduran coast and then on the mainland at Trujillo. He eventually surrendered to the British Naval Commander, Norvell Salmon, who eventually turned Walker over to Honduran authorities, who had Walker executed by a local firing squad on September 12, 1860.

Zelaya Rosales, José Manuel (1952–) Son of a wealthy businessman, Zelaya engaged in the family's ranching and timber interests before entering politics in Catacamas, Olancho Province. He served as president from January 27, 2006 until June 28, 2009. A conservative when elected President of Honduras in 2005 as the Liberal Party candidate, Zelaya moved to the left and identified with Venezuelan President Hugo Chavez and the Castro brothers in Cuba. Owing to the global economic downturn that paralleled Zelaya's presidential tenure, thousands Hondurans lost their jobs, and the government debt increased to 5 percent of the nation's GDP. Still, Zelaya could count significant progressive achievements, including an 80 percent increase in the minimum wage, introduction of free education for all children, guaranteed school lunches for over 1.6 million poor children, a 10 percent reduction in poverty, free electricity to the most needy, and direct state help to 200,000 impoverished families. At the same time, he doubled military spending. By 2008, he appeared to flaunt his popularity among the Honduran lower classes, and it appeared that he intended to extend his presidency through extra constitutional means. Early in the morning of the voting day, June 29, 2009, the military arrested and deported Zelaya to Costa Rica over the ouster of a constitutionally elected president. Despite numerous efforts to return Zelaya to office, the interim government held firm, and in November 2009, PNH candidate Porfirio Lobo Sosa was elected President. Following Lobo's inauguration in January 2010, Zelaya agreed to relocate to the Dominican Republic.

Zemurray, Samuel (1877–1961) Zemurray came to the United States from Bessarabia in 1892 and shortly thereafter began selling ripened discarded fruit to local dealers, first in Mobile, Alabama, and then in New Orleans, Louisiana. In 1910, with a $100,000 bank account, Zemurray headed for Honduras where he bought 2,000 acres of property on the Cuyamel River.. After financing the 1911 revolution against President Manuel Bonilla, Zemurray continued to receive concessions for expanding his banana operations and by the early 1920s rivaled the United Fruit Company. In 1929, he accepted a $30 million offer from UFCO and returned to New Orleans. Given the impact of the Great Depression, Zemurray's UFCO stock dropped to $10 share, prompting him to return to Honduras and assume control of UFCO. He became company president in 1938. Whereas he was largely criticized for his business tactics and influence in Honduran political affairs, Zemurray invested heavily in solving problems of the banana industry: the sigatoka and other diseases; soil erosion; sanitation, and so on.

Bibliographic Essay

This bibliographic essay represents some of the most important works on Honduras written in the English language. For those wishing to pursue Spanish language sources, a good starting point would be the bibliographies found in the historical surveys of Central America and Honduras. The reader should also be aware that many of the works go beyond Honduras to include all of Central America, in which the country is treated as part of the region. For the purpose of this selected bibliographic essay, Central America is defined to include the contemporary nations of Costa Rica, El Salvador, Guatemala, Honduras and Nicaragua. This determination is based upon the historic facts that these countries comprised an administrative unit of the Spanish colonial system; that Belize, despite its linkage to Guatemala, is a former British colony and is treated as part of its Caribbean community; and that Panama was administered by Peru and Colombia until its independence in 1903, followed by its special relationship with the United States. Finally, other than the reference works cited immediately below, the citations are placed in the same sequential order as the book is presented to the reader.

ELECTRONIC REFERENCE WORKS

The following two sources provide daily and weekly news summaries of contemporary events events in Honduras: Honduras News: www.honduras.com and *Honduras Weekly:* www.hondurasweekly.com. The following references provide contemporary information on all aspects of Honduran life—political, economic, and social—and are updated annually: *CIA World Fact Book:* https://www.cia.gov/library/publications/the-world-factbook/index.html; The Records of Contemporary States, Honduras: www.fco.gov.uk/en/; and *United Nations Economic Commission for Latin America (ECLAC)* www.un.org/popin/regions/eclac.html. The United States Department of State (USSD) *Background Notes* provide a brief summary of contemporary issues in U.S.-Honduran relations: www.state.gov/www/background_notes/honduras_1099_bgn.html.

ENCYCLOPEDIAS, HISTORICAL DICTIONARIES, OTHER PRINT REFERENCE WORKS

Encyclopedias about Latin America contain numerous entries on Honduras. A chronological approach is Leslie Bethel's, general editor, *The Cambridge Encyclopedia of Latin America and the Caribbean* (New York: Cambridge University Press, 1984–2008) 11 volumes, Thomas M. Leonard, general editor, *Encyclopedia of Latin America* (New York: Facts on File, 2010), four volumes is divided by time periods each volume with its own specialist editor: (1) Amerindians/Foreign Colonization; (2) Colonies/Independence; (3) Nineteenth Century; and (4) the Twentieth and Twenty-First Century. John Middleton, editor in chief, *Encyclopedia of Latin American History and Culture* (Farmington Hills, Michigan, 2008 2nd ed.) six volumes is an A to Z encyclopedia that updates of the original work directed by Barbara Tennenbaum and published in 1996. Although dated, *Historical Dictionary of Honduras* (Lanham, Md. Scarecrow Press, 1994) compiled by Harvey K. Meyer and Jessie H. Meyer, provides brief descriptions of events individuals and places.

Among the specialized reference works that are germane to the study of Honduras include: Victor Bulmer-Thomas, John H. Coatsworth, Roberto Cortés Conde, editors, *The Cambridge Economic History of Latin America* (Cambridge: Cambridge University Press, 2006) that provides an analytical discussion of the various time periods and economic pursuits in the Latin American experience. David Carrasco, editor, *The Oxford Encyclopedia of Meso-American Culture of Mexico and Central America* (New York: Oxford University Press, 2001), 3 volumes provides information on the various indigenous and other groups that inhabit Central America. Diana Kapiszewski, editor, *Encyclopedia of Latin American Politics* (Westport, CN Oryx Press for the Center for Latin American Studies, Georgetown University, 2002) provides a historical overview of Honduran politics.

The most detailed cartographic source is Carolyn Hall and Héctor Pérez Brignoli, with cartographer John V. Cotter, *Historical Atlas of Central America* (Norman: University of Oklahoma Press, 2003). Finally, Janet N. Gold, *Cultures and Customs of Honduras* (Westport, CN: Greenwood, 2009), provides the readers with a guide to the literature, dance, the arts, education, and other contributions to the Honduran milieu.

HISTORICAL STUDIES: HONDURAS AND CENTRAL AMERICA

Several historical surveys of Central America place Honduras in its regional context from its earliest times to the present. Ralph Lee Woodward, Jr., considered the dean of U.S. Central American historians, produced a most detailed work: *Central America: A Nation Divided* (New York: Oxford University Press, 2nd ed., 1999). A more brief and social science approach is John A. Booth and Thomas W. Walker, *Understanding Central America* (Boulder: Westview Press, 3rd edition, 1999). Two important works that provide a Central American perspective are Hector Perez-Brignoli, translated by Ricardo B. Sawrey A. and Susana Stettri de Sawrey, *A Brief History of Central America* (Berkeley: University of California Press, 1989) and Edelberto Torres Rivas, translated by Douglas Sullivan-González, *History and Society in Central America* (Austin: University of Texas Press, 1993).

Often referred to as the initial detailed history of Honduras since independence is William Stokes, *Honduras: An Area Study in Government* (Madison: University of Wisconsin Press, 1950). Otherwise, most of the important works focusing solely upon Honduras are the result of interest in the region during the Central American Wars of the 1980s. The most complete work is Tim Merrill, editor, *Honduras: A Country Study* (Washington, D.C.: Federal Research Division, Library of Congress, 3rd ed., 1995). Two works emphasize the twentieth century: Alison Acker, *Honduras: The Making of a Banana Republic* (Boston: South End Press, 1988) and James A. Morris, *Honduras: Caudillo Politics and Military Rulers* (Boulder: Westview Press, 1984). An interesting group of essays and primary materials that trace the course of Honduran history is Nancy Peckenham and Amy Street, editors, *Honduras: Portrait of A Nation* (New York: Praeger, 1985). An important study of the emergence of the Honduran North Coast into national politics is Darío A. Euraque's *Banana Republic: Reinterpreting the Region and State in Honduras, 1870–1972* (Chapel Hill: University of North Carolina Press, 1996)

HISTORICAL STUDIES: HONDURAS AND INTERNATIONAL AFFAIRS

The Central American Wars of the 1980s significantly contributed to numerous studies of the region's relationships with the international community. The following volumes place Honduras within the historical context: John F. Findling, *Close Neighbors, Distant Friends: United States and Central American Relations* (Westport, CN: Greenwood Press, 1987); Thomas M. Leonard, *The United States and Central America: The Search for Stability* (Athens: University of Georgia Press, 1991); and the earlier but excellent, study by Mary W. Williams, *Anglo-American Isthmian Diplomacy, 1815–1915* (New York: American Historical Association, 1916).

The British, Germans and French also demonstrated significant interest in Central America during the nineteenth and twentieth centuries and are the subject of the following works: J. Fred Rippy, *British Investments in Latin America 1822–1949* (London: Routledge, Taylor and Francis Division, 2nd. ed., 2000); Thomas D. Schoonover, Germany In Central America: Competitive Imperialism, 1821–1929 (Tuscaloosa: University of Alabma Press, 1998); and Thomas D. Schoonover, *The French in Central America: Culture and Commerce, 1820–1930* (Wilmington, DE.: Scholarly Resources, 2000).

HONDURAS: PRE-COLOMBIAN PERIOD

For an introductory essay about the indigenous groups in Honduras see: John B. Glass, "Archaeological Survey of Western Honduras," in Gordon F. Ekholm and Gordon R. Willey, editors, *Handbook of Middle American Indians: Volume 4, Archaeological Frontiers and External Connections*, 157–179 (Austin: University of Texas Press, 1966). The Mayans, who dominated the Honduran region are the subject of Francis Robiscek's *Copán: Home of the Mayan Gods* (New York: Museum of the American Indian, 1972) whereas the *Instituto Antropolgía y Historía, Proyecto Arqueológico Copán, Honduras* (Tegucigalpa: Imprenta nacional, 1983) provides an excellent introduction to the excavations at Copán.

THE SPANISH COLONIAL PERIOD

The Spanish conquest of Honduras is the subject of Robert S. Chamberlin's, *The Conquest and Colonization of Honduras, 1502–1550,* (Washington: Carnegie Institution, 1966). Detailed examinations of Spanish colonial rule over its Honduran colony are pursued by Murdo J. MacLeod and Miles Wortman in their respective works *Spanish Central America: A Socio-Economic History 1520–1720* (Berkeley: University of California Press, 1973) and *Government and Society in Central America, 1680–1840,* (New York: Columbia University Press, 1982). Gene A. Müller examines the weaknesses of the Catholic Church in colonial Honduras in "The Church in Poverty: Bishops, Bourbons and Tithes in Spanish Honduras, 1700–1821," Unpublished PhD. dissertation, University of Kansas, 1982. The impact of Spanish colonization upon the Honduran indigenous population is the subject of

Linda Desmond's "The Indian Population of Colonial Honduras," *Meso America* 9:1 (1985), 23–40 and Linda Newson's *The Cost of Conquest: Indian Decline in Honduras under Spanish Rule* (Boulder: Westview Press, 1986. Troy S. Floyd examines the European struggle for control of the ill-defined Mosquito Coast in *The Anglo-Spanish Struggle for Mosquitia* (Albuquerque: University of New Mexico Press, 1967)

THE NINETEENTH CENTURY

In addition to the William F. Stokes 1950 study cited in the historical survey section above, readers should also see Charles Cecil, *Honduras: Land of Great Depth* (New York: Rand McNally Co., 1890) for a general understanding of Honduras throughout the nineteenth century. Among the important descriptive travel accounts are E. George Squier's *Honduras: A Historical and Statistical Description* (London: Tubner, 1870) and his *Notes on Central America: Particularly the States of Honduras and El Salvador* (New York: AMS Press, 1871); Arthur Morelet, *Travels in Central America (New York: Loypoldt, Holt and Williams, 1871)*; John L. Stephens, *Incidents of Travel in Central America, Mexico and Yucatán* (New York: Dover, 1841 and reprinted several times since); and William V. Wells, *Explorations and Adventures in Honduras, Comprising Sketches of Travel in the Gold Regions of Olancho and A Review of the History and General Resources of Central America* (New York: Harper and Brothers, 1857)

For an understanding of the Honduran participation in Central America's independence from Spain in 1821 and then Mexico in 1823, and the subsequent struggle to create a political union among the states see: Mario Rodríguez, *The Cádiz Experiment in Central Amrica, 1808–1826* (Berkeley: University of California Press, 1978); Thomas L. Karnes, *The Failure of Union: Central America, 1824–1960* (Chapel Hill: University of North Carolina, Chapel Hill, 1961); Franklin D. Parker, "Jose Cecilio Del Valle: Scholar and Patriot, *Hispanic American Historical Review 32:4 (1952)*, 516–539; and the Miles Wortman volume cited in the section of the Spanish colonial period.

Two important works for understanding Honduras within the broader framework of the nineteenth century include Lowell Gudmundson and Hector Lindo-Fuentes, *Central America: 1821–1871: Liberalism Before Liberal Reform* (Tuscaloosa: University of Alabama Press, 1995) and Robet H. Holden, *Armies Without Nations: Public Violence and State Formation in Central America, 1821–1960* (New York: Oxford University Press, 2004). Gudmundson and Lindo-Fuentes demonstrate the movement toward liberal economic and political policies prior to the emergence of liberal politicians in the latter part of the nineteenth century; while Holden examines the transformation of the military from an institution serving the state into one that served its own interests.

As explained by Robert A. Naylor in "The British Role in Central America prior to the Clayton-Bulwer Treaty of 1850," *Hispanic American*

Historical Review 40:3 (1960), 361–382; Mario Rodríguez in his *A Palmerstonian Diplomat in Central America* (Tucson: University of Arizona Press, 1964); and Charles L. Stansifer, "United States-Central American Relations, 1824–1850," in T. Ray Shurbutt, *United States-Latin American Relations, 1800–1850: The Formative Years* (Tuscaloosa: University of Alabama Press, 1991, the British were the first to establish diplomatic and trade relations with the Central American nations following its independence in 1823 and devolvement into separate states in 1840.

Mid-nineteenth century U.S. excursions into Honduras included the search for a place to locate a trans-isthmian canal as explained by Charles L. Stansifer, "E. George Squier and the Honduras Inter-Oceanic Railway Project," *Hispanic American Historical Review* 46:1 (1966), 1–27 and William Walker's vision of a personal empire in the region. See: Albert Z. Carr, *The World and William Walker* (New York: Harper and Row, 1962)

With the exception of Washington S. Valentine's silver mining pursuits, U.S. investors found Honduras an inhospitable place for investment. See Charles V. Finney, "Rosario and the Election of 1888: The Political Economy of Mining in Honduras, *Hispanic American Historical Review* 59:1 (1979), 81–107 for a discussion of Valentine. Charles A. Brand, "The Background of Capitalist Underdevelopment: Honduras to 1913," Unpublished Ph.d. dissertation, University of Pittsburgh, 1972, explains the conditions in Honduras that limited foreign investment, while Thomas D. Schoonover, *The United States in Central America, 1860–1911: Episodes of Social Imperialism and Imperial Rivalry in the World System* (Durham: Duke University Press, 1991) finds U.S. businessmen more aggressive than is commonly accepted.

THE TWENTIETH CENTURY TO 1954

A contemporary analysis of Central America, including Honduras, is the subject of Frederick Parker's *Central America and Its Problems*, (New York: Oxford University Press, 1913). Contemporary travel accounts that provide personal perspectives of Honduran life in the early twentieth century include Harry A. Franck, *Tramping Through Mexico, Guatemala and Honduras* (London: Fisher Unwin, 1916) and Charles H. Harris and Louis R. Sadler, *The Archaeologist Was A Spy: Sylvanus G. Morley and the Office of Naval Intelligence* (Albuquerque: University of New Mexico Press, 2004). Political parties, as they are known today, did not develop in Honduras until the twentieth century. A discussion of their formation can be found in Ernesto Paz Aguilar, "The Origin and Development of Political Parties in Honduras in Louis W. Goodman, William M. Leo Victor Bulmer-Thomas, *The Political Economy of Central America Since 1920* (Cambridge: Cambridge University Press, 1987) and in William Leo Grande and Johanna Mendelson Forman, editors, *Political Parties and Democracy in Central America* (Boulder: Westview Press, 1992). The dominant political figure of the time period was Tiburcio Carías, who ruled Honduras for 16 years. Thomas J. Dodd's *Tiburcio Carías: Portrait of a Honduran Political Leader* (Baton Rouge: Louisiana State University Press, 2005) is an excellent analytical study of his administration.

Victor Bulmer-Thomas, *The Political Economy of Central America Since 1920* (Cambridge: Cambridge University Press, 1987) provides an excellent overview of the region's economy, including the role of bananas in each of the five republics. An early stinging criticism of the banana company's business practices is Charles D. Kepner and Henry Jay Soothill, *The Banana Empire: A Case Study of Economic Imperialism* (New York: Vanguard Press, 1935).

Honduras, which became known as a banana republic because of the importance of the fruit to the national economy is examined by several authors. Stacy May and Galo Plaza, *The United Fruit Company in Latin America* (Washington: National Planning Association, 1958) provide a positive view of the company's operations, but it contrasts sharply with the works of Thomas P. McCann, *An American Company: Tragedy of the United Fruit Company* (New York: Crown, 1976) and Thomas L. Karnes, *Tropical Enterprise: Standard Fruit and Steamship Company in Latin America* (Baton Rouge: Louisiana State University Press, 1978). Because a biography of Samuel Zemurray has yet to appear, these volumes are the best sources for discussion of him and his Cuyamel Fruit Company.

The adverse impact of the banana industry upon the Central American societies is the subject of Charles D. Kepner, Jr., *Social Aspects of the Banana Industry* (New York: AMS Press, 1967) and Darío A. Euraque, "The Threat of Blackness to the Mestizo Nation: Race and Ethnicity in the Honduran Banana Ecomomy, 1920s–1930s, in Steve Striffler and Mark Modero, editors, *Banana Wars: Power, Production and History in the Americas* (Durham: Duke University Press, 2003). The immediate impact of the Great Depression upon Honduras is explained by: Great Britain, Department of Overseas Trade, *Economic Conditions in the Republics of Guatemala, Honduras and Nicaragua, 1930* (London: His Majesty's Printing Office, 1931).

As the banana industry came to dominate Honduran affairs in the early twentieth century, the United States assumed a leader role in Central American affairs. The broader policy reasons are explained in the historical survey in the International Affairs section above. Although historian Walter La Feber would argue that U.S. policies were economically motivated (see: Walter La Feber, *Inevitable Revolutions: The United States in Central America* (New York: W. W. Norton, 1983), U.S. policymakers at the time demonstrated primary concern with keeping the Europeans out of the Caribbean and in bringing democratic principles and financial responsibility to the governments of Central America. For example, see Dana G. Munro's, *Intervention and Dollar Diplomacy in the Caribbean, 1900–1921* (Princeton: Princeton University Press, 1964) and his *The United States and the Caribbean Republics, 1921–1933* (Princeton: Princeton University Press, 1974). Academic studies that reach the same conclusion include

George W. Baker, "Ideals and Realities in the Wilson Administration's Relations With Honduras" *The Americas* 21:5 (1964), 3–19 and Thomas M. Leonard, *U.S. Policy and Arms Limitation in Central America: The Washington Conference of 1923* (Los Angeles: Center for the Study of Armament and Disarmament, California State University at Los Angeles, 1982).

The development of the Good Neighbor that led to U.S. non-intervention in Central America during the 1930s and 1940s is discussed by Bryce Wood, *The Making of the Good Neighbor Policy* (New York: Columbia University Press, 1961). The application of the Good Neighbor policy to Honduran politics is discussed by Thomas M. Leonard in "The Declining Use of the Non-Recognition Policy in United States-Central American Relations, 1933–1949 (Coral Gables, Florida: Occasional Paper Series, Florida International University, Latin American and Caribbean Center, 1982).

HONDURAS: SINCE 1954

Three readings that provide an excellent introduction for the post 1954 time period are: Kent Norsworthy with Tom Barry, *Inside Honduras: The Essential Guide to Its Politics, Economy, Society and Environment* (Albuquerque: Resource Center Press, 1994) and Neale J. Pearson, "Honduras," in Jack W. Hopkins, editor, *Latin America and the Caribbean Contemporary Record, 1981–1982* (New York: Holmes and Meier, 1983), 439–454 and Victor Bulmer-Thomas, "Honduras Since 1930," in Leslie Bethell, editor, *Central America Since Independence*, (Cambridge: Cambridge University Press, 1991).

For 46 years after the end of World War II in 1945, the United States engaged in a Cold War with the Soviet Union, each attempting to prevent the other from extending its influence to various parts of the world. By the early 1950s, the Cold War settled into all Latin America. The recent study by Alan McPherson, *Intimate Ties, Bitter Struggles: The United States and Latin America Since 1945* (Washington, D.C.: Potomac Books, 2006) illustrates the shifting of U.S. policy. An examination of shifting Cold War attitudes in Central America is Thomas M. Leonard, *The United States and Central America, 1944–1949: Perceptions of Political Dynamics* (Tuscaloosa: University of Alabama Press, 1984. The climax in U.S. policy change came with the 1954 Central Intelligence Agency's (CIA) sponsorship of the invasion of Guatemala to restore the old order that had its repercussions in Honduras (See: Richard H. Immerman, *The CIA in Guatemala: The Foreign Policy of Intervention* (Austin: University of Texas Press, 1982); and Stephen Schlesinger and Stephen Kinzer, *Bitter Fruit: The Untold Story of an American Coup in Guatemala* (New York: Anchor, 1983).

The fundamental question throughout this time period centered around the legitimacy of the demands for socioeconomic and political change traditionally based upon oligarchic rule and the extent, if any, international communist influence in the drive for change. Charles D. Brockett, *Land, Power and Poverty: Agrarian Transformation and Political Conflict in Central*

America (Boston: Unwin Hyman, 1990) provides a broad overview of the problem. Thomas P. Anderson, *The War of the Dispossessed: Honduras and El Salvador, 1968* (Lincoln: University of Nebraska Press, 1981) and William H. Durham, *Security and Survival in Central America: Ecological Origins of the Soccer War* (Stanford: Stanford University Press, 1979) explain the impact of Salvadoran outmigration into Honduras and its impact upon the limited land available for distribution to peasants, native and foreign. The changing nature of the banana industry at the start of the twenty-first century is the subject of John Soluri, *Banana Cultures: Agriculture, Consumption and Environmental Change in Honduras and the United States* (Austin: University of Texas Press, 2006)

Robert MacCameron, *Bananas, Labor and Politics in Honduras, 1954–1963* [Foreign and Comparative Studies: Latin American Series No. 5] (Syracuse: Syracuse University Press, 1983) traces the various proposals for land distribution reform and the response by the landless and landowners. The provisions of the 1962 Honduran reform law are analyzed in "Agrarian Reform Law in Honduras," *International Labour Review*, 87:6 (1962), 573–580; Neale J. Pearson, "Peasant Pressure Groups and Agrarian Reform in Honduras, 1962–1977," in Willliam Avery, editor, *Rural Change and Public Policy in Eastern Europe, Latin America and Australia* (New York: Pergamon Press, 1980), 297–320 provides an international comparative perspective on Honduran land reform over a 15-year period. David J. Glover, Agrarian Reform and Agro-Industry in Honduras, Canadian *Journal of Development Studies*, 7:1 (1986), 21–35. J. Mark Rudd, The Honduran Agrarian Reform Program Under Suazo Cordova, 1982–1985, *Inter-American Economic Affairs*, 39:3 (1985), 68–130 examines the land reform process while the military stood over the civilian government's shoulder.

The changing patterns and impact of foreign sponsored economic development programs in Honduras are explained by William S. Stokes, "Honduras: Dilemna of Development, *Current History*, 49:2 (1962), 83–88; and James A. Morris and Steve C. Ropp, "Corporatism and Dependent Development: A Honduran Case Study," *Latin American Research Review* 12:2 (1977), 27–68.

Throughout the Cold War, the Honduran military increased its position as keeper of the internal peace and played a larger role in identifying and detaining communists, real or imagined. Part of the later came via U.S. military training programs as described by Don L. Etchison in *The United States and Militarism in Central America* (New York: Praeger, 1975), and the impact upon civilian life is assessed by Neale J. Pearson, "The Impact of U.S. Military Presence on Honduran Politics," *Texas Journal of Political Studies*, 8:2 (1986), 77–107 and Steve C. Ropp, "The Honduran Army in the Sociopolitical Evolution of the Honduran State," *The Americas* 30:4 (1974), 504–528.

Mark B. Rosenberg's two essays provide a comparative study at a five year interval: "Honduras: The Reluctant Democracy," *Current History*

85:12 (1986), 417–420+ and "Honduras" in Howard J. Wiarda and Harvey F. Kline, editors, *Latin American Politics and Development* (Boulder: West-view Press, 1990, 519–534. As the Central American Wars of the 1980s were winding down, Rosenberg and Philip Shepherd, editors, produced a collection of essays *Honduras Confronts Its Future: Contending Perspectives on Critical Issues*, (Boulder: Lynne Reiner Publishers, 1986) that illustrate the myriad of problems challenging the country at that time.

Several specialized studies add to our understanding of Honduran socio-economic and political dynamics. Women are the subject of Elvis Alvarado, *Don't Be Afraid Gringo: A Honduran Woman Speaks From the Heart* (San Francisco: Food First Books, 1987) and the Women's International Resource Exchange, *Honduran Women: The Marginalized Majority* (New York: WIRE, 1986). An interesting study of the Catholic clergy and their place in peasant reform is Harry Maurer, "The Priests in Honduras, Radical Agitators," *Nation*, 222 (March 6, 1976), 266–269. The violence that mars Honduran urban areas today is described by Adrienne Pine, *Working Hard, Drinking Hard: On Violence and Survival in Honduras* (Berkely: University of California Press, 2008).

Excellent summaries of the June 2009 overthrow of President Juan Maduro and its aftermath are Peter J. Meyer, "Honduras Political Crisis, June 2009–January 2010," (Washington, D.C.: Congressional Research Service, February 1, 2010) http://opencrs.com/ and Mark P. Sullivan, Honduras: Political and Economic Situation (Washington, D.C.: Congressional Research Service, February 1, 2010) www.crs.gov.

HONDURAS AND THE CENTRAL AMERICAN CRISIS: 1980S

The violent conflicts that plagued Central America during the 1980s set off a serious debate in the United States, Latin America, and Europe whether the rebel movements were legitimate nationalistic responses to the region's socioeconomic and political institutions, or if they were part of the international communists to a gain a foothold in the western hemi-sphere beyond Cuba. A plethora of literature was produced. Three collec-tions of essays provide an excellent starting point for understanding the debate:

Robert S. Leiken, editor, *Central America: Anatomy of a Conflict* (New York: Pergamon press for the Carnegie Endowment for International Peace, 1984); Steve C. Ropp and James A. Morris, editors, *Central America: Crisis and Adaptation* (Albuquerque: University of New Mexico Press, 1984); Stan-ford Central America Action Network, *Revolution in Central America* Boulder: Westview Press, 1982); and Stanford Central America Action Net-work, *Revolution in Central America* Boulder: Westview Press, 1982). The same debate in the United States, as manifested in the congressional-White House struggle over funding of the war is examined by William M.

LeoGrande, *Our Own Backyard: The United States in Central America, 1977–1992* (Chapel Hill: University of North Carolina, 1998) and Robert Kagan, *A Twilight Struggle: American Power and Nicaragua, 1977–1990* (New York: The Free Press, 1996)

As time passed international opposition to the conflict intensified, as explained in Richard E. Feinberg, editor, *Central America: International Dimensions of the Crisis* (New York: Holmes & Meier, 1982). Several countries pursued their own policies in an effort to bring peace to Central America including Mexico, Spain and Canada as found in the following studies: H. Rodrigo Jauberth, et. al., *The Difficult Triangle: Mexico, Central America and the United States* (Boulder: A PACCA book, published by Westview Press, 1992); Robin L. Rosenbert, *Spain and Central America: Democracy and Foreign Policy* (Westport, CN: Greenwood Press, 1992); and Jonathan Lemco, *Canada and the Crisis in Central America* (Westport, CN: Praeger, 1991). In what subsequently became a western hemispheric effort to negotiate a settlement to the conflict is the subject of Bruce M. Bagley's *Contadora and the Diplomacy of Peace in Central America* (Boulder: Westview Press, 1987).

Honduras became involved in the conflicts first as a U.S. sponsored and supported training program for the Nicaraugan *contras*, alleged "freedom fighters" intent on overthrowing the Sandinista regime in Nicaragua. Initially, the Argentine military provided the *contra* training for the United States as explained by Ariel C. Armony, *Argentina, the United States and the Anti-Communist Crusade in Central America, 1977–1984* (Athens: Ohio University Press, 1997). One of the early works to expose the U.S. secret role in the anti-Sandinista crusade, and the using of Honduras as staging area is Richard Lapper's, *Honduras: State for Sale* (London: Latin American Bureau, 1982). Subsequently, Donald E. Shultz produced two excellent studies about the wars and Honduras. His *The United States, Honduras and the Crisis in Central America* (Boulder: Westview Press, 1993) builds upon Lapper's earlier study in much more analytical detail. In Shultz's other study, *How Honduras Escaped Revolutionary Violence* (Washington, D.C.: U.S. Army War College, 1992) he argues that the brutality inflicted upon the people by the Honduran military, as the U.S. diplomats and military officers turned a blind eye, kept Honduras from being becoming a victim or the social revolutions afflicting the region. A much briefer discussion of the same issue can be found in Steve Levitsky, "Taming the Honduran Military," *Hemisphere*, 4:2 (1992), 36–38.

Throughout the 1980s the Honduran government was accused of widespread human rights violations, particularly its military. A good starting point for a discussion of the issue is Amnesty International, *Honduras: Civil Authority-Military Power: Human Rights Violations in the 1980s* (London: Amnesty International, 1989).

Index